THE GOSPEL RECORDS:

THEIR

GENUINENESS, AUTHENTICITY, HISTORIC VERITY, AND INSPIRATION,

WITH SOME

PRELIMINARY REMARKS ON THE GOSPEL HISTORY.

BY

WILLIAM NAST, D. D.

A REVISED EDITION OF THE AUTHOR'S GENERAL INTRODUCTION TO THE FIRST VOLUME OF HIS COMMENTARY ON THE NEW TESTAMENT.

CINCINNATI:
PUBLISHED BY POE & HITCHCOCK.

R. P. THOMPSON, PRINTER.
1866.

INTRODUCTORY NOTICE.

THE appearance of Dr. Nast's "General Introduction to the Gospel Records" in the present form, is necessitated by the fact that several institutions of learning have adopted it as a text-book of Christian evidences, and that it has also been introduced by the bishops of the Methodist Episcopal Church into the course of ministerial study. The present form will meet the wants of the student, and it is hoped also will lead to a much wider circulation among general readers. After the high authorities who have already pronounced favorably on the valuable character of this work, in its relation to the evidences of Christianity, and especially since its adoption as a text-book by the Board of Bishops, it is needless for us to commend it.

It is not designed to be an exhaustive discussion of the evidences of Christianity. Originally intended to be used only as introductory to the author's Commentary, it treats chiefly of those subjects which are most intimately connected with the historical verity of the Gospel Records. The whole argument revolves about the personality of our Lord and Savior; and herein are found its strength and opportuneness. The surest argument for the divine origin of Christianity is Christ himself. His life, as contained in the Gospels, being demonstrated as a historical reality, all else follows. If the Gospels, examined by the acknowledged laws of historical criticism, are proved to be genuine and authentic historical records, the history which they contain is itself a Divine revelation in the person of Jesus Christ, a personality utterly inexplicable without the admission of a supernatural and Divine element. Nor can any better evidence be offered for the historical verity of these sacred records than the character of the wonderful Being whose history they relate. The Christ described by the Evangelists could not possibly have been conceived by them, if they had not seen and heard what they record of him, and if so, his personality is historically proved, and that personality is God manifest in the flesh.

The opportuneness of this argument is seen in the fact that the great battle of infidelity in our day is raging about the person of Christ, so that the author's argument is not only the strongest that can be presented, but is also the one that brings him directly into antagonism with the most recent phases and objections of skepticism. This treatise, therefore, commends itself to the reader as the embodiment of the results of the most recent criticism of the historical trustworthiness of the Gospel Records, and as a fresh, and in many respects original consideration of the most recent objections of rationalism and infidelity. We have only to add that the author has in this edition made some valuable additions from Dr. Tischendorf's lately-published essay, entitled, "*When were our Gospels Composed?*" These are inserted in Part II, chapter 1.

I. W. WILEY.

CONTENTS.

PART I.

THE GENUINENESS OR INTEGRITY OF THE SACRED TEXT.

CHAPTER I.

THE HISTORY OF THE TEXT.

CHAPTER II.

THE IMPOSSIBILITY OF SUCCESS IN AN ESSENTIAL MUTILATION OR CORRUPTION OF THE GOSPEL RECORD.

PART II.

THE AUTHENTICITY OF THE GOSPEL RECORDS.

CHAPTER I.

THE OUTWARD HISTORICAL TESTIMONIES.

CHAPTER II.

THE INTERNAL EVIDENCES.

PART III.

THE HISTORIC VERITY OF THE GOSPEL RECORDS.

CHAPTER I.

A CONSIDERATION OF THE OBJECTIONS THAT HAVE BEEN RAISED AGAINST THE CREDIBILITY OF THE EVANGELISTS.

CHAPTER II.

THE CREDIBILITY OF THE EVANGELISTS.

CHAPTER III.

THE DIVINE SEAL STAMPED UPON THE GOSPEL HISTORY BY ITS SUBJECT—THE PERSON OF JESUS CHRIST.

PART IV.

THE ATTACKS OF MODERN CRITICISM ON THE INSPIRATION OF THE FIRST THREE GOSPELS.

PART V.

REMARKS ON THE GOSPEL HISTORY.

PART I.

THE GENUINENESS OR INTEGRITY OF THE SACRED TEXT.

THE

GOSPEL RECORDS.

PART I.

THE GENUINENESS OR INTEGRITY OF THE SACRED TEXT.

§1. INTRODUCTORY REMARKS.

It is to be regretted that nearly all English writers on the Evidences are in the habit of using the words "genuine" and "authentic" as synonyms, and sometimes even of attaching to the word "authentic" the popular sense of "true" or "credible," by which the whole argumentation is obscured. A book is to be called genuine, if it has remained in all material points the same as it was when it proceeded from its author. It is authentic, if it has proceeded at all from the person whose name it bears, or, where the name of the author was not assigned with certainty at the time of its origin, if it originated at the time and under the circumstances it professes to have done. A book may be genuine and authentic, and yet its contents may lack credibility.

We propose, in the order named, to inquire into the genuineness, the authenticity, and the credibility of the Gospel records, and then to consider their inspired character. The object of Part I is to show that the text of the four canonical Gospels has been preserved in its integrity—is genuine or uncorrupted. The investigation into the genuineness or integrity of the inspired writings is legitimate and of great importance. For though we may have the most satisfactory proofs that they proceeded at first from the apostles or evangelists whose names they bear, they may have been so altered since that time as to convey to us very false information with regard to their original contents. It is admitted on all hands that the original manuscripts disappeared at a very early time, owing to the frailty of the material on which the apostles wrote, and to the frequent use which was made of them by being read in the Churches and constantly transcribed, and that, in common with all other ancient writings, the original text of the New Testament has been exposed to the accidents to which all works preserved by transcription are liable. We will, therefore, consider, first, the history of the text, as the German writers call it—that is, the changes to which the original was unavoidably subjected in the process of transcription—and then prove that all these changes have not impaired the integrity of the original.

CHAPTER I.

THE HISTORY OF THE TEXT.

§ 2. THE CHANGE OF THE ORIGINAL TEXT WITH REGARD TO ITS OUTWARD APPEARANCE.

INASMUCH as our present mode of publishing books is very different from that of ancient times, we can not but expect that the outward appearance of the original text underwent great changes by being transcribed from century to century, and a consideration of these external changes claims our attention first. The following points are of general interest:

1. The authors of the New Testament used the charta—ὁ χάρτης, 2 John, 12—paper made of layers of the papyrus, a plant that was very common in Egypt. Of this paper there were, in the apostles' times, several kinds in use, differing from each other in strength and durability. Of the existing manuscripts, however, none are written on papyrus, but on vellum or parchment and on paper of later origin. Vellum was the most durable, but also the most costly material. The manuscripts on paper are of a date posterior to the seventh century.

2. As to the external form of the manuscripts, the ancients made use of rolls in their writings; yet as this form was unhandy in several respects, the custom arose to write on large sheets, which were folded up like maps in an atlas, four, five, six, or eight fold, of different sizes. This is the form of all manuscripts extant.

3. The Greek manuscripts were mostly written without division of words, in capital letters—which, in the time of Jerome, were called *uncials*—till the ninth century, when the so-called cursive handwriting—that is, writing with small letters, and capitals only at the head of certain words—came into use, as requiring less space and being better adapted for fast writing. The separation of words from each other by a point or empty space did not become general before the ninth century.

4. Punctuation marks were seldom used by the ancients. The numerous mistakes of the fathers, or their uncertainty, how particular passages were to be read and understood, clearly prove that there was no regular or accustomed system of punctuation in use in the fourth century. Toward the middle of the fifth century Euthalius, of Alexandria, wrote the Pauline epistles, and afterward the Gospels, stichometrically; that is, in lines regulated by the sense, so that each terminated where some pause was to be made; when the line was not filled, the remainder was, at first, left empty, but afterward, in order to save space, it was filled up, and a point was made to indicate the pause. The lines of the books were generally numbered and the number marked at the end. Although some full points are to be found in the Codex Alexandrinus, the Codex Vaticanus, and the Codex Bezæ—as they also are in inscriptions four hundred years before the Christian era—yet there is abundant evidence that our present system of Greek punctuation was not fully adopted before the ninth century.

5. The same remarks apply to the *accents*, *spiritus*—breathings—and the so-called *iota subscriptum*. The *accents* were gradually introduced. Some of the oldest

manuscripts have them, others not, and it is only toward the end of the tenth century that they became general. The rough breathing—*spiritus asper*—was anciently a full letter in the form of the Latin H, and so it is found on monuments—e. gr., *Hoι=όι*. Afterward the first half of the letter (Ͱ) was used for the rough breathing, and the other half (ͱ) for the smooth breathing, and from these two signs the modern form of breathings (‘’) arose. According to the oldest manuscripts, it seems that the writers of the New Testament did not use these two signs, at least not uniformly. The *iota subscriptum* was anciently written as a letter in the line—*iota postscriptum*—afterward entirely omitted, but came into general use as *iota subscriptum* with the introduction of the cursive characters. Whether a word was originally meant for *ἀυτῇ*, *ἀυτή*, or *αὕτη*, must be determined by the context alone.

6. Our present division of the sacred text into chapters and verses is of still more recent date. The first general division was made in the thirteenth century, in all probability, by the Cardinal Hugo Carensis, and the latter by Robert Stephanus in 1551, after a variety of other divisions had been in partial use before. Tertullian already speaks of *capitula* in portions of the New Testament Scriptures. But this division did neither extend over all the books of the New Testament, nor was it in general use, as far as it went. In early use was the division into *κεφάλαια*, portions much smaller than our chapters and larger than our verses. The Gospel of Matthew had 355 such *κεφάλαια*, that of Mark 234, that of Luke 341, that of John 231, altogether 1,162. This division was introduced by Ammonius, of Alexandria, in his Gospel Harmony—*τὸ*

διὰ τεσσάρων ἐυγγέλιον—and afterward completed by Eusebius. A later division was that into *τίτλοι*—*tituli*—introduced in the fifth century. The Gospel of Matthew was divided into 68, that of Mark into 48, that of Luke into 83, and that of John into 18 such tituli. Our present division has, of course, no claims whatever to the authority of the text, and being, in a number of instances, certainly faulty, the reader must take care not to be misled by it; yet, as it is in universal use, and is of great advantage for the purpose of reference, it is not expedient to make a change. Besides the older divisions, which we have named, selections of the New Testament Scriptures—*pericopæ*—were made for the public reading on each Sunday in the ecclesiastical year. The time and manner of their introduction are uncertain. Those from the Acts and the Epistles were probably first introduced by Euthalius; but those from the Gospels were undoubtedly earlier, at least in the Latin Church. These selections were often bound up separately, in their regular order, and are also of moment in Biblical criticism.

7. The inscriptions or titles of the various books of the New Testament, it is generally admitted, were not originally written by the apostles, but were subsequently added as the seal which the Church stamped upon them in settling the canon. The subscriptions annexed to some of the Epistles are manifestly spurious. They are altogether wanting in some ancient manuscripts of the best note, and in others they are greatly varied. Some contain false assertions.

§ 3. Some General Remarks on the Existing Manuscripts.

1. The autographs—manuscripts of the New Testament which were written either by the apostles them-

selves or by amanuenses under their immediate inspection, (Rom. xvi, 22; Gal. vi, 11; 2 Thess. iii, 17; 1 Cor. xvi, 21,) have long since perished, and we have no information whatever concerning their history. It has been thought that Ignatius and Tertullian appealed to them. Ignatius in his letter to the Philadelphians says that he heard some say: "If I do not find it ἐν τοῖς ἀρχαίοις, I do not believe it in the Gospel;" but τὰ ἀρχαῖα can here mean only the Old Testament writings, since the context shows, that the objection quoted came from Judaizers, who were unwilling to believe any thing in the Gospels that was not contained in the Old Testament. Tertullian appeals to the *autenticæ literæ* of the apostles as being read at his time in the Churches at Corinth, Philippi, Ephesus, etc. From this passage it might seem as if the autographs were referred to; but from another passage in the same author it plainly appears, that not autographs, but correct copies of them, *in the original language*, made and preserved by the respective Churches, were meant. If the autographs had existed at that time, the Church fathers would certainly have appealed to them in their controversies with the heretics on the genuineness of disputed passages.

2. No existing manuscript of the New Testament can be traced higher than the fourth century. The number of manuscripts that have thus far become known is about seven hundred. They belong to different centuries, from the fifth, perhaps the fourth, down to the sixteenth, and are accordingly written in different characters, the *oldest* in uncials, *by far the most* in cursive letters, partly without, partly with divisions into words and sections, with or without

accents, and with punctuation marks of different kinds. These very points, the shape of the letters, the material, and orthography furnish the principal data for determining the time and country, when and where the manuscripts were made. Sometimes other internal data are furnished by the manuscripts, giving, in a few instances, the name of the copyist and the year when the manuscript was made, or containing menologies, in which the festival days of the saints are mentioned, on which certain portions of Scripture are to be read in the Churches. As these menologies often designate such days as were celebrated in honor of certain saints from otherwise known dates, in certain countries, they furnish important data for determining the time and place when and where the manuscript was made.

3. Very few manuscripts contain the whole either of the Old or of the New Testament. By far the greater part—five hundred—have only the four Gospels, because they were most frequently read in the Churches; two hundred the Acts and catholic epistles; three hundred the Pauline epistles, and one hundred the Apocalypse. Almost all of them, especially the more ancient manuscripts, are imperfect, either from the injuries of time or from neglect. All manuscripts, the most ancient not excepted, have erasures and corrections; which, however, were not always effected so dextrously but that the original writing may sometimes be seen.

4. Before the invention of paper, the great scarcity of parchment in different places induced many persons to obliterate the works of ancient writers, in order to write in their place another work. Such manuscripts are termed *Codices Palimpsesti* or *Re-*

scripti. In general, a Codex Rescriptus is easily known, as it rarely happens that the former writing is so completely erased as not to exhibit some traces; in a few instances both writings are legible. Very valuable discoveries have been made in these rewritten manuscripts.

5. Besides the manuscripts which contain the whole New Testament, or certain books of it in full, there are others which contain only the selections or *pericopæ;* they are called *Codices Ecclesiastici or Lectionaria.* These selections were often prefaced with some remarks respecting the day on which they were to be read, and such remarks have, in some instances, crept into the text.

6. Some manuscripts have not only the Greek text, but are accompanied with a version, which is either interlined or in a parallel column; these are called *Codices Bilingues.* The greatest number is in Greek and Latin; and the Latin version is, in general, one of those which existed before the time of Jerome.

7. A comparative description of the different manuscripts, and an account of the various critical methods adopted to arrange them in certain classes or families, can be of interest and profit only to the professional scholar, but does not lie within our scope, and is to be sought in the special works on Biblical Text Criticism. Yet a few words of explanation may be expected by the general reader on the critical references of various readings, which he will find in the footnotes of the text in the author's Commentary. The manuscripts in *uncials* have, since Wetstein, been designated with the capital letters of the Latin alphabet, and where these do not suffice, with the Greek capitals; those in cursive characters—minuscles—

with the common Arabic ciphers. But as the manuscripts of both kinds—the uncial and cursive—are divided into four classes, namely, into codices, containing the Gospels, the Acts and catholic epistles, the Pauline epistles, and the Apocalypse, both the capital letters and ciphers commence in them four times anew. Thus, a codex, that contains the whole New Testament, comes up in the four classes with the capital or cipher peculiar to each class. As these two marks, capitals and ciphers, often vary in the different classes in the same manuscripts, and as new documents are constantly coming into the lists, it is necessary to notice—when they are simply quoted with their capitals or ciphers—to which book of the New Testament the quotations refer, in order to find them in the lists of the codices.

§ 4. A Consideration of the Variety of Readings presented by the Manuscripts of the New Testament.

Alarming as it may appear to the simple, pious Christian, to be told of fifty thousand up to one hundred and fifty thousand different readings, as they have been variously estimated, in the books of the New Testament, and much as infidels have boasted of this discovery, a slight examination of the matter will not only completely remove all apprehensions, but furnish us with the most conclusive proof that Divine Providence has provided the very best security for the integrity of the documents, upon which our faith rests.

In the first place, the number of various readings, great as it appears, is really less, in proportion, than that of the various readings extant in most classic authors, when compared with the quantity of text examined, and the number of manuscripts and other authorities collated in each particular case. Nineteen out of twenty, at least, are to be dismissed at once from consideration, because they are found in so few authorities, and their origin is so easily explained, that no critic would regard them as having any claim to be inserted in the text. Of those which remain, a very great majority are entirely unimportant. They consist in transpositions or omissions of letters, the use of different grammatical forms, the exchange of synonymous words and transpositions of words in sentences; and a very small number affects the sense of all. Only six passages have been discovered where a vital doctrine is affected by the different readings; but even in these instances the doctrine itself is not periled, because it is plainly taught in other passages.

The great value of the immense amount of labor, which has been expended for nearly a century upon the received text of the New Testament, consists not so much in the emendations of that text, as in establishing the fact, that the original text has been transmitted to us with remarkable integrity, that far the greater part of the variations among different copies are of no authority or of no importance, and that some of them are so trifling as not to admit of being made apparent in a translation.

The condition of the text, then, is such as we have to expect from the human agents through whom the documents were transmitted to posterity. The copyist was naturally exposed to mistakes of the eye by the unbroken current uncials—capitals; thus letters of similar form were interchanged, some words were omitted, others written twice, others transposed, and sometimes whole sentences were erroneously divided.

Those who copied from dictation—a common practice—were liable to errors by confounding sounds. Mistakes were also made, at a later period, by writing out abbreviations. Again, some words had been left out, and then were set as glosses in the margin; the copyist wishing to restore the original text, inserted the gloss or glosses in the text, but often in the wrong place. Errors of this kind are more frequent in the manuscripts of the New Testament than in those of other ancient writings, because the former were more frequently copied than the latter, and there were, therefore, more intermediate links between the autographs and the later copies. Other corruptions of the text arose from the efforts to correct it or make it plainer by removing the peculiarities of the New Testament diction, or by the reception of glosses into the text, which had at first been written in the margin to explain a difficulty, especially in the synoptical Gospels. The higher the authority of these writings rose, the more natural became the desire of the later copyist to amend a supposed error of an earlier one.

To have prevented such variations of the original text would have required such a continuous miracle on the part of God, as would not have been in accordance with God's dealings with man, nor consistent with the freedom of human agency. "They," says Dr. Hill, in his Lectures on Divinity, "who seem to think that the all-ruling providence of God should have preserved every copy of the original from any kind of vitiation, forget the extent of the miracle which they ask, when they demand, that all who ever were employed in copying the New Testament should at all times have been effectually guarded by the Spirit of God from negligence, and their works kept safe from the injuries of time. They forget, moreover, that the very circumstance to which they object has, in the wisdom of God, been highly favorable to the cause of truth. The infidel has enjoyed his triumph and has exposed his ignorance. Men of erudition have been encouraged to apply their talents to a subject which opens so large a field for their exercise. Their research and their discoveries have demonstrated the futility of the objection, and have shown that the great body of the people in every country, who are incapable of such research, may safely rest in the Scriptures as they are, and that the most scrupulous critics, by the inexhaustible sources of correction which lie open to them, may attain nearer to an absolute certainty with regard to the true reading of the books of the New Testament, than of any other ancient book in any language. If they require more, their demand is unreasonable; for the religion of Jesus does not profess to satisfy the careless, or to overpower the obstinate, but rests its pretensions upon evidence sufficient to bring conviction to those who with honest hearts inquire after the truth, and are willing to exercise their reason in attempting to discover it."

The Church was at all times enabled to ascertain, in all essential points, the true text of the New Testament writings, by means of the great number of old manuscripts of the very ancient versions, which were made from copies much nearer the original manuscripts than any that we have, and of the many quotations with which the works of the Christian fathers and other early writers abound. For a full description of these means, as well as for the rules in using them, the canons of criticism, which have been investigated and digested by many learned men, we must again refer the reader to the elaborate works that have been written on this subject. We will only add, that it may please Divine Providence to bring to light ancient documents, not yet discovered, an instance of which we have had but a few years ago in the discovery of the Codex Sinaiticus, by Tischendorf. However that may be, with the apparatus and the clearly-ascertained principles of criticism which we possess now, we may confidently indulge the hope of recovering the original purity of the text, where it is yet obscured. With regard to the duty of the critical examination of the correctness of the *received* text, the eminent English commentator, Dr. Ellicott, makes, in the recently-published "Aids to Faith," the following remarks, which must commend themselves to every candid mind: "Let the interpreter be seduced by no timidity or prejudices from ascertaining the true text. Let him not fall back upon the too often repeated statement, that, as readings affect no great points of doctrine, the subject may be left in abeyance. It is, indeed, most true, that different readings of such a character as 1 Tim. iii, 16, or interpolations such as 1 John v, 7, are few and exceptional. It is, indeed, a cause for devout thankfulness, that out of the vast number of various readings so few affect vital questions; still it is indisputably a fact, that but few pages of the New Testament can be turned over without our finding points of the greatest interest affected by very trivial variations of reading. On the presence or absence of an article in John v, 1, the whole chronology of our Lord's ministerial life may be said almost entirely to depend. A very slight alteration in

Mark vii, 31, would indicate a fact of deep historical interest, and is of very great significance in reference alike to commands subsequently given to the apostles to preach the Gospel, and to former prohibitions. (Matt. x, 5.) The absence of two words in Eph. i—now rendered somewhat more probable by the testimony of the Codex Sinaiticus—gives a fresh aspect to an important Epistle, disposes at once of several *prima facie* difficulties, and, further, must be taken greatly into account in the adjustment of some subordinate, but interesting questions with which the Epistle has been thought to stand in connection. (Col. iv, 16.) The presence or absence of a few words in Matt. xxviii, 9, affects considerably our ability to remove one of the many seeming discrepancies in the narratives of the first hours of the morn of the resurrection. We could multiply such examples; but perhaps enough has been said. There are, indeed, several grounds for thinking that there is an improved feeling on the whole subject; and there seem some reasons for hoping that, though no authoritative revision is likely to take place, nor, at present, perhaps, even to be desired, yet that the time is coming when there will be a considerable agreement on many of the results of modern criticism."

CHAPTER II.

IMPOSSIBILITY OF SUCCESS IN AN ESSENTIAL MUTILATION OR CORRUPTION OF THE GOSPEL RECORDS.

WE have seen that there is nothing in the various readings to shake our faith in the integrity of the sacred text. On the contrary, the very disagreement of the manuscripts shows that there could have been no collusion; but that the manuscripts were written, independently of each other, by persons separated by distance of time, remoteness of place, and diversity of opinion. This extensive independency of manuscripts on each other is the effectual check of willful alteration; which, whenever attempted, must have been immediately corrected by the agreement of copies from various and distant regions out of the reach of the interpolator. We are aware that we here enter upon an argumentation, where the question of genuineness coincides with that of authenticity. This, however, does not militate against the distinction which we have made between the two terms. We may use an argument for the genuineness of the Gospel Records, though it may also apply to their authenticity, and in doing so we furnish the reader with a natural transition and proper introduction to Part II.

The arguments which prove the Gospel Records to have remained uncorrupted have been set forth with peculiar force and clearness by Prof. A. Norton, in his "Evidences of the Genuineness of the Gospels," a work truly classic, but so learned and expensive as to be found only in the library of the professional scholar, and unadapted for general circulation in the orthodox Churches on account of the theological stand-point which the author occupies as a Unitarian. Yet the manner in which he presents the arguments on the uncorrupted preservation of the Gospel Records is unsurpassed, and we can do our readers no better service than to give them in his own language, though in a *condensed* form and separated from those arguments that bear only on the authenticity of the records, which the author does not sufficiently distinguish from genuineness in the strict sense in which we have defined this word.

§ 5. Argument from the Agreement of the Respective Copies of the Four Gospels.

That the Gospels have not been corrupted, but have remained essentially the same as they were originally composed, appears, in the first place, from the agreement among our present manuscript copies. These were written in different countries, and at different periods. They have been found in places widely remote from each other; in Asia, in Africa, and from one extremity of Europe to the other. Besides these manuscripts of the Greek text there are many manuscripts of ancient versions of the Gospels in different languages of each of the three great divisions of the world just mentioned. There are, likewise, many manuscripts of the works of the Christian Fathers abounding in quotations from the Gospels; and especially manuscripts of ancient commentaries on the Gospels, such as those of Origen, who lived in the third century, and of Chrysostom, who lived in the fourth; in which we find the sacred text quoted, as the different portions of it are successively the subjects of remark.

Now, all these different copies of the Gospels, or parts of the Gospels, so numerous, so various in their character, so unconnected, offering themselves to notice in parts of the world so remote from each other, concur in giving us essentially the same text. They vary, indeed, more or less from each other; but their variations have arisen from the common accidents of transcription; or, as regards the versions, partly from errors of translations; or in respect to the quotations by the Fathers, from the circumstance, that in ancient as in modern times the language of Scripture was often cited without regard to verbal accuracy, in cases where no particular verbal accuracy was required. The agreement among the extant copies of any one of the Gospels, or of portions of it, is essential; the disagreements are accidental and trifling, originating in causes which, from the nature of things, we know must have been in operation. The same work every-where appears; and, by comparing together different copies, we are able to ascertain the original text to a great degree of exactness. But as these professed copies thus correspond with each other, it follows that they must all be derived from one original manuscript, and that such manuscript has been faithfully copied.

Let us now consider the supposition that one transcriber, in one part of the world, would have made certain alterations in his copy, and inserted certain narratives which he had collected; and another, in another place, would have made different alterations, and inserted different narratives. Such copies, upon the supposition that this imagined license continued, would, when again transcribed, have been again changed and enlarged. Copies would have been continually multiplying, diverging more and more from the original and from each other. No generally-received text would have existed; none, therefore, could have been preserved and handed down. Instead of that agreement among the copies of each Gospel which now exists, we should have found every-where manuscripts, presenting us with different collections of narratives and sayings, and differing, at the same time, in their arrangement of the same facts and in their general style of expression. The copies of these writings would have presented the same phenomena as those of some of the apocryphal books, as, for instance, that called the Gospel of the Infancy, which appears in several different forms, this collection of fables having been remodeled by one after another according to his fancy. It is, moreover, to be taken into consideration, that the transcriber of a manuscript, making such alterations as the hypothesis supposes, could by doing so not corrupt the work itself. His copy could have had no influence upon the numerous cotemporary copies in which the true text might be preserved, or into which different alterations might be introduced. It is quite otherwise since the invention of printing. He who now introduces a corruption into the printed edition of a work, introduces it into all the copies of that edition; and if it be the only edition, into all the copies of that work.

It is evident, from the preceding statements, that the existing copies of each of the Gospels have been derived from some common exemplar, faithfully followed by transcribers. But it may be said that this exemplar was not the original work, as it proceeded from the hand of the Evangelist; that the lineage of our present copies is not to be traced so high; but that, at some period, the course of corruption which has been described was arrested, and a standard text was selected and determined upon, which has served as an archetype for all existing copies, but that this text, thus fixed as the standard, had already suffered greatly from the corruptions of transcribers, and was very different from the original. According to Eichhorn, the Church selected, at the end of the second and the beginning of the third century, out of the many Gospels then extant, four, which had the greatest marks of credibility and the necessary completeness for common use, and labored to procure their general reception among Christians, with the suppression of all other Gospels. In order properly to judge of this supposition, let us first inquire whether, at the time named, "the Church" had the power to do what is ascribed to her. There was no single ecclesiastical government which extended over Christians, or over a majority of Christians, or over any considerable portion of their number. They had no regular modes of acting in concert, nor any effectual means whatever of combining together for a common purpose. Neither the whole body, nor a majority of Christians, ever met by delegation to devise common measures. Such an event did not take place till a hundred and twenty years after the end of the second century, when Christianity had become the established religion of the Roman Empire, and the first general council, that of Nice, was called together by the Emperor Constantine. At the time of which we are speaking, the Christians were disturbed and unsettled by frequent cruel persecutions. Exclusively of those generally considered heretics, they were alienated from each other by differences of religious opinion; for it was before the end of the second century that Victor, Bishop of Rome, had excommunicated the Eastern Churches. This was the state of the Church at the end of the second century, and yet it is supposed that she came to an agreement to select four out of the many manuscript Gospels then in existence, all of which had been exposed to the license of transcribers. Of these four no traces are said to be discovered before that time; but it was determined to adopt them for common use, to the prejudice, it would seem, of others longer known. There was, as it is supposed, a universal and silent compliance with this proposal. Copies of the four new manuscripts and translations of them were at once circulated through the world. All others ceased to be transcribed, and suddenly disappeared from common notice. Copyers were at the same time checked in their former practice of licentious alteration. Thus a revolution was effected in regard to the most important sacred books of the Christians, and at the same time better habits were introduced among the transcribers of those books.

Now, who can suppose that any such series of events took place at the end of the second century? It is intrinsically incredible. Let us consider for a moment what an effort would be required, and what resistance must be overcome, in order to bring into general use among a single nation of Christians at the present day, not other Gospels, but simply a new and better translation of our present Gospels. In the case under consideration, allowing the supposed change to have been possible, it must have met with great opposition; it must have provoked much discussion; there must have been a great deal written about it at the time; it must have been often referred to afterward, especially in the religious controversies which took place; it would have been one of the most important events in the history of Christians, and the account of the transaction must have been preserved. That there are no traces of it whatever is alone conclusive evidence that it never took place.

Lastly: our present Gospels, it is conceded, were in common use among Christians about the end of the second century. The number of manuscripts then in existence bore some proportion to the number of Christians. The number of Christians can be safely set down at three millions. As few possessions could have been valued by a Christian so highly as a copy of the records of that Gospel, for which he was exposing himself to the severest sacrifices, and as a common copy of the Gospels could not have been very expensive, to judge from a remark of Juvenal respecting the cost of books in ancient times, there can be little doubt that copies of the Gospels were owned by a large portion of Christians; and, in supposing one copy for every fifty Christians, the estimate is probably much within the truth. This proportion would give us sixty thousand copies of the Gospels for three millions of Christians. But whether more or less, if there had been important discrepancies among the large number of copies, in common use and dispersed over the world, no series of events could either have destroyed the evidence of these discrepancies or could have produced the present agreement among existing copies, derived, as they are, from those in use at the period in question. The agreement, then, at the end of the second century, among the numerous copies of the respective Gospels, proves that an archetype of each Gospel had been faithfully followed by the transcribers. This archetype, as we have seen, there is no ground for imagining to have been any other than the original work of the author of that Gospel. It follows, therefore, that in the interval between the composition of these works and the end of the second century, their text did not suffer, as has been fancied, from the licentiousness of transcribers.

§ 6. Arguments Drawn from Other Considerations.

1. It would have been inconsistent with the common sentiments and practice of mankind for transcribers to make such alterations and additions as have been imagined in the sacred books which they were copying. Such license has never been attributed to the transcribers of the ancient classics, and what we apprehend so little concerning other writings, is still less to be apprehended concerning the Gospels, on account of their sacred character. Let us adduce a few testimonies in proof of this fact, and in refutation of the assertion made by Eichhorn, that, "before the invention of printing, in transcribing a manuscript, the most arbitrary alterations were considered as allowable, since they affected only an article of private property, written for the use of an individual."

Justin Martyr, in the dialogue which he represents himself as having held with Trypho, an unbelieving

Jew, charges the Jews with having expunged certain passages of the Old Testament relating to Christ. To this Trypho answers that the charge seems to him incredible. Justin replies, "It does seem incredible; for to mutilate the Scriptures would be a more fearful crime than the worship of the golden calf, or than the sacrifice of children to demons, or than slaying the prophets themselves." Is it credible that, when such sentiments existed with regard to the heinousness of attempting an adulteration of the Old Testament writings, the Christian Churches would suffer a tampering with their own sacred books?

Some of the heretics in the second century made, or were charged with making, alterations in the Christian Scriptures, in order to accommodate them to their own opinions. Of such corruptions of Scripture Dionysius, who was Bishop of Corinth about the year 170, thus speaks: "I have written epistles at the desire of the brethren. But the apostles of the devil have filled them with darnel, taking out some things and adding others. Against such a woe is denounced. It is not wonderful, therefore, that some have undertaken to corrupt the Scriptures of the Lord, since they have corrupted writings not to be compared with them." The meaning of Dionysius is, that the persons spoken of having shown their readiness to commit such a crime, it was not strange that they should even corrupt the Scriptures, these being works of much higher authority than his epistles, and from the falsification of which more advantage was to be gained. From the manner in which Dionysius denounces the guilt of some "apostles of the devil," in corrupting the Scriptures, we may confidently infer that the Christian

Churches were not guilty of such a practice. And yet this very passage of Dionysius is quoted by Eichhorn in support of his supposition. Equally groundless is his appeal to a saying of Celsus. "Celsus," says he, "objects to the Christians that they had changed their Gospels three and four times and oftener, as if they were deprived of their senses." If the charge of Celsus were correctly represented, the first obvious answer would be, that such a charge is as little to be credited, upon the mere assertion of Celsus, as various other calumnies of that writer against the Christians, which no one at the present day believes. But Celsus does not say what he is represented as saying. He does not bring the charge against the Christians generally, but against *some* Christians. His words are preserved in the work composed by Origen, in reply to Celsus; and, correctly rendered, are as follows: "Afterward Celsus says, that some believers, like men driven by drunkenness to commit violence on themselves, have altered the Gospel history, since its first composition, three times, four times, and oftener, and have refashioned it, so as to be able to deny the objections made against it." To this the whole reply of Origen is as follows: "I know of none who have altered the Gospel history, except the followers of Marcion, of Valentinus, and I think also those of Lucan. But this affords no ground for reproach against the religion itself, but against those who have dared to corrupt the Gospels. And as it is no reproach against philosophy that there are Sophists, or Epicureans, or Peripatetics, or any others, who hold false opinions, so also it is no reproach against true Christianity that there are those who have altered the Gospels and introduced heresies foreign from the teaching of Jesus." It is evident that Origen regarded the words of Celsus not as a grave charge against the whole body of Christians, but as a mere declamatory accusation, which he was not called upon to repel by any elaborate reply. Celsus compares the conduct of those whom he charges with altering the Gospels to that of men impelled by drunkenness to commit violence on themselves. To this comparison no objectien is to be made; for the question, whether the early Christians altered the Gospels, really resolves itself into the question, whether they acted like men intoxicated to the evident ruin of their cause.

To return, then, to the positive testimonies against the supposition of a corruption of the Gospel Records having been suffered by the Christian Churches—"we have not received," says Irenæus, (contra Hær., l. ii, c. 1,) "the knowledge of the way of our salvation by any others than those through whom the Gospel has come down to us, which Gospel they first preached, and afterward, by the will of God, transmitted to us in writing, that it might be the foundation and pillar of our faith." He immediately proceeds to speak particularly of the composition of the four Gospels, referring them to the authors to whom they are commonly ascribed. These books he afterward represents as the most important books of Scripture, (Ib., l. iii, c. 11, § 8,) and the Scriptures he calls "oracles of God." (Ib., l. i, c. 8, § 1.) He says, "We know that the Scriptures are perfect, as dictated by the Logos of God and his Spirit." (Ib., l. ii, c. 28, § 2.)

Clement, of Alexandria, also calls the Scriptures divinely inspired, and speaks of the four Gospels, in contradistinction from all other accounts of Christ, as having been handed down to the Christians of his age. (Stromat., l. iii, § 13.) Tertullian manifests the same reverence for the Scriptures, and especially for the Gospels, as his cotemporaries, Irenæus and Clement. He, like them, quotes the Gospels as works of decisive authority, in the same manner as any modern theologian might do. He wrote much against the heretic Marcion, whom he charges with having rejected the other Gospels, and having mutilated the Gospel of Luke, to conform it to his system. This leads him to make some statements which have a direct bearing on the present subject. "I affirm," says Tertullian, "that not only in the Churches founded by apostles, but in all which have fellowship with them, *that* Gospel of Luke, which we so steadfastly defend, has been received from its first publication." "The same authority," he adds, "of the apostolic Churches will support the other Gospels, which, in like manner, we have from them, conformably to their copies." (Adv. Marcion, l. iv, § 5.) "They," he says, "who were resolved to teach otherwise than the truth, were under a necessity of new modeling the records of the doctrine." "As they could not have succeeded in corrupting the doctrine without corrupting its records, so we could not have preserved and transmitted the doctrine in its integrity, but by preserving the integrity of its records." (De Præser. Hæret., § 28.)

The passages quoted show the state of opinion and feeling among Christians during the first two centuries, and it is clear that those who entertained these sentiments would neither make nor permit intentional alterations in the Gospels.

2. About the close of the second century, different

Christian writers express strong censure of the mutilations and changes which they charge some heretics, particularly Marcion, with having made in the Gospels and other books of the New Testament. Some passages to this effect have been quoted; it is unnecessary to adduce others, because the fact is well known and universally admitted. But if our Gospels had not existed in their present form till the close of the second century, if before that time their text had been fluctuating, and assuming in different copies a different form, such as transcribers might choose to give it, those by whom they were used could not have ventured to speak with such confidence of the alterations of the heretics.

3. We happen to have, in the words of a single writer, decisive evidence that no such differences as would imply a mutilation or corruption of the text ever existed in the manuscripts of the canonical Gospels. Origen was born A. D. 185, and flourished during the first half of the third century. He was particularly skilled in the criticism of the Scriptures. He had the means of consulting various manuscripts of the Gospels, of which he made a critical use, noticing their various readings. His notices are principally found in his Commentaries on the Gospels. If transcribers had indulged in such licentious alterations as have been supposed, he could not have been ignorant of them. But the various readings he adduces give a convincing proof that the manuscripts of his time differed, to say the least, as little from each other as the manuscripts now extant, and, consequently, that before his time there was the same care to preserve the original text as there has been since. This conviction is not weakened by a passage

in his writings, which may seem at first view to favor the opposite opinion. Origen expresses his doubts in the genuineness of the words, "Thou shalt love thy neighbor as thyself," (Matt. xix, 19,) and says: "But if it were not that in many other passages there is a difference among copies, so that all those of the Gospel of Matthew do not agree together, and so also as it regards the other Gospels, it might well seem irreverent in any one to suspect that the precept has been inserted here without its having been mentioned by the Savior. But it is evident that there exists much difference among copies; partly from the carelessness of some transcribers, partly from the rashness of others in altering improperly what they find written, and partly from those revisers who add or strike out according to their own judgment." (Com. in Matt., tom. xv, § 14.) In this passage there is no reference to the intentional corruptions of the heretics, in which case another Greek word would have been used for "altering" and for "revisers;" it refers only to the well-known, common causes of error in the transcription of manuscripts. We learn from it that transcribers were sometimes careless; that they sometimes improperly altered from conjecture a reading in the copy before them, which they fancied to be erroneous; and that those whose business was to revise manuscripts after transcription, for the purpose of correcting errors, did sometimes, in the want of proper critical apparatus, rely too much upon their mere judgment concerning what was probably the true text. His language in speaking of the difference among the manuscripts is even not as strong as that used by some modern critics concerning the disagreement among our present copies, which we know does not involve any essential mutilation or corruption. The passage of Origen, then, shows, on the one hand, that he did not regard the Gospels as having been exposed to any other causes of error than those common in the transcription of manuscripts; on the other hand, that he had no disposition to keep out of view or to extenuate the differences among the copies extant in his time. We may, therefore, be satisfied that none of more importance existed than what we find noticed by him.

We may reason in a similar manner from all the notices in ancient writers relating to the text of the Gospels. Nothing can be alleged from their writings to prove any greater difference among the copies extant in their time than what is found among those which we now possess. It may here be proper to refer to an objection which Eichhorn makes. He says: "Clement, of Alexandria, at the end of the second century, speaks of those who corrupted the Gospels, and ascribes it to them; that at Matthew v, 10, instead of the words, '*for theirs is the kingdom of heaven*,' there was found in some manuscripts, '*for they shall be perfect;*' and in others, '*for they shall have a place where they shall not be persecuted.*'" This statement is erroneous. Clement does not speak of those who corrupted, but of those who paraphrased the Gospels; nor does he give the words alleged by him, as various readings in manuscripts of the Gospels. Quoting the original text incorrectly, from memory, in these words, "blessed are they who are persecuted for righteousness' sake, for they shall be called the sons of God," he adds, "or as some, who have paraphrased the Gospels, express it: Blessed are they who are persecuted for righteousness' sake, for they shall be perfect; and blessed are they who are persecuted for my sake, for they shall attain a place where they shall not be persecuted." Clement evidently expresses no indignation against those of whom he speaks, as he would have done if the passages quoted had assumed three such different forms in the manuscripts which he had seen; for that would prove a general license of corruption in his time.

4. If our present Gospels had been the result of successive additions, made by different hands to a common basis, there would have been a marked diversity of style in different portions of the same Gospel, so that these works would have been very unlike what they are now. We should have perceived clear traces of different writers, having greater or less command of expression, and accustomed to a different use of language. But when we examine the Gospels, there is nothing which discovers marks of their having been subjected to such a process of interpolation. On the contrary, there is decisive evidence that each is the work of an individual, and has been preserved, as it was written by him. The dialect, the style, and the modes of narration in the Gospels, generally, have a very marked and peculiar character. Each Gospel, also, is distinguished from the others by individual peculiarities in the use of language, and other characteristics exclusively its own.

5. In those cases in which we have good reason to suspect an ancient writing of being spurious altogether, or of having received spurious additions, the fact is almost always betrayed by something in the character of the writing itself. Spurious works and

interpolations in authentic works are discovered by something not congruous to the character of the pretended author, by a style different from his own, by an implied reference to opinions or events of a later age, or by some other bearing and purpose not consistent with the time when they are pretended to have been written. Traces of the times when they were really composed are almost always apparent. This must have been the case with the Gospels if they had been subjected to alterations and additions from different editors and transcribers with different views and feelings, more or less affected by opinions and circumstances which had sprung up in their own times. But no traces of a later age than that which we assign for their composition appear in the Gospels.

PART II.

THE AUTHENTICITY OF THE GOSPEL RECORDS.

PART II.

THE AUTHENTICITY OF THE GOSPEL RECORDS.

§ 7. INTRODUCTORY REMARKS.

By the *authenticity* of the Gospels we understand that *they were written by the men whose names they bear, who were partly eye-witnesses, partly persons cotemporaneous with the events narrated.* To declare the Gospels authentic in this sense has been pronounced by infidels to be "an assumption originating from the titles which the Biblical books bear in our canon." We grant that little reliance can be placed on these titles or headings, but it is absurd to say that these headings originated the belief that the books were written by the men whose names they bear; for before the titles were attached, the belief must have existed. There is not the slightest pretense for insinuating that there was ever any doubt as to the authorship of any one of the historical books of the New Testament; which are as uniformly ascribed to the writers whose names they bear as the "Return of the Ten Thousand" to Xenophon, or the "Lives of the Cæsars" to Suetonius. There is, indeed, *far* more and stronger testimony concerning the authenticity of the four Gospels than exists with respect to the works of almost any classical writer; for it is a rare occurrence for classical works to be distinctly quoted, or for their authors to be mentioned by name within a century of the time of their publication.

CHAPTER I.

THE OUTWARD HISTORICAL TESTIMONIES.

§ 8. The Testimony of the Apostolical Fathers.

By the Apostolical Fathers we understand those early Christian writers who lived wholly or in part in the very age of the apostles, and were more or less conversant with them. These are: *Clement*, of Rome, mentioned (Phil. iv, 3) as a fellow-laborer of Paul, afterward Bishop of Rome; *Barnabas*, of Cyprus. frequently mentioned in the New Testament as a co-laborer of Paul; *Ignatius*, Bishop of Antioch in Syria; *Polycarp*, a disciple of John, ordained by him Bishop of Smyrna, where he died a martyr. Of these Apostolical Fathers we have only a few writings and some fragments.

The learned Dr. Lardner has carefully collated all the passages in which these writers have made any allusion to the canonical books of the New Testament. Their allusions to the Epistles are far more numerous and direct than those to the Gospels. The latter have been subjected by Eichhorn and others to a very rigid scrutiny, for the purpose of destroying the evidence they furnish that our Gospels were known to the Apostolical Fathers. It is said, that "by far the greater part of them are so general in the allusions they are supposed to make to passages occurring in the Gospels, that no weight can be attached to them." To this it might be sufficient to reply, that the very peculiarity of these allusions, instead of invalidating the evidence, furnishes a very strong argument in favor of the existence of the Gospels in their day. "When does an author," says Dr. W. L. Alexander, in his *Christ and Christianity*, "feel himself at liberty to deal in general allusions to other writings, and, instead of formally citing them, to invigorate his own style, or point his own sentences, by a few words borrowed from them, or a passing hint at something they contain? Is it not when he may safely take for granted the familiarity of his readers with the authors he thus passingly lauds? and does not this feature in the writings of any author invariably prompt the inference, that he has assumed the fact of such familiarity? . . . . What confirms this inference is, that exactly in the same way of general allusion and partial citation do these Apostolic Fathers frequently make use of the writings of the Old Testament and of the Epistles of the New."

It is true, that with the exception of the direct appeals to Paul's Epistles to the Corinthians, Ephesians, and Philippians, by Clement, Ignatius, and Polycarp, the Apostolic Fathers bear no formal testimony of the existence of the canonical books of the New Testament; but their indirect testimony is sufficiently strong to satisfy every reasonable demand. How fully it accords with the very nature of their position is very clearly set forth by Westcott, in his excellent work on the Canon of the New Testament, from which we shall draw most of what we have to say *in this whole chapter*.

"That the Apostolical Fathers," he says, "do not appeal to the Apostolic Writings more frequently and more distinctly, springs from the very nature of their position. Those who had heard the living voice of apostles were unlikely to appeal to their written words. It is an instinct which always makes us prefer any personal connection to the more remote relationship of books. . . . . The words of Scripture are inwrought into the texture of the books, and not parceled out into formal quotations. They are not arranged with augmentative effect, but used as the natural expression of Christian truths. Now, this use of the Holy Scripture shows at least that they were even then widely known, and so guarded by a host of witnesses—that their language was transferred into the common dialect—that it was as familiar to those first Christians as to us, who use it as unconsciously as they did in writing or conversation. If the quotations of the Old Testament in the Apostolic Fathers were uniformly explicit and exact, this mode of argument would lose much of its force. With the exception of Barnabas, it does not appear that they have made a single reference by name to any one of the books of the Old Testament. Clement uses the general formula, 'It is written,' or, even more frequently, 'God saith,' or, simply, 'One saith.' The two quotations from the Old Testament in Ignatius are simply preceded by 'It is written.' Exactness of quotation was foreign to the spirit of their writing."

Respecting the coincidences between the Apostolic Fathers and the canonical Gospels, in particular, Mr. Westcott says: "From the nature of the case, casual coincidences of language can not be brought forward in the same manner to prove the use of a history as of a letter. The same facts and words, especially if they be recent and striking, may be preserved in several narratives. References in the sub-apostolic age to the discourses or actions of our Lord, as we find them recorded in the Gospels, show that what they relate was then so far held to be true; but it does not necessarily follow that they were already in use, and the precise source of the passage in question. On the contrary, the mode in which Clement refers to our Lord's teaching, 'the Lord said,' not 'saith,' seems to imply that he referred to tradition, and not to any written accounts, for words most closely resembling those which are still found in our Gospels. The testimony of the Apostolic Fathers is to the substance, and not to the authenticity of the Gospels. And in this respect they have an important work to do. They witness that the great outlines of the life and teachings of our Lord were familiarly known to all from the first: they prove that Christianity rests truly on a historic basis. The 'Gospel' which the Fathers announce includes all the articles of the ancient creeds. 'Christ,' we read, 'our God, the eternal Word, the Lord and Creator of the world, who was with the Father before time began, at the end humbled himself, and came down from heaven, and was manifested in the flesh, and was born of the Virgin Mary, of the race of David, according to the flesh; and a star of exceeding brightness appeared at his birth. Afterward, he was baptized by John, to fulfill all righteousness; and then, speaking his Father's message, he invited not the righteous, but sinners, to come to him. At length, under Herod and Pontius Pilate, he was crucified, and vinegar and gall was offered him to drink. But on the first day of the week he rose from the dead, the first-fruits of the grave;

and many prophets were raised by him for whom they had waited. After his resurrection he ate with his disciples, and showed them that he was not an incorporeal spirit. And he ascended into heaven, and sat down on the right hand of the Father, and thence he shall come to judge the quick and the dead.' Such, in their own words, is the testimony of the earliest Fathers to the life of the Savior. Round these facts their doctrines are grouped; on the truth of the incarnation, and the passion, and the resurrection of Christ, their hopes were grounded."

Mr. Westcott, in conclusion, makes the following remarks on the age of the Apostolic Fathers: "If the extent of the evidence of the Apostolic Fathers to the books of the New Testament is exactly what might be expected from men who had seen the apostles, who had heard them, and who had treasured up their writings as the genuine records of their teaching, the character of their evidence is equally in accordance with their peculiar position. It will be readily seen that we can not expect to find the New Testament quoted in the first age as authoritative, in the same manner as the Old Testament. There could not, indeed, be any occasion for an appeal to the testimony of the Gospels, when the history of the faith was still within the memory of many; and most of the epistles were of little use in controversy, for the earliest heretics denied the apostleship of St. Paul. The Old Testament, on the contrary, was common ground; and the ancient system of Biblical interpretation furnished the Christian with ready arms. When these failed it was enough for him to appeal to the death and resurrection of Christ, which were at once the sum and the proof of his faith. . . .

The successors of the apostles did not, we admit, recognize that the written histories of the Lord, and the scattered epistles of his first disciples, would form a sure and sufficient source and test of doctrine, when the current tradition had grown indistinct or corrupt. Conscious of a life in the Christian body, and realizing the power of its Head, as later ages can not do, they did not feel that the apostles were providentially charged to express once for all in their *writings* the essential forms of Christianity, even as the prophets had foreshadowed them. . . . . But they had certainly an indistinct sense that their work was essentially different from that of their predecessors. They attributed to them power and wisdom to which they themselves made no claim. Each one of those teachers, who stood nearest to the writers of the New Testament, plainly contrasted his writings with theirs, and definitely placed himself on a lower level."

To these general remarks we add the positive results which the testimony of the Apostolic Fathers gives us. In the letters which Ignatius composed while he was conveyed to Rome, between the years 107 and 115, there are found unmistakable references to John vi, 41, 48, 51, 54, and to Matt. iii, 15, xvi, 26. In like manner, the short letter of Polycarp, written soon after the death of Ignatius, about 115, refers to Matt. vi, 13, and xxvi, 41. Polycarp quotes also from the first Epistle of John the words: "Every one that confesseth not that Jesus Christ is come in the flesh, is antichrist." This is of importance, inasmuch as the Epistle and the Gospel of John must have been the work of one and the same author. The authentication of the Epistle, therefore, serves at the same time for that of the Gospel. But a testimony of Polycarp respecting the writings of John, considering the intimate relation in which he stood to that apostle, possesses a value so extraordinary as hardly to admit any further objection against the authenticity of the fourth Gospel.

A testimony of the highest significance to the authenticity of the Gospels has lately been rendered by the epistle of Barnabas, for which we are indebted to the important discovery of the Sinai Manuscript, by Dr. Tischendorf. For two centuries past the Christian Church has occupied itself much with this epistle; but, unfortunately, in all the manuscripts of the Greek text extant in European libraries, the first five chapters are wanting. An ancient, but very imperfect, Latin translation alone supplied the defect. In this Latin translation there is the following passage: "Let us, therefore, beware that we be not found, *as it is written*, 'many called, but few chosen.'" The expression, "as it is written," is used throughout the New Testament when a quotation is made from the Old Testament Scriptures. To the writings composed by apostles this formula could evidently not be applied before these writings had attained a footing of equal authority with those of the Old Testament. If we find, therefore, in the ancient writings of the Church passages quoted from the Gospels with the same formula, then it follows that, at the time when these writings were composed, the Gospels must have had a co-ordinate authority with the Old Testament. To obviate this conclusion, Dr. Credner asserted "the argument was not valid before the formula could be found in the original Greek text." And in the order of Divine Providence, the entire epistle of Barnabas, in the original Greek text, was discovered among the old parchment books of a Greek convent, in an Arabian desert, and the original text now gives the proof that the important formula, "as it is written," was prefixed to the passage quoted from Matthew by the author of the epistle, and not by the tranlator. This result is of no small importance, for the epistle of Barnabas can not be placed later than at the beginning of the second century. Opinion formerly wavered between the first and second decades of years in that century, but the Sinai Manuscript has induced most scholars to go back to the last decade of years in the first century. In this venerable work, which, at the close of the second century, Clement, of Alexandria, reckoned as a part of Holy Scripture, there are found several obvious references to the Gospel of Matthew; and one with the formula accustomed to be employed only for citations from Holy Writ. Hence, it follows that at the beginning of the second century the Gospel of Matthew possessed already the authority of sacred Scripture. This fact becomes the more significant if it can be proven, as we shall show in the course of our investigation, by the testimony of Justin and Irenæus, and even by that of heretics, that the Gospel of Matthew could not be taken into the number of the sacred books by itself alone, but only in connection with the other three Gospels.

We must not pass over to the next section without considering the testimony of Papias, who has been erroneously supposed to have been a pupil of the apostle John, and, therefore, has been reckoned, by some, among the Apostolic Fathers, and whose testimony has been perverted by those who deny the apostolic origin of our Gospels. Dr. Tischendorf, in his lately-published essay, "When were our Gospels Composed?" sets the whole question in the clearest light:*

"The obscurity which rests upon the man himself, as well as upon his testimony, disqualifies him to become an independent witness, or even to be placed in antagonism to other witnesses; yet this has happened. Through Eusebius, (iii, 39,) we know that he wrote a work in five books, which he styled, "An Exposition of the Sayings of the Lord." In collecting materials for this work, he entertained the idea that his purpose would be better served by the living word of tradition than by what he might find in 'books.' His sources of information, therefore, according to his assurance, were such oral reports as were capable of being traced to the apostles. His own language in regard to these sources is as follows: 'I shall collect what I have learned from the elders (presbyters) and have retained in memory, at the same time confirming their truth by my own explanations.' Again: 'Also when I fell in with any one who had had intercourse with the elders, I made inquiry concerning the communications of the elders, what Andrew or Peter had said, or what Philip, or what Thomas, or James, or what John or Matthew, or what any other of the disciples of the Lord.' Who the elders referred to in these words were is not entirely clear. Those men of letters who would make the term refer to the apostles themselves are certainly in the wrong. We are rather to understand by it venerable men who had had personal inter-

*We quote from the translation, by Dr. H. Smith, Professor in Lane Theological Seminary. See the "Eclectic," No. 10, 1866.

course with the apostles. So Eusebius, whose judgment rested upon a knowledge of the entire work of Papias, understood the word, and expressed himself upon the point in still more definite terms. He testifies expressly that Papias by no means claims to be a man who had himself heard and seen the holy apostles, but a pupil of Aristion, and of the presbyter, or elder, John, to whose testimony also he most frequently appealed. Even Eusebius regarded it as an error in Irenæus, that he had characterized him as a 'hearer of John and a companion of Polycarp,' a passage in which Irenæus must have confounded presbyter John, mentioned by Papias as his teacher, with the apostle of the same name. This is confirmed by the circumstance that Irenæus derives an extravagant tradition touching the millennial kingdom expressly, 'from the mouth of the elders, who had seen John, the disciple of the Lord.' In this passage, beyond doubt, Irenæus distinguishes the elders from the apostles; but since he appeals to Papias for the tradition concerning the millennial kingdom, he leaves no room to doubt that the elders of whom he speaks were no others than those mentioned by Papias.

"According to Eusebius, Papias declared that he learned much more in the form of oral tradition, 'also some unheard-of (strange)* parables and teachings of the Lord, and some other matter partaking too much of the fabulous.' Of this character, Eusebius pronounces the doctrine of a millennial kingdom, which, after the resurrection of the dead, in a sensuous way, should exist upon this earth. Eusebius

*The Greek word has both senses. Eusebius appears to have expressed by it his own judgment touching the pretended discourses of our Lord.

thereupon remarks that Papias, as a man of very limited intelligence, which his whole book proves, had gathered them from misunderstood expressions of the apostles. He then proceeds to say that still other reports, springing from Aristion and the presbyter John, are to be found in the book of Papias, but refers those who feel an interest in them to the book itself. He then remarks that he will add to his previous quotations his tradition concerning Mark. His language is: 'And this said the presbyter: Mark, the interpreter of Peter, wrote down carefully what he remembered; not, however, in the order in which Christ had spoken or acted, for neither had he heard the Lord nor did he follow him; but, as already said, Peter, who delivered his discourses according to occasion, but did not wish to collect, in an orderly way, the discourses of the Lord. Mark, therefore, was not in fault when he wrote down any thing as he remembered it. On one thing only was he intent, not to omit any thing which he had heard, and not to falsify any thing.' To this statement of Papias, Eusebius immediately annexes another concerning Matthew, proceeding to say: 'This, then, Papias writes concerning Mark, but of Matthew he says: Now Matthew wrote the discourses of the Lord in the Hebrew language, but each one interpreted them as he could.' In these sentences there is much which is obscure. It is doubtful, for instance, whether we have rightly translated the expression, 'the discourses of the Lord;' for that which Papias had previously spoken concerning Mark—we mean the words, 'which Christ had spoken or acted—makes it probable that discourses and actions both are to be understood. Now, do these statements of the presbyter and Papias refer to our two Gospels which are named after Matthew and Mark? Even if the expression 'discourses of the Lord' should be correct, it can not thence be inferred that a historical clothing of the discourses is excluded, for neither Eusebius nor any theologian of Christian antiquity has supposed that the expressions of Papias stand opposed to the two Gospels. If, on the other hand, any in our time have built upon this—the conclusion that our Gospel of Mark is to be regarded as the proper book of Mark only in the second degree, and that it sprung from a later revision of the book written by Mark—this supposition is obviously nothing but a groundless speculation. It serves only to deliver over our investigations touching the origin and mutual relations of our first three Gospels a prey to endless conjectures. This is true of Mark, and it is not less true of Matthew. The statement of Papias concerning the latter has its point in this: that he ascribes to Matthew only a Hebrew text. If there is any truth in this statement, then, especially if we accept the other, that every one interpreted it as he could, a wide field of conjecture is opened between the primeval Hebrew text and the Greek text in our possession. That Hebrew text must have been lost in the very earliest times, for not a single one of the earliest Church Fathers had seen or used it. For our part, we are fully satisfied, and rest quietly in the conviction, that the supposition of a primary Hebrew text of Matthew, on the part of Papias, originated entirely in a misconception. Perfectly to establish the truth of this conviction would require an elaborate and learned discussion, for which this is not the proper place. We will barely indicate to the reader the source of the error into which Papias fell. We learn even from the Epistle of Paul to the Galatians the existence of vexatious party strifes arising from Judaizing teachers. After the destruction of Jerusalem they seem to have manifested themselves with ever-increasing violence. There were two chief parties. One, which we may call that of the Nazarenes, was of a more simple character than the other, that of the Ebionites. Both used a Gospel named after Matthew; the first in the Hebrew, the other in the Greek language. That they did not hesitate to alter the text which came into their hand according to their own taste, is a fact springing from their very posture—that of mere arbitrary sects; and what has come to our actual knowledge on the subject proves at once a very great similarity to our Matthew, and an arbitrary departure from him in particular passages. When now, at a later day, it was repeated that the Nazarenes, who had sprung from the oldest Christian stock, possessed a Matthew in Hebrew, what was more natural than that the one or the other should assume, perhaps in accordance with the pretense of the sect itself, that Matthew wrote in Hebrew, and that the Greek text was a translation? How widely these texts differed from each other was a matter which no one knew accurately or inquired into. Moreover, the remote position of the sect of the Nazarenes, who resided chiefly near the Dead Sea, would not prompt such an investigation.

"In this explanation of the statement of Papias, we are supported by Jerome. Jerome, who—a singular accomplishment in his day—was acquainted with Hebrew, in the fourth century actually got possession of the Hebrew Gospel of the Nazarenes, and at once cried out that he had the original Hebrew text of Matthew. After a closer investigation, however, he said only that many held this Hebrew text to be the real Matthew. He translated it into Greek and Latin, and published some observations derived from it. From these observations of Jerome, as well as from other ancient sources, it can now be proved that the view of Papias, shared by many learned men in modern times, that the so-called Hebrew Gospel is more ancient than our Matthew, must be directly reversed; for that Hebrew book was rather borrowed from our Greek Matthew, with arbitrary variations of the text. The same remarks are applicable to the Greek text of the Hebrew Gospel, already mentioned, which was used by the Ebionites. In a word, this was better known in the Church than the Hebrew, simply because it was Greek; but in the earliest times it was also regarded as only another text of Matthew. With this agrees what Papias has written concerning the various interpretations of Matthew.

"But we have something more to say of Papias and his compilation. As touching his efforts in collecting materials, he wrote that he believed he should be less aided by that which was found in books. What books? Did he refer to our Gospels? From the expression, this is not impossible, but, from the whole character of his book, it is very improbable; for manifestly he aimed, on the basis of what at that time—perhaps A. D. 130 or 140—was still orally related concerning the Savior, to produce a kind of supplement of the Gospels. These last, therefore, he could not have regarded as sources—as presenting materials for his collection. By the books referred to, he must rather have understood the unauthorized apocryphal delineations of Christ, so many of which made their appearance from the earliest times onward. These he placed in contrast with his oral sources, the genuineness of which appeared to him perfectly established, since, equally with the Gospels themselves, they had been derived from the apostles, although through the testimony of the elders.

"Now, can any important historical information touching our Gospels be derived from all that Papias and his book have to offer upon the subject? Even though a man of intellect, with much to support him, has actually answered this question in the affirmative, we can not but give it an unconditional denial. The judgment of Eusebius, touching the man, that he was a person of limited understanding, is confirmed by the fact that his pretended enrichment of evangelical literature was entirely disregarded by the Church. What value would not a single parable of the Lord have had, if it could lay claim to credibility? But no one has taken the least notice of all those described by Papias. The fabulous character of which Eusebius, a man not distinguished for critical acumen, speaks, without doubt belonged to the entire work.

"Nevertheless, in our century, Papias has grown into a torch-bearer, and that, too, among men who claim special eminence in acute criticism. Why? Papias is silent in respect to the Gospel of John. This silence is arrayed by Strauss, Renan, and other critics of like spirit, in opposition to the faith of the Church touching the genuineness of John's Gospel, as a fact suggesting the very gravest doubts. It is maintained that Papias could have known nothing of John's

Gospel, because he does not mention it. Of course, herewith would be gained nothing less than a decisive testimony against the genuineness of this Gospel; for Papias, the Bishop of Hierapolis, resided in the vicinity of Ephesus, whence the Gospel of John must have gone forth to the world, and the earliest information places the martyr-death of Papias at the same time with that of Polycarp; that is, in the sixteenth year of the second century.

"Now, a more groundless and frivolous affirmation could hardly be made, than that the silence of Papias concerning the Gospel of John yields "a strong proof against its genuineness." For, in the first place, to bear a testimony concerning John's Gospel, is a matter entirely aside from the plan and object of Papias; in the second place, from the circumstance that Eusebius has quoted nothing from the book of Papias concerning the Gospel of John, we are by no means able to infer that nothing in reference to John existed in that book. The notices touching Mark and Matthew are not given by Eusebius as testimonies for the genuineness of their Gospels, but on account of particular circumstances mentioned in them. Concerning John, therefore, and this is the only conclusion yielded by the silence of Eusebius, no similar notices were found. But Eusebius is as silent concerning the writings of Luke and the Pauline Epistles, in citing from Papias, as concerning John's Gospel. Is it not an absurdity to suppose that Papias knew nothing of all these? Yet this absurd affirmation must necessarily be made, side by side, with that concerning John's Gospel.

"But we have not yet mentioned that Eusebius, at the conclusion of his article concerning Papias, observes that he cited proof-texts from the 1st Epistle of John and the 1st Epistle of Peter. Does not this make against us, if we deny any significance to his silence concerning Luke, Paul, and the Gospel of John? No, the reverse. The genuineness of the four Gospels and of the Pauline Epistles was doubted by no one in the Church; therefore Eusebius could not have conceived the idea of gathering ancient testimonies to establish it. The case was different with the Catholic Epistles, with the Apocalypse, and with the Epistle to the Hebrews. To collect ancient witnesses to these writings was a matter of importance to him. But may it not be alleged that this is a mere arbitrary representation? We have at hand two vouchers for the correctness of our view, which will entirely exclude the charge of arbitrariness. Of Polycarp's letter to the Philippians, Eusebius (iv, 14) says nothing, except that it contains proof-texts from the 1st Epistle of Peter, and yet this very letter is full of citations from Paul. In like manner he proceeds to say (iv, 26) that Theophilus, in his book to Autolycus, used the Apocalypse, and makes no mention of the fact that these very books distinguish themselves by the citation of a passage from John's Gospel containing even a mention of the name of John. All this, a blind zeal against the Gospel of John has overlooked. One thing in this connection we must not leave untouched. Eusebius testifies that Papias used the 1st Epistle of John. Now, inasmuch as, upon grounds of the most convincing power, that Epistle and Gospel must have had the same author, the testimony of Papias to the Epistle is at the same time a testimony for the Gospel of John."

§ 9. The Testimony of the Fathers in the Sub-Apostolic Age, from A. D. 120–170.

In this age the Church had to maintain its ground amid systematic persecution, organized heresies, and philosophic controversy. The apostolic tradition was insufficient to silence or condemn false teachers who had been trained in the schools of Athens or Alexandria, but new champions were raised up to meet the emergency; and some of these did not scruple to maintain the doctrines of Christianity in the garb of philosophers. As Christianity was shown to be the true completion of Judaism before the Church was divided from the Synagogue, so it was well that it should be clearly set forth as the center to which old philosophers converged before it was declared to supersede them. This, then, was one great work of the time, that apologists should proclaim Christianity to be the Divine answer to the questionings of heathendom, as well as the antitype to the law and to the hope of the prophets. To a great extent the task was independent of the direct use of Scripture. Those who discharged it had to deal not so much with the words as with the thoughts of the apostles, not so much with the records as with the facts of Christ's life. Even the later apologists abstained from quoting Scripture in their addresses to heathens; and the practice was still more alien from the object and position of the earliest. The arguments of philosophy and history were brought forward first, that men might be better prepared for the light of revelation. The literature of this age included almost every form of prose composition—letters, chronicles, essays, apologies, visions, tales; but although it was thus varied, the fragments of it which are left scarcely do more than witness to its extent. Omitting what can be gathered from the scanty fragments of the Athenian Apologists, Quadratus and Aristides, from the letter to Diognetus, from the Jewish Apologists, from Dionysius, Hermas, Hegesippus, etc., we will confine ourselves to the all-sufficient testimony of Justin Martyr, to whom the first rank must be assigned among the apologetical writers of the second century. He was of Greek descent, but his family had been settled for two generations in the Roman colony of Flavia Neapolis, near the site of the ancient Sichem, where he was born at the close of the first century. He died as martyr in the year 166. After he had, as as a heathen, successively sought after truth in the various philosophical systems, he became, in the thirtieth year of his life, a convert to Christianity, which, while continuing to wear his philosopher's cloak, he enthusiastically defended by writings and discussions.

Eusebius has given a list of such books of his as had come to his own knowledge. Of the writings which bear his name now, two, Apologies and the Dialogue with Trypho, are genuine beyond all doubt. They exhibit a mass of references to the Gospel narratives. The first thing that must strike any one who examines a complete collection of the passages in question is the general coincidence in range and contents with our Gospels. Nothing, for instance, furnished wider scope for apocryphal narratives than the history of the infancy of our Lord; yet Justin's account of the infancy is as free from legendary admixture as it is full of incidents recorded by the Evangelists. He does not appear to have known any thing more than they knew. The style and language of the quotations which he makes from Christ's teaching agree no less exactly with those of the Evangelist. He quotes frequently from memory; he interweaves the words which we find separately given by Matthew, Mark, and Luke; he condenses, combines, transposes the language of our Lord as they have recorded it; he makes use of phrases characteristic of different Gospels; yet, with very few exceptions, he preserves through all these changes the marked peculiarities of the New Testament phraseology, without the admixture of any foreign element. We have observed that the quotations from the Gospel history in the early Fathers are almost uniformly anonymous; the words of Christ were as a living voice in the Church, apart from any written record. Justin likewise habitually represents Christ as speaking, and not the Evangelist as relating, his discourses; but he is the first who distinctly refers to what he calls "The Memoirs of the Apostles," in which he found written "all things concerning Jesus Christ."

The peculiar objects which he had in view in his extant writings did not suggest, even if they did not exclude, any minute description of these records. It would have added nothing to the vivid picture of Christianity which he drew for the heathen to have quoted with exact precision the testimony of this or that apostle, even if such a mode of quotation had been usual. One thing they might require to know, and that he tells them that the words of Christ were still the text of Christian instruction, that the "Memoirs of the Apostles" were still read, together with the writings of the prophets, in their weekly services, (Ap., i, 87.) So, on the other hand, the great difficulty in a controversy with a Jew was to show that the humiliation and death of Christ were reconcilable with the Messianic prophecies. The chief facts were here confessed; and in other points it was enough for the apologist to assert, generally, that the Memoirs which he quoted rested upon apostolic authority, (Dial., c. 103.) The manner in which Justin alludes to the Memoirs of the Apostles in his first Apology, and in his Dialogue with Trypho, confirms what has just been said. If his mode of reference were not modified by the nature of the subject, it would surely have been the same in both. As it is, there is a marked difference, and exactly such as might have been expected. In the Apology, which contains nearly fifty allusions to the Gospel history, he speaks only twice of the apostolic authorship of his Memoirs, and in one other place mentions them generally. (Ap., i, 86; 87; 33.) In the Dialogue, which contains about seventy allusions, he quotes them ten times as "the Memoirs of the Apostles," and in five other places as "the Memoirs."

This difference is still more striking if examined closely. Every quotation of our Lord's words in the Apology is simply introduced by the phrases, "Thus Christ said," or "taught," or "exhorted." His words were their own witness. For the public events of his life Justin refers to the Enrollment of Quirinius, and the Acts of Pilate. He quotes the "Gospels" only when he must speak of things beyond the range of common history. Standing before a Roman emperor as the apologist of the Christians, he confines himself, as far as possible, to common ground; and if he is compelled for illustration to quote the books of the Christians, he takes care to show that they were recognized by the Church, and no private documents of his own. Thus, in speaking of the Annunciation, he says: "And the angel of God, sent to the Virgin at that season, announced to her glad tidings, saying, Behold thou shalt conceive of the Holy Spirit, and bear a son, and he shall be called the Son of the Highest; and thou shalt call his name Jesus, for he shall save his people from their sins, as those who have written memoirs of all things concerning our Savior Jesus Christ taught us, whom we believed, since also the prophetic Spirit said that this would come to pass." (Ap., i, 33.) So, again, when explaining the celebration of the Eucharist, he adds: "The apostles, in the Memoirs made by them, which are called Gospels, have handed down that it was thus enjoined on them." (Ap., i, 66.) And once more, when describing the Christian service, he notices that "the Memoirs of the Apostles, or the writings of the prophets, are read as long as the time admits." (Ap., i, 67.)

There is no further mention of the Memoirs in the Apology. In the Dialogue the case was somewhat different. Trypho was himself acquainted with the Gospel, (Dial., c. 10,) and Justin's language becomes proportionally more exact. The words of our Lord are still quoted very often, simply as His words, without any acknowledgment of a written record; but from time to time, when reference is made to words of more special moment, so to speak, it is added that they are so "written in the Gospel." In one passage the contrast between the substance of Christ's teaching and the record of it is brought out very clearly. After speaking of the death of John the Baptist, Justin adds: "Wherefore also our Christ when on earth told those who said that Elias must come before Christ: 'Elias indeed will come, and will restore all things; but I say to you that Elias has come already, and they knew him not, but did to him whatsoever they listed.' And it is written, 'Then understood the disciples that he spake to them concerning John the Baptist.'" (Dial., c. 49; Matt. xvii, 13.) In another place it appears that Justin refers particularly to one out of the Memoirs. "The mention of the fact," he says, "that Christ changed the name of Peter, one of the apostles, and that the event has been written in his (Peter's) Memoirs, together with His having changed the name of two other brethren, who were sons of Zebedee, to that of Boanerges, tended to signify that He was the same through whom the surname Israel was given to Jacob, and Joshua to Hoshea." (Dial., c. 106; Mark iii, 16, 17.) Now, the surname given to James and John is only found at present in one of our Gospels, and there it is mentioned in immediate connection with the change of Peter's name. That Gospel is the Gospel of Mark, which, by the universal voice of antiquity, was referred to the authority of Peter. That Justin found in his Memoirs facts at present peculiar to Luke's narrative, is equally clear. "And Jesus, as he gave up his spirit upon the cross," he writes, "said, Father, into thy hands I commend my spirit, as I learned from the Memoirs."

But this is not all: in his Apology, Justin speaks of the Memoirs generally as written by the apostles. In the Dialogue his words are more precise: "In the Memoirs, which I say were composed by the apostles and those who followed them, [it is written] that sweat as drops (of blood) streamed down (from Jesus), as He was praying and saying, Let this cup, if it be possible, pass away from me." The description, it will be seen, precedes the quotation of a passage found in Luke, the follower of an apostle, and not an apostle himself. Some such fact as this is needed to explain why Justin distinguishes at this particular time the authorship of the records which he used. And no short account would apply more exactly to our present Gospels than that which he gives. Two of them were written by apostles, two by their followers. There were many apocryphal gospels, but it is not known that any one of them bore the name of a follower of the apostles. The application of Justin's words to our Gospels seems indeed absolutely necessary when they are compared with those of Tertullian, who says, (Adv. Marcion, iv, 2:) "We lay down as a principle, first, that the Evangelic Instrument has apostles for its authors, on whom this charge of publishing the Gospel was imposed by the Lord himself: that if [it includes the writings of] apostolic men also, still they were not alone, but [wrote] with [the help of] apostles and after [the teachings of] apostles. . . . . In fine, John and Matthew out of the number of the apostles implant faith in us, Luke and Mark out of the number of their followers refresh it." This, then, is the sum of what Justin says of the Memoirs of the apostles. They were many, and yet one: they were called gospels: they contained a record of all things concerning Jesus Christ: they were admitted by Christians generally: they were read in their public services: they were of apostolic authority, though not exclusively of apostolic authorship: they were composed in part by apostles, and in part by their followers. And further than this, we gather that they related facts only mentioned at present by one or other of the Evangelists: that thus they were intimately connected with each one of the synoptic Gospels: that they contained nothing, as far as Justin expressly quotes them, which our Gospels do not now substantially contain. Up to this point of our inquiry the identification of his Memoirs with our Gospels seems to be as reasonable as it is natural. But on the other hand, it is said that there are objections to this identification; first, that Justin no where mentions the Evangelists by name. It has been already shown that there were peculiar circumstances in Justin's case which rendered any definite quotation of the Evangelists unlikely and unsuitable, even if such a mode of quotation had been common at the time. But in fact, when he referred to written records of Christ's life and words he made an advance beyond which the later Apologists rarely proceeded. Tatian, his scholar, has several allusions to passages contained in the Gospels of Matthew and John, but they are all anonymous. Athenagoras quotes the words of our Lord, as they stand in Matthew, four times, and appears to allude to passages in Mark and John, but he no where mentions the name of an Evangelist. Theophilus, in his books to Autolycus, cites five or six precepts from "the Gospel," or the "Evangelic Voice," and once only mentions John as "a man moved by the Holy Spirit," quoting the prologue to his Gospel; though he elsewhere classes the Evangelists with the prophets as all inspired by the same Spirit. The usage of Tertullian is very remarkable. In his other books he quotes the Gospels continually, and, though rarely, mentions every Evangelist by name; but in his Apology, while he gives a general view of Christ's life and teaching, and speaks of the Scriptures as the food and the comfort of the Christian, he no where cites the Gospels, and scarcely exhibits any coincidence of language with them. Clement of Alexandria, as is well known, investigated the relation of the synoptic Gospels to that of John, and his use of the words of Scripture is constant and extensive; and yet in his "Exhortation to Gentiles," while he quotes every Gospel, and all, except Mark, repeatedly, he only mentions John by name, and that but once. (Protrep., § 59.) Cyprian, in his address to Demetrian, quotes words of our Lord as given by Matthew and John, but says nothing of the source from which he derived them. At a still later time Lactantius blamed Cyprian for quoting Scripture in a controversy with a heathen; and though he shows in his Institutions an intimate acquaintance with the writings of the Evangelists, he mentions John only by name, quoting the beginning of his Gospel. Arnobius, again, makes no allusion to the Gospels; and Eusebius, to whose zeal we owe most of what is known of the history of the New Testament, though he quotes the Gospels eighteen times in his "Introduction to Christian Evidences," (Præparatio Evangelica,) yet always does so without referring to the Evangelist of whose writings he made use.

It has been objected, secondly, that Justin's citations differ considerably from the corresponding passages in the Gospels. But they differ simply from his having sometimes combined two passages from different Gospels into one, or from his having given the substance of the passage rather than the exact words; for both of which practices he has the example of the apostle Paul in his citations from the Old Testament. Such modes of dealing with books are common to writers of all ages; and, as Justin exhibits the same practice in reference to the Old Testament, and to profane writers, it is groundless to urge the trifling discrepancies which exist between his quotations and the received text of the Evangelists as any evidence that it was not from them he quoted.*

The last—and, if it could be substantiated, the most weighty—objection to our identifying Justin's Memoirs of the Apostles with our four Gospels is the allegation, that he introduced apocryphal additions into his narrative. Some of his quotations, it is said, exhibit coincidences with fragments of heretical gospels. That quotations made by memory from the written Gospels should exhibit some points of partial resemblance to apocryphal gospels is very natural. For these apocryphal gospels were not mere creations of the imagination, but narratives based on the original oral Gospel, of which the written Gospel was the authoritative record. The same cause might, therefore, very naturally lead to the introduction of a common word, a characteristic phrase, or a supplementary trait. But it is further objected that Justin's quotations differ not only in language, but also in substance, from our Gospels; that he attributes sayings to our Lord which they do not contain, and narrates events which are either not mentioned by the Evangelists, or recorded by them with serious variations from his account. It is enough to

*All the quotations of Justin have been subjected to a thorough critical examination by Mr. Westcott in his "Canon," a work not published in this country, and to which we are indebted for most of the historical testimonies contained in this Part.

answer, that he never does so when he proposes to quote the Apostolic Memoirs. Like other early Fathers, he was familiar by tradition with the words of our Lord which are not embodied in the Gospel. Like them, he may have been acquainted with details of His life treasured up by such as the elder of Ephesus, who might have heard John. But whatever use he makes of this knowledge, he never refers to the Apostolic Memoirs for any thing which is not substantially found in our Gospels.

Justin's account of the baptism, which might seem an exception to this statement, really confirms and explains it. It is well known that there was a belief long current, that the heavenly voice addressed our Lord in the words of the Psalm, which have ever been applied to him: "Thou art my Son; this day have I begotten thee." Augustine mentions the reading as current in his time; and the words are found at present in the Cambridge MS., (D,) and in the old Latin version. Justin might then have found them in the MS. of Luke, which he used; but the form of his reference is remarkable. When speaking of the temptation he says: "For the devil, of whom I just now spoke, as soon as he [Christ] went up from the River Jordan,—when the voice had been addressed to him, 'Thou art my Son; this day have I begotten thee,'—is described in the Memoirs of the Apostles as having come to him and tempted him, so far as to say to him, Worship me." The definite quotation is of that which is confessedly a part of the Evangelic text; it is evident, from the construction of the sentence, that Justin gives no authority for the disputed clause.

This apparent mixture of two narratives is still

more remarkable in the mode in which Justin introduces the famous legend of the fire kindled in Jordan when Christ descended into the water: "When Jesus came to the Jordan, where John was baptizing, when he descended to the water, both a fire was kindled in the Jordan, and the apostles of Christ himself recorded that the Holy Spirit as a dove lighted upon him." Here the contrast is complete. The witness of the apostles is claimed for that which our Gospels relate; but Justin affirms, on his own authority, a fact which, however significant in the symbolism of the East, is yet without any support from the canonical history.

Justin lived at the period of transition from a traditional to a written Gospel, and his testimony is exactly fitted to the position which he held. He refers to books, but more frequently he appears to bring forward words which were currently circulated rather than what he had privately read. In both respects his witness to our Gospels is most important. For it has been shown that his definite quotations from the Memoirs are so exactly accordant with the text of the Synoptists, as it stands now, or as it was read at the close of the second century, that there can be no doubt that he was familiar with their writings as well as with the contents of them. And the wide and minute agreement of what he says of the life and teachings of our Lord with what they record of it, proves that his knowledge of the Gospel history was derived from a tradition they had molded and controlled, if not from the habitual and exclusive use of the books themselves.

He states in his First Apology, (A. D. 138,) that "the Memoirs of the Apostles," called Gospels, " were read every Sunday in the Christian assemblies in connection with the writings of the prophets." Now, who can suppose that in Justin's time other Gospels besides our own—which latter we know, with absolute certainty, that they were acknowledged as sacred and canonical a few decades after Justin—could have been in the sacred use of the Church? Is it possible to suppose, that within twenty or thirty years after his death, these Gospels should have been replaced by others similar and yet distinct? that he should speak of one set of books, as if they were permanently incorporated into the Christian services, and that those who might have been his scholars should speak exactly in the same terms of another collection, as if they had had no rivals within the orthodox pale? that the substitution should have been effected in such a manner that no record of it has been preserved, while smaller analogous reforms have been duly chronicled? The complication of historical difficulties is overwhelming; and the alternative is that which has already been justified on critical grounds, the belief that when Justin spoke of apostolic memoirs or gospels, he meant the Gospels which were enumerated in the early anonymous canon, and whose mutual relations were eloquently expounded by Irenæus.

This, then, appears to be established, both by external and internal evidence, that Justin's "gospels" can be identified with those of Matthew, Mark, and Luke. If his references to John are not so frequent, this follows from the character of the fourth Gospel. It was unlikely that he should quote its peculiar teaching in apologetic writings addressed to Jews and heathen; and at the same time he exhibits types of language and doctrine which, if not immediately drawn from John, yet mark the presence of his influence and the recognition of his authority. The sentence, which is entirely peculiar to John, "And the Word was made flesh," reappears unmistakably in several passages. The answer which, according to Justin, the Baptist gives to the interrogating messengers of the Jews, "I am not Christ, but the voice of a preacher," is a clear quotation from John i, 20, 23. The words of the prophet Zachariah, (xii, 10,) John quotes in a manner no where else to be found; and since Justin does the same, he must be considered dependent upon John. Finally, we find in Justin's First Apology (A. D. 138) the following: "Christ has said, Except ye be born again, ye can not enter the kingdom of heaven. But that it is impossible that those who have once been born should enter again into their mother's womb, is clear to every man." This is certainly a plain reference to our Lord's conversation with Nicodemus in John iii.

In addition to the Gospels, the Apocalypse is the only book of the New Testament to which Justin alludes by name. Even that is not quoted, but appealed to generally, as a proof of the existence of prophetic power in the Christian Church. But it can not be concluded from his silence that Justin was either unacquainted with the Acts and the Epistles, or unwilling to make use of them. His controversy against Marcion is decisive as to his knowledge of the greater part of the books, and various Pauline forms of expression and teaching show that the apostle of the Gentiles had helped to mold his faith and words.

§ 10. The Formation of a Canon of the Universally-Acknowledged Books of the New Testament at the Close of the Second Century.

The Latin fragment on the Canon, first published by Muratori, was discovered in the Ambrosian Library at Milan in a MS. of great antiquity, which purported to contain the writings of Chrysostom. It is mutilated both at the beginning and end; and is disfigured throughout by gross inaccuracies and barbarisms, due in part to the ignorance of the transcriber, and in part to the translator of the original text; for there can be little doubt that it is a version from the Greek. But, notwithstanding these defects, it is of the greatest interest and importance. That this catalogue was written soon after the time of the Roman Bishop Pius, (A. D. 142–157,) consequently about A. D. 170, and in all probability at Rome, we may infer from the fact that the author of the catalogue says: "The Shepherd was written *very lately, in our time*, by Hermes, in the city of Rome, while Pius, his brother, occupied the Episcopal Chair." Internal evidence fully confirms its claims to this high antiquity; and it may be regarded, on the whole, as a summary of the opinion of the Western Church on the Canon shortly after the middle of the second century. The fragment commences with the last words of a sentence which evidently referred to the Gospel of Mark. The Gospel of Luke, it is then said, stands third in order—in the Christian Canon—having been written by "Luke the physician," the companion of Paul, who, not being an eye-witness, based his narrative on such information as he could obtain, beginning from the birth of John. The fourth place is given to the Gospel of John. Though there is no trace of any reference to Matthew, it is impossible not to believe that it occupied the first place among the four Gospels of the anonymous writer. Assuming this, it is of importance to notice that he regards our canonical Gospels as essentially one in purpose, contents, and inspiration. He draws no distinction between those which were written from personal knowledge, and those which rested on the teaching of others. He alludes to no doubt as to their authority, no limit as to their reception, no difference as to their usefulness. "Though various points are taught in each of the Gospels, it makes no difference to the faith of believers, since, in all of them, all things are declared by one informing Spirit concerning the nativity, the passion, the resurrection, the conversation [of our Lord] with his disciples, and his double advent, at first in humility, and afterward in royal power as he will yet appear." This first recognition of the distinctness and unity of the Gospels, of their origin from human care and Divine guidance, is as complete as any later testimony. The fragment lends no support to the theory which supposes that they were gradually separated from the mass of similar books. Their peculiar position is clear and marked; and there is not the slightest hint that it was gained after a doubtful struggle or only at a late date. Admit that our Gospels were regarded from the first as authoritative records of Christ's life, and then this new testimony explains and confirms the fragmentary notices which alone witness to the earlier belief; deny it, and the language of one who had probably conversed with Polycarp at Rome becomes an unintelligible riddle.

Irenæus died as a martyr A. D. 202. About the year 177 he succeeded Photinus in the Bishopric of Lyons. In his youth he had sat at the feet of the venerable, aged Polycarp, who in his time had been a disciple of the Evangelist John, and he had, moreover, been acquainted with other eye-witnesses of the Gospel history. In his letter to Florinus, (see Euseb. Hist., Eccl. v, 20,) he thus writes: "I saw thee, when I was yet young, with Polycarp, in Asia Minor, when thou wast living in the splendor of the Imperial Court, and wast at pains to secure his approbation. For what happened at that period I remember better than what has recently occurred. That which we receive in youth grows with ourselves, and clings to us firmly. And so I am able now to tell where the blessed Polycarp sat in his addresses; how he came in and went out; how he lived, and how he looked; what discourses he held to the people; how he spoke of his intimate intercourse with John, and with others who had seen the Lord, and quoted their own discourses; how he rehearsed what he had heard from those who, with their own eyes, had seen the Light of the World, in full agreement with the Scripture."

Surely, the testimony of Irenæus on the authenticity of our Gospels, involving that of Polycarp, must, in the judgment of every sober-minded, candid critic, far outweigh all the scruples raised by skepticism. In his work against the heretics he availed himself throughout of our Gospels, naming each Evangelist. The number of passages in which this is done amounts, according to Tischendorf, to about four hundred, of which more than eighty are quotations from the Gospel of John. He, moreover, expressly asserts that there exist, of necessity, *four* Gospels, precisely four, neither more nor less, comparing this fact with the four quarters of the globe, the four principal winds, the four faces of the cherubim. He says, the four Gospels are the four pillars of the Church spread over the earth's surface, recognizing in their quadruplicity a special decree of the Creator. Such a testimony is utterly irreconcilable with the notion that our Gospels *began* to acquire their authority in the time of Irenæus himself, and that to the three elder a latter fourth was at that time striving to attach itself. It is asserted by the Critical School of Baur that the Gospel of John made its first appearance about the year 150, and that Polycarp never spoke of it to Irenæus. If this were the case, how is it conceivable that Irenæus should have believed this work, which appeared as the most sublime legacy of John to the Christian Church, to be genuine, and should have employed it as a sacred and safe weapon in his conflict with men who dealt in corrupt scriptures and apocryphal writings? Though Irenæus has not given us a professed catalogue of the books of the New Testament, we learn from his treatise that he received, as authentic and canonical Scriptures, not only the four Gospels, but also the Acts of the Apostles, the Epistle to the Romans, the Epistles to the Galatians, Ephesians, Philippians, and Colossians, the First and Second Epistles to the Thessalonians, the two Epistles to Timothy, the Epistle to Titus, the two Epistles of Peter, and the First and Second Epistles of John. Can it be supposed, with reason, that forgeries came into use in the time of Irenæus, which he must have been able to detect by his own knowledge? that they were received without suspicion or reserve in the Church over which he presided? Is it possible that he decided otherwise than his first master, when he speaks of the tradition of the apostles by which the canon of the Scripture was determined? (Adv. Hær., iv, 33, 8.) He appeals to the known succession of teachers in the Churches of Rome, Smyrna, and Ephesus, who held fast, up to his own time, the doctrine which they had received from the first age; and is it possible that he used writings, as authentic and authoritative, which were not recognized by those who must have had unquestionable means of deciding on their apostolic origin?

A cotemporary of Irenæus was Clement of Alexandria; he was trained in the school of Pantænus, who was personally connected with some immediate disciples of the apostles. He distinguishes the Gospel from the other writings of the New Testament, which he calls *ὁ ἀπόστολος*, and sometimes *ἀπόστολοι*, but combines them "as Scriptures of the Lord," with the Law and the Prophets, and as "ratified by the authority of one Almighty Power."

Tertullian, a presbyter of the Church of Carthage, was born 160, and died about the year 220. He became a Montanist about the year 200. But his testimony to the authority of the canonical Scriptures is exactly the same before and after he embraced the tenets of Montanus. In his numerous works, we find many hundred passages of our Gospels cited as decisive proof-texts; from the Gospel of John alone, over two hundred. He uniformly recognizes the four Gospels as written by the Evangelists to whom we ascribe them; distinguishing Matthew and John as apostles, and Mark and Luke as apostolical men, and asserting the authority of their writings as inspired books, acknowledged by the Christian Church from their original date. (Adv. Marcion, I, c. iv, 2.) He notices particularly the introduction of the word *Testament* for the earlier word "*Instrument*," as applied to the dispensation and the record, (Adv. Marcion, iv, 1,) and appeals to the New Testament, as made up of "the Gospels" and "Apostles." (Adv. Prax., 15.) This comprehensive testimony extends to the four Gospels, the Acts, 1 Peter, 1 John, thirteen Epistles of Paul, and the Apocalypse. "Tertullian," remarks Dr. Tischendorf, "presents an irrefragable principle by which the truth of the several parts of the Christian Canon and—a point on which he insists most earnestly—the genuineness of the apostolic writings are to be tested. He shows and demands that a testimony which now passes for truth should bear this test: that it was regarded as truth in former days; that from this previous authority we are to ascend to the apostles themselves; but that apostolic genuineness is to be measured by the testimony of the Apostolic Churches, the Churches which were founded by the apostles in person. (See Adv. Marcion, iv, 5.) Is it at all credible that this acute man should have fallen into an uncritical carelessness just at this point; his reception, namely, and defense of the genuineness of the four Gospels? The passages just referred to are in his famous work against Marcion, who, following the bent of his heretical humor, had arbitrarily tampered with the Evangelical text. Of the four Gospels he had entirely suppressed three, and in the fourth, Luke, he had made such changes as suited him. Now Tertullian, in his work against him, appeals expressly to the testimony of the Apostolic Churches for the four collective Gospels. Is this assurance in the mouth of a man like Tertullian to pass for nothing? At the time when he wrote it, scarcely more than a hundred years had yet passed since the death of John. At that time the testimony of the Apostolic Church of Ephesus, to which he appeals—a Church in which John had long labored, and in whose bosom he died—was, in fact, perfectly decisive, as touching the genuineness or the spuriousness of the Gospel of John; and the task of ascertaining the judgment and testimony of this Church was perfectly easy. In this connection, it is a point not to be overlooked that we have not here to do with a mere man of letters, dealing in learned observations, but with a man with whom this was a question of deep and holy solemnity touching his faith; yea, touching the salvation of his soul. The foundation Scriptures of Christianity, claiming for themselves an apostolic origin, books which even at that time awoke the universal opposition of that wordlly wisdom, from whose school Tertullian himself had proceeded, is it possible to believe that he would have accepted these books with an unscrupulous credulity? But now, since he, in addition, expressly assures us that in his decisive defense of the apostolic origin of all four of the Gospels, he goes back to the warrant of the Apostolic Churches, it would plainly fall into the category of contemptible quibbling, to pretend to cherish doubts touching his conscientious investigation of the apostolic origin of the Gospels."

All the Fathers, at the close of the second century, from opposite quarters of Christendom, agree in appealing to the testimony of antiquity as proving the authenticity of the Gospels, and other books which they used as Christian Scriptures. The appeal was made at a time when it was easy to try its worth. The links which connected them with the apostolic age were few and well known; and, if they had not been continuous, it would have been easy to expose the break. But their appeal was never gainsayed. We need, therefore, not descend to later testimonies.

Let us, in conclusion, bear in mind that the admitted universal reception of the Gospels, toward the close of the second century, conveys to us the testimony of a communion not only fully qualified to arrive at a sound judgment on the authenticity of the Gospels, but also deeply interested in ascertaining the truth upon the question at issue, inasmuch as the early Christians, by believing the Gospels to be the authentic productions of the men whose names they bear, exposed themselves to the fiercest persecutions—from which it follows that they must have come to them with an evidence of their authenticity such as could not be gainsayed.

§ 11. The Early Versions of the New Testament.

Of the utmost importance is the fact that already in the second half of the second century our four Gospels had received a common translation into Latin, as well as into Syriac.

THE PESHITO.

Almost universal opinion assigns the Peshito, or "simple" Syriac, (Aramaic,) version to the most remote Christian antiquity. The Syriac Christians of Malabar even now claim for it the right to be considered as an Eastern original of the New Testament;

and though their tradition is wholly unsupported by external evidence, it is not, to a certain extent, without all plausibility. The dialect of the Peshito, even as it stands now, represents in part, at least, that form of Aramaic which was current in Palestine. In this respect it is like the Latin Vulgate, which, though revised, is marked by the provincialisms of Africa. Both versions appear to have had their origin in districts where their languages were spoken in impure dialects, and afterward to have been corrected and brought nearer to the classical standard. In the absence of an adequate supply of critical materials it is impossible to construct the history of these recensions in the Syriac; the analogy of the Latin is at present our only guide. But if a conjecture be allowed, it is probable that the various facts of the case are adequately explained by supposing that versions of separate books of the New Testament were first made and used in Palestine, perhaps within the apostolic age, and that shortly afterward these were collected, revised, and completed at Edessa. Many circumstances combine to give support to this belief. The early condition of the Syrian Church, its wide extent and active vigor, lead us to expect that a version of the Holy Scriptures into the common dialect could not have been long deferred; and the existence of an Aramaic Gospel was in itself likely to suggest the work. Differences of style, no less than the very nature of the case, point to separate translations of different books; and, at the same time, a certain general uniformity of character bespeaks some subsequent revision. Whatever may be thought of the alleged intercourse of Abgarus with our blessed Lord, Edessa itself is signalized in early Church history by many remarkable facts. It was called the "holy" and "blessed" city, (Horæ Syriacæ;) its inhabitants were said to have been brought over by Thaddeus, in a marvelous manner, to the Christian faith; and, "from that time forth," Eusebius adds, (Euseb., H. E., ii, 1,) "the whole people of Edessa has continued to be devoted to the name of Christ, exhibiting no ordinary instance of the goodness of the Savior;" in the seaond century it became the center of an important Christian school, and long afterward retained its preëminence among the cities of this province. As might be expected, tradition fixes on Edessa as the place whence the Peshito took its rise. Gregory Bar Hebræus, one of the most learned and accurate of Syrian writers, relates that the New Testament Peshito was "made in the time of Thaddeus, and Abgarus, King of Edessa;" when, according to the universal opinion of ancient writers, the apostle went to proclaim Christianity in Mesopotamia.

No other direct historical evidence remains to determine the date of the Peshito; and it is impossible to supply the deficiency by the help of quotations occurring in early Syrian writers. No Syrian works of a very early period exist. Still it is known that books were soon translated from Syriac into Greek, and while such an intercourse existed it is scarcely possible that the Scriptures remained untranslated. Again, the controversial writings of Bardesanes necessarily imply the existence of a Syriac version of the Bible. Tertullian's example may show that he could hardly have refuted Marcion without the constant use of Scripture. And more than this, Eusebius tells us that Hegesippus "made quotations from the Gospel according to the Hebrews, and especially from [writings in] the Hebrew language, showing thereby that he was a Christian of Hebrew descent." (Euseb., H. E., iv, 22.) This testimony is valuable as coming from the only Greek writer likely to have been familiar with Syriac literature: and may we not see in the two Gospels thus mentioned, two recensions of Matthew—the one disfigured by apocryphal traditions, and the one written in the dialect of Eastern Syria? Ephrem Syrus, himself a deacon of Edessa, treats the version in such a manner as to prove that it was already old in the fourth century. He quotes it as a book of established authority, calling it "Our Version;" he speaks of the "Translator" as one whose words were familiar, (Horæ Syriacæ;) and, though the dialects of the East are proverbially permanent, his explanations show that its language, even in his time, had become partially obsolete. Another circumstance serves to exhibit the venerable age of this version. It was universally received by the different sects into which the Syrian Church was divided in the fourth century, and so has continued current even to the present time. The respect in which the Peshito was held was further shown by the fact that it was taken as the basis of other versions in the East. The text, even in its present corrupt state, exhibits remarkable agreement with the most ancient Greek MSS., and the earliest quotations. The very obscurity which hangs over its origin is a proof of its venerable age, because it shows that it grew up spontaneously among Christian congregations, and was not the result of any public labor. It is almost universally referred to the end of the second century, but some competent scholars have fixed its date within the first half of the second century.

THE OLD LATIN VERSION.

At first it is natural to look to Italy as the center of the Latin literature of Christianity, and the original source of that Latin version of the Holy Scriptures which, in a later form, has become identified with the Church of Rome, yet, however natural such a belief may be, it finds no support in history. Rome itself, under the emperors, was well described as a "Greek city;" and Greek was its second language. As far as we can learn, the mass of the poorer population—every-where the great bulk of the early Christians—was Greek, either in descent or in speech. Among the names of the fifteen bishops of Rome, up to the close of the second century, four only are Latin; but in the next century the proportion is nearly reversed. When Paul first wrote to the Roman Church he wrote in Greek; and in the long list of salutation to its members, with which the Epistle is concluded, only four Latin names occur. Shortly afterward, Clement wrote to the Corinthians in Greek in the name of the Church of Rome; and at a later date we find the bishop of Corinth writing in Greek to Soter, the ninth in succession from Clement. Justin, Hermas, and Tatian published their Greek treatises at Rome. The Apologies to the Roman emperors were in Greek. Modestus, Caius, and Asterius Urbanus bear Latin names, yet their writings were Greek. Meanwhile, however, though Greek continued to be the natural, if not the sole language of the Roman Church, the seeds of Latin Christianity were rapidly developing in Africa. Nothing is known in detail of the origin of the African Churches. At the close of the second century Christians were found in that country in every place and of every rank. They who were but of yesterday, Tertullian says about the year 200, (Apol., i, 37,) already fill the palace, the senate, the forum, and the camp, and leave their temples only to the heathen. To persecute the Christians was even then to decimate Carthage. These fresh conquests of the Roman Church preserved their distinct nationality in their language. Carthage—the second Rome—escaped the Graecism of the first. In Africa Greek was no longer a current dialect. A peculiar form of Latin, vigorous, elastic, and copious, however far removed from the grace and eloquence of a classical standard, fitly expressed the spirit of Tertullian. It is, then, to Africa we must look for the first traces of the "Itala." "Before the end of the second century it had already acquired," says Tischendorf, "a degree of public authority for the Latin translator of the great Greek work of Irenæus *against the heretics,* who is to be placed at about the close of the second century—and this translator is followed by Tertullian in his citations from Irenæus—as well as Tertullian himself, at the close of the same century, follow the text of the Itala. This authority of the Latin translation of the Gospels, at the end of the second century, necessarily presupposes that at that time it had an age of several decades of years." Not only is the character of the version itself a proof of its great antiquity, but the mutual relations of different parts of it show that it was made originally by different hands; and if so, that it was coeval with the introduction of Christianity into Africa, and the result of the spontaneous efforts of African Christians.

§ 12. The Testimony of Apocryphal and Heretical Writings.

Before we inquire into the relation which the heretical and apocryphal writings bear to our canonical Gospels, let us take a survey of the heretical sects which arose in the first two centuries, and their relation to the great body of Christians called the Catholic Christians, or the Catholic Church. They may be arranged under two great principles: "That well-known pharisaical Judaism whose shibboleth was that the Gentiles should be constrained to observe the ceremonial law, and which continued to attack Paul in his missionary labors, produced *Ebionism*, in the general sense of this term; the desire to amalgamate with Christianity Grecian and Oriental theosophy, and an opposition to Judaism, inclusive of the Old Testament, on the part of Gentile philosophers converted to Christianity, introduced *Gnosticism*. These two directions were, however, also combined into a Gnostic-Ebionism, a system for which the doctrines of the Essenes seem to have served as a point of transition and connecting link. This 'opposition of science falsely so called' (1 Tim. vi, 20) began to intrude into Christianity during the latter years of Paul's labors. Against it Paul uttered a prophetic warning in his farewell address at Miletus. (Acts xx, 29, 30.) Afterward he opposed it in the Epistles to the Ephesians and to the Colossians, and especially in his pastoral letters, even as Peter combated it in his First Epistle. It assumed many and varied forms. It appeared in the shape of Oriental theosophy, magic, and theurgy, in voluntary asceticism with reference to meats and marriage, in fancied mysteries about the nature and subordination of heavenly powers and spirits, and in the transformation of certain fundamental doctrines of Christianity—such as that of the resurrection, 2 Tim. ii, 18—into a mere idealism. These seeds of evil had already borne abundant fruit when John came to take up his residence in Asia Minor. Accordingly, in his First Epistle, the apostle opposed the growing heresy, and more especially that form of Gnosis, in which the incarnation of God in Christ was denied." (See Kurtz's Church History, pp. 71 and 72.)

The *Ebionites* proper—as distinguished from the Nazarenes, who, though they held themselves bound still to observe the ceremonial law, believed in the Divinity of Christ, and did not reject Paul entirely—deemed the observance of the ceremonial law indispensably necessary for salvation; they saw in Jesus nothing but a human Messiah, whom, at his baptism, God had endowed with supernatural powers. His Messianic activity they limited to his teaching, by which he had enlarged and perfected the law, adding to it new and more strict commandments. The death of Christ was an offense to them, under which they consoled themselves with the promise of his return, when they expected that he would set up a terrestrial kingdom. They, of course, repudiated the apostle Paul entirely, and in order to have some basis for their monstrous heresies, they *mutilated and interpolated the Gospel of Matthew.* A similar position to the Gospels was taken by the *Gnostics.* Though their doctrines were as irreconcilable with the contents of our Gospels as those of the Ebionites, they did not assail their authenticity, but rejected them only as carnal apprehensions of Jesus and his doctrine, while

Marcion boldly *mutilated the Gospel of Luke*, and declared this to be the only true Gospel. With regard to the evidence the Gnostics give for the authenticity of our Gospels, they may be divided into two principal classes: the theosophic (or Valentinian) Gnostics, and the Marcionites.

Now, if it can be proved that the theosophic Gnostics appealed to our canonical Gospels as freely and confidently as did the Catholic Christians, that they did not pretend to possess any Gospel, in any way contradictory to the account of Christ's ministry contained in our Gospels, and that the Gospel used by the Marcionites was essentially the same with that of Luke, we have an argument of uncommon strength in favor of the authenticity of our Gospels. For these early heretics were, in their opinions and feelings, so widely separated from the Catholic Christians, that they present themselves as an independent class of witnesses, and they lived at a time, when, upon the supposition that our Gospels were not written by the authors whose names they bear, it must have been very easy to them to prove the fact. Could they have rejected the authority of the Gospels *on this ground*, they would certainly have done it. And had they done so, it is altogether incredible that the fact should not have been conspicuous throughout the controversial writings of Irenæus and Tertullian, the two principal writers against the Gnostics. From their works it does not appear that the Valentinians, the Marcionites, or any other Gnostic sect, adduced *in support of their opinions* a single narrative relating to the public ministry of Christ, besides what is found in the Gospels, or that any sect appealed to the authority of any history of our Lord's ministry besides the

Gospels, except so far as the Marcionites, in their use of the interpolated and mutilated copy of Luke's Gospel, may be regarded as forming a verbal exception. The Fathers were eager to urge against the Gnostics the charge of corrupting and perverting the Scriptures, and of fabricating apocryphal writings, but they never brought forward the far graver allegation, that the Gnostics pretended to set up other histories of Christ *in opposition to those received* by the great body of Christians. Had they been guilty of this, the fact neither would nor could have remained unnoticed. On the contrary, Irenæus says: "There is such assurance concerning the Gospels, that the heretics themselves bear testimony to them, so that each one of them, taking the Gospels as his starting-point, endeavors thereby to maintain his own teaching." (Adv. Hær., III, xii, 7.) And Tertullian says: "They profess to appeal to the Scriptures; they urge arguments from the Scriptures—as if they could draw arguments about matters of faith from any other source than the records of faith." (De Præscr. Hær., c. xiv.) He takes in this treatise, moreover, especial pains to prove that they had no right at all to appeal to the Scriptures as they do.

But the question naturally arises, how could the Gnostics defend their strange doctrines, and yet appeal to our Gospels? This important question is more fully answered by Mr. Norton than by any other writer on this subject. We will, therefore, give to the reader the benefit of a brief condensation of his argument: 1. The theosophic Gnostics, in common with the Catholic Christians, applied the allegorical mode of interpretation to the New Testament. Neglecting the proper meaning of words, they educed from them mystical senses. Their whole system of interpretation was, besides, arbitrary, and unsupported by any correct principle. The vocabulary of the theosophic Gnostics, like that of other erring sects, consisted, in great part, of words from the New Testament, on which they had imposed new senses. It thus became easy for them, on the one hand, to find supposed references to their theory; and, on the other, to explain away much that was inconsistent with it. Like other false expositors of Scripture, they detached particular passages from their connection, and infused a foreign meaning into the words. Irenæus, after saying they appealed to unwritten tradition as a source of their knowledge, goes on to remark, that, "twisting, according to the proverb, a rope of sand, they endeavor to accommodate, in a plausible manner to their doctrines, the parables of the Lord, the declarations of the prophets, or the words of the apostles, so that their fiction may not seem to be without proof. But they neglect the order and connection of the Scriptures, and disjoin, so far as they are able, the members of the truth. They transpose and refashion, and, making one thing out of another, they deceive many by a fabricated show of the words of the Lord which they put together. (Cont. Hæres., lib. I, c. viii, § 1.) 2. They maintained a principle similar to a fundamental doctrine of the Roman Catholics; namely, that religious truth could not be learned from the Scriptures alone, without the aid of the oral instructions of Christ and his apostles, as preserved by tradition. "When," says Irenæus, "they are confuted by proofs from the Scriptures, they turn and accuse the Scriptures themselves, as if they were not correct, nor of authority;

they say that they contain contradictions, and that the truth can not be discovered from them by those who are ignorant of tradition. For that it was not delivered in writing, but orally; whence Paul said, 'We speak wisdom among the perfect, but not the wisdom of this world.'" (Lib. III, c. ii, § 2.) "The heretics," says Tertullian, "pretend that the apostles did not reveal all things to all, but taught some doctrines openly to every one, some secretly and to a few only." (De Præscr. Hær., c. xxv.) What was peculiar in their own doctrines they regarded as that esoteric teaching which had come down to them by oral tradition. This notion of a *secret* tradition is not found in Justin Martyr, Irenæus, or Tertullian. When the two latter speak of tradition, they mean that traditionary knowledge of the history and doctrines of Christianity which necessarily existed among Christians. It is described by Irenæus as a "tradition manifest throughout the world, and to be found in every Church." (Lib. III, c. iii, § 1.) By it, he says, a knowledge of our religion was preserved without books among believers in barbarous nations. (Ibid., c. iv, § 2.) At the end of about a century from the preaching of the apostles, there must have been, throughout the communities which they had formed, a general acquaintance with what they had taught, even had no written records of our religion been extant. In regard likewise to facts—important in their reference to Christianity, as, for example, the genuineness of the books of the New Testament—the Christians of the last half of the second century must have relied on the testimony of their predecessors. It is this traditionary knowledge concerning Christianity—not secret, but open to all—which

Irenæus and Tertullian appeal to with justifiable confidence in their reasoning against the heretics, when they distinguish between the evidence from tradition and the evidence from Scripture. 3. In connection with their notion of a secret tradition, some of the Gnostics said, according to Irenæus, "that the apostles, practicing dissimulation, accommodated their doctrine to the capacity of their hearers, and their answers to the previous conceptions of those who questioned them, talking blindly with the blind, weakly with the weak, and conformably to their error with those who were in error; and that thus they preached the Creator to those who thought the Creator was the only God, but to those able to comprehend the unknown Father, they communicated this unspeakable mystery in parables and in enigmas." (Lib. III, cap. v, § 1.) "Some," says Irenæus, "impudently contend that the apostles, preaching among the Jews, could not announce any other God but him in whom the Jews had believed." (Ib., cap. xii, § 6.) 4. Some of the Gnostics, especially the Marcionites, maintained that Paul was far superior to the other apostles in the knowledge of the truth—"the hidden doctrine having been manifested to him by revelation." (Ibid., c. xiii, § 1.) They represented the other apostles as having been entangled by Jewish prejudices from which he was in a great measure free. Marcion regarded the Gospels as expressing the false Jewish opinions of their writers. But among the Gospels he conceived that there was ground for making a choice; and he selected for his own use, and that of his followers, the Gospel of Luke. This he further adapted to his purpose by rejecting from it what he viewed as conformed to those opinions. Nor did he consider Paul himself as wholly free from Jewish errors, but likewise struck out, from those of his epistles which he used, the passages in which he thought them to be expressed. Sometimes, according to Irenæus, the Gnostics apparently, without making an exception in favor of Paul, charged the apostles generally with Jewish errors and ignorance concerning the higher truths and mysteries of religion. "All those," he says, "who hold pernicious doctrines have departed in their faith from him who is God, and think that they have found out more than the apostles, having discovered another God. They think that the apostles preached the Gospel while yet under the influence of Jewish prejudices, but that their own faith is purer, and that they are wiser than the apostles." He states that Marcion proceeded *on these principles* in rejecting the use of some of the books of Scripture, and of portions of those which he retained. (Lib. III, c. xii, § 12.) "The heretics," says Tertullian, "are accustomed to affirm that the apostles did not know all things; while, at other times, under the influence of the same madness, they turn about and maintain that the apostles did indeed know all things, but did not teach all things to all." (De Præscr. Hær., c. xxii.) 5. Add to this the belief of the theosophic Gnostics in their own infallible spiritual knowledge. This they conceived of as the result of their spiritual nature. "They object to us," says Clement of Alexandria, "that we are of another nature, and unable to comprehend their peculiar doctrines." (Stromat., vii, § 16.)

After these introductory remarks we will proceed to the examination of the testimony of heretical writers, as Westcott gives it in his Canon, and we shall find it strictly analogous to that of the Fathers in its progressive development. As the New Testament recognizes the existence of parties and heresies in the Christian society from its first origin, so the earliest false teachers witness more or less clearly to the existence and reception of our canonical Gospels.

SIMON MAGUS AND CERINTHUS.

The heretics that arose in the apostolic age were Simon Magus and Cerinthus. The former seems to have been the first representative of the antichristian element of the Gentile world, the latter that of the antichristian element in Judaism. In the lately-discovered parts of a work of Hippolytus, a disciple of Irenæus, (Philosophumena, or a refutation of all heresies, book VI,) there are preserved several quotations from a writing named "The Great Announcement," which contains an account of the revelation Simon Magus professed to be intrusted with, and which seems to have been compiled from his oral teaching by one of his immediate followers. In the fragments, which Hippolytus quotes of this work, there are coincidences with words recorded in the Gospel of Matthew. Reference is also made to the First Epistle of Paul to the Corinthians in terms which prove that it was placed by the author on the same footing as the books of the Old Testament. "The Cerinthians," Epiphanius says, "make use of Matthew's Gospel, (the Gospel according to the Hebrews,) like the Ebionites, on account of the human genealogy, though their copy is not entire. . . . . The apostle Paul they entirely reject on account of his opposition to circumcision." But of the most importance is the relation of Cerinthus to John. While we find in the New Testament no reference to the *later* developments of Gnosticism by Valentinus or Marcion—another proof of the authenticity of the apostolical writings, for if they had been written after the apostolical age, an entire ignoring of the heresies of the second century would be inexplicable—some of the prominent features in the false systems of Simon Magus and of Cerinthus are exposed in the Epistle to the Hebrews and in the introduction to John's Gospel. Nothing, indeed, can be more truly opposite to Cerinthianism than the theology of John. The character of his Gospel was evidently influenced by prevailing errors; though it is not a mere controversial work, we can not but feel that it was written to satisfy some pressing want of the age, and to meet some false philosophy, which had already begun to fashion a peculiar dialect. Cerinthus upheld a ceremonial system, and taught only a temporary union of the Logos with the man Jesus. St. John proclaimed that Judaism had passed away, and set forth clearly the manifestation of the Eternal Word in His historic Incarnation. The teaching of John is doubtless far deeper and wider than was needed to meet the errors of Cerinthus, but it has a natural connection with the period in which he lived.

THE OPHITES.

This sect, into which some Christian ideas were infused, Hyppolytus places in the age next succeeding that of the apostles. Although they are said to have made use of the Gospel according to the Egyptians, and of the Gospel of Thomas, the passages given from their books contain clear references to the Gospels of Matthew, Luke, and John, and to several Epistles. Irenæus speaks of the Ophites as the first source of the Valentinian school, the original "hydra-head from which its manifold progeny was derived."

BASILIDES.

He stood at the head of one of the Gnostic sects, and lived, according to Eusebius, (Hist. Ecc., IV, 7,) not long after the times of the apostles. He is said to have been a younger cotemporary of Cerinthus, and a follower of Menander, who was himself the successor of Simon Magus. Clement of Alexandria and Jerome fix the period of his activity in the time of Hadrian, and he found a formidable antagonist in Agrippa Castor. All these circumstances combine to place him in the generation next after the apostolic age, between Clement of Rome and Polycarp. Clement of Alexandria, Origen, and Epiphanius give specimens of the teaching of Basilides, exactly accordant with the more important quotations of Hippolytus. The mode in which the books of the New Testament are treated in these fragments, show that the earliest heretics sought to recommend their doctrines by forced explanations of apostolic language. And more than this, they contain the earliest undoubted instances in which the Old and New Testaments are placed on the same level; the Epistles of Paul are called "Scripture," and quotations from them are introduced by the well-known form: "It is written." Since Basilides lived on the verge of the apostolic times, it is, however, not surprising that he claimed other sources of Christian doctrine besides the canonical books. The belief in Divine inspiration was still fresh and real; and Eusebius relates that he set up imaginary prophets, Barcabbas and Barcoph, (or Parchor,) "names to strike terror into the superstitious." At the same time he appealed to the authority of Glaucias, who is said to have been, like Mark, an interpreter of Peter; he also made use of certain "Traditions of Matthias," which claimed to be grounded on private intercourse with the Savior. The author of the Homilies on Luke, which have been ascribed to Origen, speaks of a "Gospel according to Basilides." But there is no mention of it by Irenæus or by Clement of Alexandria, nor by Epiphanius, nor by Eusebius, nor by Theodoret. Why should we not have heard as much of a gospel written by Basilides as of the defective Gospel of Luke used by the Marcionites? The notion that Basilides wrote a gospel probably arose from the fact that he wrote a commentary on the Gospels. However that may be, he admitted the historic truth of all the facts contained in the canonical Gospels, and used them as scripture. In the fragments of his writings which we find in Hippolytus, there are definite references to the Gospels of Matthew, Luke, and John, as well as to several Epistles; and Bunsen is of opinion, "that his whole metaphysical development is an attempt to connect a cosmogonic system with John's prologue and with the person of Christ." (Bunsen's Hippolytus, vol. I, p. 87.) We possess in Basilides a witness to the existence of these Gospels as early as between 128 and 130 A. D.

VALENTINUS.

Shortly after Basilides began to propagate his doctrines, another system arose at Alexandria. Its author, Valentinus—after the example of the Christian teachers of his age—went to Rome, which he chose as the center of his labors. Irenæus relates, that "he came there during the episcopate of Hyginus, was at his full vigor in the time of Pius, and continued there till the time of Anicetus." His testimony, therefore, *in point of age*, is as venerable as that of Justin, and he is removed, by one generation only, from the time of John. Just as Basilides claimed, through Glaucius, the authority of Peter, Valentinus professed to follow the teaching of Theodas, a disciple of Paul. This circumstance is important; for it shows that at the beginning of the second century, alike within and without the Church, the sanction of an apostle was considered to be a sufficient proof of Christian doctrine. The fragments of his writings which remain show the same natural and trustful use of Scripture as any other Christian works of the same period. He cites the Epistle to the Ephesians as "Scripture," and refers clearly to the Gospels of Matthew, Luke, and John. The Valentinians, however, are said to have added a new gospel to the other four: "Casting aside all fear, and bringing forward their own compositions, they boast that they have more gospels than there really are. For they have advanced to such a pitch of daring as to entitle a book, which was composed by them not long since, 'the Gospel of Truth,' though it accords in no respect with the Gospels of the apostles; so that the Gospel, in fact, can not exist among them without blasphemy. For if that which is brought forward by them is the Gospel of Truth, and still is unlike those which are delivered to us by the apostles—they, who please, can learn *how* from the writings themselves—it is shown at once that that which is delivered to us by the apostles is not the Gospel of Truth." (Iren. Adv. Hær., III, xi, 11, 9.) What, then, was this gospel? If it had been a history of our Blessed Lord, and yet wholly at variance with the canonical Gospels, it is evident that the Valentinians could not have received these—nor, indeed, any one of them—as they undoubtedly did. And here, then, a new light is thrown upon the character of some of the early apocryphal gospels, which has been in part anticipated by what was said of the gospel of Basilides. The gospel of Basilides or Valentinus contained their system of Christian doctrine, their view of the Gospel, philosophically, and not historically. The writers of these new gospels in no way necessarily interfered with the old. They sought, as far as we can learn, to embody their spirit and furnish a key to their meaning, rather than to supersede their use. The Valentinians had *more* gospels than the Catholic Church, since they accepted a doctrinal gospel.

The titles of some of the other Gnostic gospels confirm what has been said. Two are mentioned by Epiphanius in the account of those whom he calls "Gnostics," as if that were their specific name, the *Gospel of Eve*, and the *Gospel of Perfection*. Neither of these could be historic accounts of the life of Christ, and the slight description of their character which he adds, illustrates the wide use of the word "gospel." The first was an elementary account of Gnosticism, "based on foolish visions and testimonies," called by the name of Eve, as though it had been revealed to her by the serpent. The second was "a seductive composition." (Epiph. Hær., xxvi, 2.)

The analogy of the title of this "Gospel of Perfection" leaves little doubt as to the character of the "Gospel of Truth." Puritan theology can furnish numerous similar titles. And the partial currency of such a book among the Valentinians offers not the slightest presumption against their agreement with catholic Christians on the exclusive claims of the four Gospels as records of Christ's life. These they took as the basis of their speculations; and by the help of commentaries endeavored to extract from them the principles which they maintained.

HERACLEON.

Origen says that "he was reported to have been a familiar friend of Valentinus," (Comm. in Joan., tom. ii, § 8.) Assuming this statement to be true, his writings can not well date later than the first half of the second century; and he claims the title of the first commentator on the New Testament. Fragments of his commentaries on the Gospels of Luke and John have been preserved by Clement of Alexandria and Origen. The fragments contain allusions to the Gospel of Matthew, to the Epistles of Paul to the Romans, and Corinthians, (I,) and to the Second Epistle to Timothy; but the character of the Commentary itself is the most striking testimony to the estimation in which the apostolic writings were held. The sense of the inspiration of the Evangelists—of some providential guidance by which they were led to select each fact in their history, and each word in their narrative—is not more complete in Origen. The first commentary on the New Testament exhibits the application of the same laws to its interpretation as were employed in the Old Testament. The slightest variation of language was held to be significant. Numbers were supposed to conceal a hidden truth. The whole record was found to be pregnant with spiritual meaning, conveyed by the teaching of events in themselves real and instructive. It appears, also, that differences between the Gospels were felt, and an attempt made to reconcile them, (Orig. in Joan., x, § 21;) and it must be noticed that authoritative spiritual teaching was not limited to our Lord's own words, but the remarks of the Evangelist also were received as possessing an inherent weight. The introduction of commentaries implies the strongest belief in the authenticity and authority of the New Testament Scriptures; and this belief becomes more important when we notice the source from which they were derived. They took their rise among heretics, and not among catholic Christians. Just as the earliest Fathers applied themselves to the Old Testament, to bring out its real harmony with the Gospel, heretics endeavored to reconcile the Gospel with their own systems. Commentaries were made where the want for them was pressing. But unless the Gospels had been generally accepted, the need for such works would not have been felt. Heracleon was forced to turn and modify much that he found in John, which he would not have done if the book had not been raised above all doubt. And his evidence is the more valuable because it appears that he had studied the history of the apostles.

PTOLEMÆUS.

Ptolemæus, like Heracleon, was a disciple of Valentinus. Epiphanius has preserved an important letter which Ptolemæus addressed to an "honorable sister

Flora," in which he maintains the imperfect character of the Law. In proof of this doctrine he quoted words of our Lord recorded by Matthew, the prologue to John's Gospel, and passages from Paul's Epistles to the Romans, Corinthians, (I,) and Ephesians. Many other fragments of the teachings, if not of the books, of Ptolemæus have been preserved by Irenæus, (Adv. Hær., I, 1sqq; and though they are full of forced explanations of Scripture, they recognize, even in their wildest theories, the importance of every detail or doctrine. He found support for his doctrine in the parables, the miracles, and the facts of our Lord's life, as well as in the teaching of the apostles. In the course of the exposition of his system quotations occur from the four Gospels, and from the Epistles of Paul to the Romans, Corinthians, (I,) Galatians, Ephesians, and Colossians.

THE MARCOSIANS.

"The Marcosians," Irenæus writes, "introduce with subtilty an unspeakable multitude of apocryphal and spurious writings, (*γραφαί*,) which they forged themselves to confound the foolish and those who know not the Scriptures (*γράμματα*) of truth." (Adv. Hær., I, xx, 1.) In the absence of further evidence, it is impossible to pronounce exactly on the character of these books; it is sufficient that they did not supplant the canonical Scriptures. At the same time their appearance in this connection is not without importance. Marcus, the founder of the sect, was probably a native of Syria; and Syria, it is well known, was fertile in those religious tales which are raised to too great importance by the title of gospels. Whatever the apocryphal writings may have been, the words of Irenæus show that they were easily distinguishable from Holy Scripture; and the Marcosians themselves bear witness to the familiar use of our Gospels. The formularies which Marcus instituted contain references to the Gospel of Matthew, and perhaps to the Epistle to the Ephesians, (Adv. Hær., I, xiii, 3.) The teaching of his followers offers coincidences with all four Gospels. These Gospel quotations present various remarkable readings, but there is no reason to suppose that they were borrowed from any other source than the canonical books. Irenæus evidently considered that they were taken thence; and while he accuses the Marcosians of "adapting" certain passages of the Gospels to their views, the connection shows that they tampered with the interpretation and not with the text.

MARCION.

Hitherto the testimony of heretical writers to the New Testament has been confined to the recognition of detached parts, by casual quotations or characteristic types of doctrine. Marcion, on the contrary, fixed a definite collection of apostolic books as the foundation of his system. Paul only, according to him, was the true apostle; and Pauline writings alone were admitted into his canon. This was divided into two parts: "The Gospel" and "The Apostolicon." The Gospel was a recension of Luke, with numerous omissions and variations from the received text. The Apostolicon contained ten epistles of Paul, excluding the pastoral epistles and that to the Hebrews. Tertullian and Epiphanius agree in affirming that Marcion altered the text of the books which he received to suit his own views; and they quote many various readings in support of their assertion. Those which occur in the Epistles are certainly insufficient to prove the point. With the Gospel the case was different. The influence of oral tradition, by the form and use of the written Gospels, was of long continuance. The personality of their authors was, in some measure, obscured by the character of their work. The Gospel was felt to be Christ's Gospel—the name which Marcion ventured to apply to his own—and not the particular narration of any Evangelist. And such considerations as these will explain, though they did not justify, the liberty which Marcion allowed himself in dealing with the text of Luke. There can be no doubt that Luke's narrative lay at the basis of his Gospel; but it is not equally clear that all the changes which were introduced into it were due to Marcion himself. Some of the omissions can be explained at once by his peculiar doctrines, but others are unlike arbitrary corrections, and must be considered as various readings of the greatest interest, dating, as they do, from a time anterior to all other authorities in our possession.

TATIAN.

The history of Tatian throws an important light on that of Marcion. Both were naturally restive, inquisitive, impetuous. They were subject to the same influences, and were for a while, probably, resident in the same city. (Tat. ad Gr., 18; Just. Ap., i, 26.) Both remained for some time within the Catholic Church, and then sought the satisfaction of their peculiar wants in a system of stricter discipline and sterner logic. Both abandoned the received canon of Scripture; and together they go far to witness to its integrity. While they witness to the existence of a critical spirit among Christians of the second century, they point to a Catholic Church as the one center from which their systems diverged.

The earliest mention of the Diatessaron of Tatian is in Eusebius. "Tatian," he says, "the former leader of the Encratites, having put together, in some strange fashion, a combination and collection of the Gospels, gave this name of the Diatessaron, and the work is still partially current." The words evidently imply that the canonical Gospels formed the basis of Tatian's Harmony. The next testimony is that of Epiphanius, who writes that "Tatian is said to have been the author of the Harmony of the four Gospels, which some call the Gospel according to the Hebrews." (Epiph. Hær., xlvi, 1.) The express mention of the four *Gospels* is important as fixing the meaning of the original titles. Not long afterward, Theodoret gives a more exact account of the character and common use of the book. "Tatian also composed the gospel called 'Diatessaron,' and all the other passages which show that Christ was born of David according to the flesh. This was used not only by the members of his own party, but even by those who followed the Apostolic doctrine, as they did not perceive the evil design of the composition, but used the book in their simplicity for its conciseness. And I found also myself more than two hundred such books in our Churches, (in Syria,) which had been received with respect; and having gathered all together, I caused them to be laid aside, and introduced in their place the Gospels of the four Evangelists." (Theod. Hær., lib. I, 20.) Not only, then, was the Diatessaron grounded on the four canonical Gospels, but in its general form it was so orthodox as to enjoy a wide ecclesiastical popularity. The heretical character of the book was not evident upon the surface of it, and consisted rather in faults of defect than in erroneous teaching. Theodoret had certainly examined it, and he, like earlier writers, regarded it as a compilation from the four Gospels. He speaks of omissions which were, in part at least, natural in a Harmony, but notices no such apocryphal additions as would have found place in any gospel not derived from canonical sources.

THE APOCRYPHA OF THE NEW TESTAMENT.

In the preceding quotations from the heretical writings various gospels have been referred to and characterized, such as the Gospel according to the Hebrews,* the Ebionite Gospel, the Gospel of Corinth;

* In order to enable the reader to make a comparison between the Gospel according to the Hebrews and the Gospel of Matthew, we will copy a few quotations. The following quotation is made by Origen, (Comm. on Matt., tom. XVI, § 14:)

"Another rich man said to him, Master, what good thing shall I do to live? He said to him: Fulfill the law and the prophets. He answered him: I have fulfilled them. He said to him: Go, sell all that thou possessest and distribute to the poor, and come, follow me. But the rich man began to scratch his head, and it did not please him. And the Lord said to him: How sayest thou, I have fulfilled the law and the prophets, since it is written in the law, thou shalt love thy neighbor as thyself; and lo! many of thy brethren, sons of Abraham, are clothed in filth, dying of hunger; and thy house is full of many goods, and nothing at all goes out of it to them! And he turned and said to Simon, his disciple, who was sitting by him: Simon, son of Jonas, it is easier for a camel to enter the eye of a needle than for a rich man to enter into the kingdom of heaven."

In Jerome we find the following quotations:

"So the mother of the Lord, and his brethren said to him: John the Baptist is baptizing for the remission of sins; let us go and be baptized by him. But he said to them: What sin have I committed that I should go and be baptized by him? Unless, perchance, this very word which I have spoken is (a sin of) ignorance." (Hieron. Adv. Pelag., III, 2.)

"Now, it came to pass when the Lord had come up out of the water, the Holy Spirit with full stream came down and rested upon him, and said to him: My

all of which were falsifications and mutilations of a translation of the original Greek Gospel of Matthew into Aramaic Hebrew, or such as the mutilated edition of Luke's Gospel by Marcion.

Of a somewhat different character is the so-called "Gospel according to the Egyptians." On this Mr. Norton remarks: "It was an anonymous book extant in the second century, and probably written in Egypt, in the dark and mystical style that prevailed in that country. In judging of its importance we must compare the writers who recognize its existence with the far greater number to whom it was unknown, or who were not led by any circumstance to mention it. It was a book of which we should have been ignorant, but for a few incidental notices afforded by writers, none of whom give evidence of having seen it. Neither Clement nor any other writer speaks of it as a Gnostic gospel. The Gnos-

Son, in all the prophets I was waiting for thee, that thou shouldest come, and I might rest in thee. For thou art my rest; thou art my first-born Son, who reignest forever." (Hieron. in Isaiah, IV, xi, 2.)

"Now the Lord, when he had given the cloth to the servant of the priest, went to James and appeared to him. For James had taken an oath that he would not eat bread from that hour on which he had drunk the cup of the Lord, till he saw him risen from the dead. Again, a little afterward, the Lord says, Bring a table and bread. Immediately, it is added, he took bread, and blessed, and brake, and gave it to James the Just, and said to him, My brother, eat thy bread, for the Son of man has risen from the dead." (Hieron. de Vir., Illust., II.)

"In the Gospel which the Nazarenes and Ebionites use," says Jerome, on Matt. xii, 13, "the man with the withered hand is described as a mason, who sought the help of Christ with words to this effect: I was a mason, seeking a livelihood by the labor of my hand. I pray thee, Jesus, to restore to me my health, that I may not beg my bread in disgrace."

These extracts show us clearly how little any other age than that of the apostles was able to originate or even to reproduce the simple grandeur of inspired language, and what might have been expected from writings founded on tradition, even when shaped after an apostolic pattern. In no sense can the apocryphal gospels of the Judaizing sects bear any comparison with ours, neither in form nor in matter. They are destitute of spirit, life, good taste, sublimity, and authority.

tics did not appeal to it in support of their fundamental doctrines; for had they done so, we should have been fully informed of the fact. The only argument for believing it to have been a history of Christ's ministry is, that it contained a narrative of a pretended conversation of Christ with Salome, but that might as well have been inserted in a merely doctrinal book. And if the book had been a historical gospel, the representation of Christ—to judge from the words ascribed to him in the conversation with Salome—must have been so foreign in its character from that in our Gospels, that it could not have existed in the last half of the second century without having been an object of far greater attention than what this book received."

The same may be said concerning the so-called "Gospel according to Peter." From the account which Serapion, Bishop of Antioch about the close of the second century, gives of it, as quoted by Eusebius, (Hist. Eccl., lib. VI, c. xii,) it appears clearly that it did not pretend to be a history of Christianity. Had this been the case, Serapion could not have regarded it with such indifference as he first manifested. It is impossible that the existence of such a history should not have been notorious, that it should not have been a frequent subject of remark. When we recollect the abundant notices of Marcion's Gospel, it can not be believed that there was another historical book extant among the heretics, of which the notices are so scanty, and which is never mentioned as a historical book. It belongs to the same class of writings as the Gospel of Basilides, the traditions of Matthias, the Gospel according to Thomas, the True Gospel, the Gospel of Eve, the Gospel of

Perfection, which, as we remarked above, were doctrinal tracts, not historical accounts of Christ's ministry; or, at least, so very obscure ones, that no sect for a moment pretended to set them up in opposition to our canonical Gospels. Norton remarks very fitly: "About the beginning of the last century a manuscript was made known of a gospel ascribed to Barnabas, in the Italian language, but supposed to be translated from the Arabic. It is the work of a Mohammedan, or a work interpolated by a Mohammedan. Much more has been written about this book than all that is to be found in the Christian writers of the first three centuries concerning apocryphal gospels; yet it is a book of which, probably, few of my readers have ever heard. It is easy to apply this fact to assist ourselves in judging of the importance to be attached to the notices of apocryphal gospels found in the Fathers." Nor would we have devoted so much attention to the consideration of these apocryphal gospels, had not the latest German school of destructive criticism set up the monstrous claim, that *the Ebionitic and Gnostic Gospels were the original histories of our Lord, and our canonical Gospels later productions, written for the express purpose to improve upon them!* To critics who can maintain that the Gospel according to the Hebrews or the Gospel of Marcion are respectively the originals of Matthew and Luke, it is sufficient to apply the word of the apostle: "Professing themselves to be wise, they became fools." The authors of our four canonical Gospels, who stood infinitely above all the authors of the second century, are assumed to have written toward the close of that century, under the fictitious names of Matthew, Mark, Luke, and John, and to have remained undiscovered, although they succeeded in revolutionizing the whole Christian literature of that age, and substituting their products in the place of the original histories of Christ's ministry, so that none of the critical writers at the close of the second century could discover the least trace of the unheard-of legerdemain!

From all the above-named productions, bearing the name of Gospels, must be distinguished some books of high antiquity, which were not imitations of the canonical Gospels, but aimed to supplement the narratives concerning the Savior, Mary and Joseph, and the apostles. They bore on their face, falsely, the names of apostles or other men highly esteemed in the Church. But, though they were esteemed and used by many persons in early antiquity, when men did not so readily know how to distinguish counterfeits from that which was genuine and true, they were repudiated by the Church. These are the *New Testament Apocrypha*, in the proper sense of the word, and they were also as strong witnesses for the early acceptance of our Gospels. It is not necessary to mention more than the two oldest ones, *the so-called Gospel of James*, and the *Acts of Pilate.* Tischendorf contends that both were composed in the first ten years of the second century, and makes the following argument:

"In his work of the year 138, as well as in his Dialogue, written somewhat later, Justin makes several statements touching the birth of Jesus, the origin of which can be traced only to the Gospel of James. Justin relates that the birth of Jesus took place in a grotto at Bethlehem. Such a statement is found only in the Gospel of James. In the annunciation to

Mary, Justin concludes with the words: 'And thou shalt call his name Jesus,' adding directly to them, 'for he shall save the people from their sins.' So precisely does it stand in the Gospel of James. In Matthew, on the other hand, the words are spoken to Joseph, and in Luke the last clause is wanting altogether. The dependence of Justin upon the book of James admits of no objection. Not only does Origen, after the expiration of the second century, make mention of the Book of James; not only is his constant subsequent use of it beyond a doubt, we have now, in addition, more than fifty manuscripts of the Greek text, written from the ninth century onward—nay, even a Syriac manuscript of the sixth century. It is only the desire to evade the conclusion that even Justin employed it, which prompts men to lose themselves in the realm of idle conjectures.

"But now the work named after James stands in such a relation to our Gospels that they must have been in long and general use before the fictitious writing was produced. Matthew and Luke had asserted that Mary was a virgin mother; still there were sects, diverging from the Church doctrine, who fancied Jesus to be the son of Joseph and Mary. That the brethren of Jesus are mentioned in the Gospels seemed, at least, to prove a later marriage of Joseph and Mary. Learned Jews threw suspicion upon the correctness of the translation of the prophetic passage touching the Virgin in Matthew i, 23; nay, both Jews and heathen poured contempt and calumny upon the Son of the Virgin. This took place in the first half of the second century, and the Gospel of James was composed to meet it. In this it was shown, in a historical form, that, from her birth onward, Mary had always maintained the highest character; that the virgin-birth was a matter of demonstration, and that she sustained a relation to Joseph far above that of marriage. If this work really falls into the first decade of years in the second century, the composition of the Gospels of Matthew and Luke, to which, as a pretended supplement, it refers, must certainly fall into the last ten years of the first century.

"The case is similar with the *Acts of Pilate*, save that this work refers as distinctly to John as to the first Gospels. For this production, also, Justin is our oldest guarantee. It professes to have been written under Pilate, and by the allegation of wonderful occurrences before, during, and after the crucifixion, to deliver a strong testimony for the divinity of Christ. That it must have originated with a Christian hand, engaged in a work of pious fraud, was indeed not discovered by Justin, nor was it detected by Tertullian and others. On the contrary, in his work of A. D. 138, Justin appeals to it twice. First, he mentions the prophecies touching the events heralding the crucifixion, (Isa. lxv, 2, and lviii, 2 Ps. xxi, 16, 18,) and says: 'That they really occurred, you may learn from the Acts composed under Pontius Pilate.' Then, again, he appeals to the miraculous cures of Jesus, predicted by Isaiah, (xxxv, 4, 6,) and adds: 'That Jesus really did these things, you may learn from the Acts composed under Pontius Pilate.' The testimony of Tertullian is rendered in still more ample terms, (Apologetic, 21) for he says that Jesus, from envy, was delivered by the Jewish scribes to Pilate, and by him, yielding to the pressure of the accusers, delivered to crucifixion; that, hanging upon the cross, with a loud cry, he yielded up the ghost; that, at the same moment, the full day was interrupted by the obscuration of the sun; that, as Jesus had predicted his resurrection, a watch of soldiers was set at the grave to prevent the abstraction of the corpse by the disciples; but that upon the third day the earth suddenly quaked, and the stone which had been rolled before the grave was removed; that nothing but grave-clothes was found in the grave; that a report was spread abroad by the authorities that the disciples had taken the body; but that Jesus himself spent forty days with his disciples, in Galilee, instructing them, and that after he had charged them with the duty of preaching, he was transported to heaven in a cloud. This full report Tertullian concludes with the words: 'All this did Pilate himself, forced by conscience to become a Christian, report of Christ to the reigning Emperor, Tiberius.'

"Such are the testimonies of Justin and Tertullian touching the *Acts of Pilate.* A work answering to these quotations, and bearing also the same title as in Justin, we possess at present, in many ancient Greek, Latin, and other original manuscript documents. Is it the same which was read by Justin and Tertullian? The affirmative answer has been resisted in many ways. It has been said that the old work itself is lost, and that the extant one is only an imitation of it. Has this opinion any solid foundation? By no means. True, indeed, the oldest text, when subsequently transcribed, was in many passages altered, as touching the expression; nay, more, in the middle ages, the Latins exchanged the title, *The Acts of Pilate*, for the title, 'The Gospel of Nicodemus,' and added a preface. We have, also, in connection with the elder Greek text, a more modern revision, but, upon the whole, we have decisive grounds for believing that our *Acts of Pilate*, with its elder text, in the main, really contains the work used by Justin and Tertullian. By our own researches in the European libraries, important proofs of this position have been discovered; namely, a manuscript written in the Egyptian language, on paper of the oldest kind, (papyrus,) of the fifth century; and, also, a parchment manuscript, with the Latin text, of the same century, which, although washed out about a thousand years ago, and replaced by a new inscription upon the parchment, thus cleansed, remaining, for good eyes, still legible. These two ancient documents, with an Egyptian and a Latin translation, insure the high antiquity of our Greek text, from which they were derived; for if, even in the fifth century, there existed such translations, the work itself, as highly esteemed, must have existed long before. But we must present the matter with still greater exactness. The primitive work was very precious to Christians. The example both of Justin and Tertullian proves it. Justin makes his appeal to the Roman Cæsar, upon this basis, as if it were a work of decisive weight. This high estimation of it naturally continued. Eusebius and Epiphanius prove this, as touching the fourth century. We learn from the former that, at the beginning of the fourth century, the Emperor Maximin, who was bitterly hostile to Christianity, caused spurious *Acts of Pilate*, full of scoffing and calumny, to be published, and even to be distributed in the schools, plainly in order to suppress and counteract the work held in such esteem by the Christians. In this state of facts, is it in the smallest degree credible, that precisely at this period, from the fourth or fifth century forward, the old work, so remarkably serviceable, should have been entirely revised; and that precisely at this period, the ancient and famous work itself having entirely disappeared, the revision should have been every-where distributed—should have been translated and preserved to our day? The supposition is in flat contradiction to a sound judgment. It contradicts the work itself as we have it, inasmuch as it unites a very peculiar freedom of narrative with a dependence upon the Gospels. Our *Acts of Pilate* not only presupposes the narratives of the first three Gospels, but also absolutely and very especially the Gospel of John. For while its report of the crucifixion and resurrection connects itself with the first, that of the trial, in its entire complexion, depends upon the narrative of John. What is the inference as touching our question? If the so-called *Acts of Pilate*, for the reason that Justin, as early as the year 138, so earnestly emphasizes its value, must be admitted to have been written at the beginning of the second century, then the Gospel of John and the rest, since they are so completely presupposed, must be admitted to have been written in the *first* century."

§ 13. The Testimonies of Heathen Adversaries.

To the external evidences for the authenticity of the Gospels is to be added the testimony of avowed enemies. The learned Lardner says in his collection of Jewish and heathen testimonies, (on the New Testament canon:) "Of all the testimonies on the writings of the New Testament, which we meet with in the first centuries of the Christian era, none are weightier and more important than those of the learned philosophers who wrote against Christianity; namely, of Celsus, in the second, Porphyry, in the third, and Julian the Apostate, in the fourth century."

Celsus, a philosopher, who flourished about 176 A. D., proposed to himself the formal task of setting forth how dangerous the Christian religion would prove to the State. His learned argument against the Christians is *the first heathen testimony as to the existence of New Testament writings.* This work, entitled "The True Word," has unfortunately been lost, but in Origen's reply to it there are more copious extracts from it than from any other book of antiquity that has been lost. In these extracts we have almost an abridgment of the Gospel history. They contain about eighty quotations from the New Testament, which amply prove that Celsus was acquainted with the writings of Matthew, Luke, and John, and some of the Epistles of Paul. He mentions nearly all the leading events in the life of Christ from his birth to his death; of course, only in order to make them ridiculous. His whole argument, however, is based on the admission that the writings of the Christians were the productions of their professed authors, though he refers to some alterations of the Gospels made by the Marcionites and other heretics. From the testimony, then, of this most malignant enemy of the Christian religion, who was, at the same time, a man of considerable learning and influence, it appears, that the writings of the Evangelists existed in his time, the first period succeeding the apostolic age, and that these writings were then acknowledged, even by enemies, to be authentic.

The next witness is Porphyry, who was born 230 A. D., and wrote against Christianity about 270 A. D. From the few fragments left of this work it appears that he was acquainted with our Gospels and some other of the New Testament writings. This work enjoyed a high reputation among the heathen, and Eusebius and other learned Christians deemed it worth their while to refute it. In what we have left of it there are direct references to the Gospels of Matthew, Mark, and John, the Acts, and the Epistles to the Galatians. Speaking of the Christians, he calls Matthew their Evangelist. This man was every way qualified, both by education and his position in society, to find out whether the New Testament writings were authentic, or whether, after the death of the apostles and Evangelists, spurious works were, as their writings, palmed upon the Christians. But we discover not even a hint at a suspicion of this kind; yea, Porphyry appears to have had no doubt whatever as to the authenticity of these writings. From the attempt of this ingenious writer that the book of Daniel was an *ex post facto* prophecy, we see how well he knew to estimate an argument against the authenticity of a book of the New Testament, and how eagerly he would have made use of it against the Christians, if he had had but the least data for forming one.

One hundred years after Porphyry, flourished the Emperor Julian, (A. D. 331–363,) surnamed the Apostate, from his renunciation of Christianity after he mounted the imperial throne. Though he resorted to the most artful political means for undermining

Christianity, yet, as a writer against it, he was every way inferior to Porphyry. From various extracts of his work against the Christians, transcribed by Jerome and Cyril, it is evident that he did not deny the truth of the Gospel history, as a history; though he denied the Divinity of Jesus Christ asserted in the writings of the Evangelists, he acknowledged the principal facts in the Gospels, as well as the miracles of our Savior and his apostles. Referring to the difference between the genealogies recorded by Matthew and Luke, he noticed them by name, and recited the sayings of Christ in the very words of the Evangelists. He also bore testimony to the Gospel of John being composed later than the other Evangelists, and at a time when great numbers were converted to the Christian faith both in Italy and Greece; and alluded oftener than once to facts recorded in the Acts of the Apostles. By thus quoting the four Gospels and Acts of the Apostles, and by quoting no other books, Julian shows that these were the *only* historical books received by the Christians as of authority, and as containing authentic memoirs of Jesus Christ and his apostles, together with the doctrines taught by them. But Julian's testimony does something more than represent the judgment of the Christian Church in his time; it discovers also his own. He himself expressly states the early date of these records; he calls them by the names which they now bear. He all along supposes, he no where attempts to question, their genuineness or authenticity; nor does he give even the slightest intimation that he suspected the whole or any part of them to be forgeries.

We have seen that none of these avowed enemies of Christianity has expressed the least suspicion as to the authenticity of the New Testament writings, and we would ask, in conclusion, who will deny that in the writings of a Celsus, Porphyry, and Julian, all of whom were learned men and zealous adversaries and persecutors of the Christians, and whose testimonies cover the period from 176 to 361 of the Christian era, every reasonable demand of testimony borne by enemies is fully met, and that this testimony, in the wise providence of God, makes the external evidence for the Gospel history as complete as it possibly can be from the nature of the case?

CHAPTER II.

THE INTERNAL EVIDENCES.

§ 14. The Peculiar Dialect of Greek in which the Evangelists have Written.

As we remarked in § 5, that some arguments for the genuineness or integrity of the Sacred Text were, at the same time, arguments for the authenticity of the records, so we can not entirely separate the internal evidences for the authenticity from the arguments for the credibility or historic verity of the Gospel Records, which will be the subject of investigation in our next Part. In the case of such compositions as the Gospels, the proof of their having been written by apostles, and by those who received their accounts immediately from the apostles, is at the same time, as we shall further show in the next Part, the proof of their historic verity. But, though the arguments for their authenticity and their credibility are thus intimately blended together, and though the ultimate purpose of both is the same, it is, nevertheless, desirable to consider the former separately, and simply with reference to their bearing upon the question of authenticity. They will thus form a natural transition and proper introduction to Part III.

The Greek language, in which the New Testament writings originally appeared—as is universally admitted, with the exception of the Gospel of Matthew, and the Epistle to the Hebrews*—is not the classical Greek, such as was written by Plato, Aristotle, and other eminent Greek writers. Had the Evangelists and apostles written in pure, elegant, classical Greek, thoughtful minds would have found considerable difficulty in believing them to be the authors of those productions, and we should lack one important evidence of the authenticity of New Testament Scripture—its being written in the style natural to the persons by whom, and to the age in which it was produced.

The basis of the New Testament Greek is the common or Hellenic dialect—the name given to that form of the Greek language which came into general use after the Macedonian conquest. It was called *common*, because it originated in a sort of fusion of the particular dialects which had prevailed in earlier times; and this fusion of dialects had its origin chiefly from the fusion of the several States of Greece into the one great Macedonian Empire. In this fusion of dialects, however, the Attic still prevailed as the model form of the Greek language. This common dialect we find in the New Testament writings—in some of them to a greater extent than in others—intermixed with the free and frequent use of forms derived from the Aramaic or Syro-Chaldaic dialect of the Hebrew language, which had become the vernacular language of the Jewish people in the

* The Epistle to the Hebrews is now held, by all men of competent learning, to have been originally composed in Greek. And as to the Gospel of Matthew, though the opinions of the learned are still divided, yet the conviction has of late been growing in favor of the proper originality of the present form, which was certainly in current use before the close of the apostolic age. (Fairbairn's Hermeneutical Manual.)

time of the Savior. This Hebraistic influence* in the style of the New Testament writers appears, as Fairbairn shows by many examples, 1, in the various features of grammatical construction peculiar to the Hebrew language, as, (1,) in the more frequent use of the

*Against the frequent misuse of the so-called Hebraisms in the interpretation of the New Testament, Fairbairn, in his Hermeneutical Manual, has very justly protested, showing, in the first place, that they are not nearly so numerous as they were at one time represented to be. They occur only so far as rendered necessary by the circumstances of the writers. Though the Greek syntax differs in many things from the Hebrew, we find the New Testament writers accommodating themselves far more to the foreign idiom than has been generally allowed; as, for instance, in the discriminating use of the aorist and perfect tenses—the aorist as denoting the historic past, and the perfect as denoting the past in its relation to the present, the past continuing with its effects and consequences to the present. John carefully observes this distinction when he says, (c. i, 3:) ἐγένετο οὐδὲ ἓν ὃ γέγονεν, that is, nothing whatever that has been made, and is still in being, was made without Him. So, also, in Colossians i, 16; iii, 3. In the second place, we should beware not to attach arbitrary meanings to the real Hebraisms which we find in the New Testament, as if the Hebrews had contravened the laws of all human language. For a long time the opinion was prevailing among commentators and lexicographers, that the prepositions, when handled by a Hellenistic Jew, might express almost any relation whatever. So Schleusner assigns to the preposition εἰς twenty-four, and to ἐν thirty distinct uses and meanings. In a few instances, even the authorized English version and that of Luther have suffered from the too prevalent notion of Hebraistic laxity. Thus, in the prayer of the converted malefactor, (Luke xxiii, 42:) "Remember me when thou comest ἐν τῇ βασιλείᾳ σου"—not *into* thy kingdom, which might seem to point to the glory into which the Lord was presently going to enter, but *in* thy kingdom; namely, when the time comes for thee to take to thyself thy great power, and to reign among men; for this future manifestation of glory was undoubtedly what the faith of the penitent man anticipated and sought to share in, not the glory which lay within the vail, which only the answer of Christ brought within the ken of his spiritual vision. From the real or alleged Hebraisms of the New Testament we must distinguish a class of expressions not in themselves absolutely new, but still fraught with an import which could not attach to them as used by any heathen writer, nor even in the production of any Greek-speaking Jew prior to the birth of Christ. With the marvelous events of the Gospel age, old things passed away, all things became new; and the change which took place in the Divine dispensation could not fail to impress itself on those words and forms of expression which bore respect to what had then for the first time come properly into being. We refer to such terms as λόγος, (word,) βασιλεία τοῦ Θεοῦ, (kingdom of God,) αἰὼν μέλλων, (world to come,) δικαιοσύνη, (righteousness,) ζωή, (life,) θάνατος, (death,) χάρις, (grace,) etc. In so far as these terms embodied the distinctive facts or principles of Christianity, their former and common usage could only in part exhibit the sense now acquired by them; for the full depth and compass of meaning belonging to them in their new application, we must look to the New Testament itself, comparing one passage with another, and viewing the language used in the light of the great things which it brings to our apprehension.

prepositions for marking relations, which were wont to be indicated in pure Greek by means of cases; (2,) in the paucity of conjunctions which existed in the Hebrew, while the Greek possessed a great abundance—of which, however, the New Testament writers did not avail themselves. (3.) A further Hebraistic turn appears in the frequent use of the genitive pronouns instead of the possessives. This naturally arose from the inspired writers being used to the Hebrew suffixes. (4.) Another pronominal peculiarity, arising from assimilation to the Hebrew, is occasionally found in the New Testament. In Hebrew there is only one relative pronoun, and this is without any distinction as to number, gender, or case; on which account, to make the reference explicit, it is necessary to add the suffixes of the personal pronouns, or these pronouns themselves with a preposition. Hence such expressions as the following: "The land in which ye dwell upon it," "the place in which ye sojourn in it," and so on. As the Greek language possesses a declinable relative pronoun, and adverbs derived from it, there was no need for this kind of awkward circumlocution. Yet the Evangelists were so accustomed to the Hebrew usage that they indulged in it occasionally, though not so frequently as the Septuagint. (5.) Again, the Hebrew was as remarkable for the fewness, as the Greek for the multiplicity, of its forms to express time—the one having its simple past and future tenses, while the other had its present, imperfect, perfect, pluperfect, its two aorists, first and second future, and paulo-post future. There can be no doubt that the New Testament writers were well acquainted with the principal tenses of the Greek verb; at the same time there are occasional anomalies, with a manifest preference for the simple past and future of the Hebrew, and a tendency to use the future, as expressive of necessity and continued action (*must* and *is wont*) somewhat more frequently than is usual in ordinary Greek. 2. In the use of words and phrases which have their correspondence only in Hebrew, but are not found in profane Greek writers, whether of the earlier or of the later periods. We mention, first, such words as *ἄββα*, (abba,) *ἀμήν*, (amen,) *γεέννα*, (hell,) *Σατᾶν*, (Satan,) etc. These are Oriental words in Greek letters, or with a Greek termination, and their meaning must be determined simply by a reference to their Oriental use. There are, again, words and phrases in themselves strictly Greek, but used in a sense different from what would naturally be put upon them by a simply Greek reader. For instance, the phrase *πᾶσα σάρξ*, (all flesh,) for "all men," is quite a Hebraism, for native Greek writers never used *σάρξ* in the sense of "*men;*" and such an expression, if employed by them, would have meant not all mankind, but the whole flesh—of a man or an animal, as it might happen.

On the whole, we may say the New Testament Greek has about as many Hebraisms as a work written in English by a German in this country, who, though familiar with the English language, is not a thorough scholar, or a work translated from the German, and referring to modes of thought peculiar to German mind, will exhibit, more or less, the idiom of the German language. Thus, the Hebraisms we find in the Gospels show the Evangelists to have been Jews by birth, and men in humble stations, who were not ambitious of seeking an exemption from the dialect they had once acquired, and we need not wonder to find the Hebraistic elements also in the writings of so learned a man as Paul. Great as his erudition was, it was the erudition of a Jewish, not of a Grecian, school. His argumentations were those of a Jewish convert to Christianity, confuting his brethren on their own ground. How clearly can we recognize in his writings the Saul of Tarsus, who was educated at the feet of Gamaliel! There was, moreover, apart from the relation the New Testament writers bore to their country and nation, as Fairbairn remarks, "a necessity for a certain departure from the pure, classical style, and calling in the aid of Jewish idioms and forms of speech, in order to exhibit in the most distinct and appropriate manner the peculiar truths of the Gospel. The native language of Greece, though in some respects the most perfect medium for the communication of thought which has ever been employed by the tongue of man, yet from being always conversant with worldly things, adapted to express every shade of thought and every variety of relationship within the human and earthly sphere—but still *only* these—it was not fully adequate to the requirements and purposes of Christian authorship. For this higher end it needed to borrow something from the sanctuary of God, and to be, as it were, baptized in the modes of thought and utterance which were familiar to those who had enjoyed the training of the Spirit. Thus the writings of the Old Testament formed a necessary preparation for the language of the New, as did also the history and institutions of the one for the religious ideas of the other. Nor is it too much to say, that a Gospel in pure Greek, or even an apostolic epistle in pure Greek, is inconceivable. The canonical and the Hebrew are most intimately connected." Fairbairn adds to this: "It is perfectly consistent with all this, and no less true, that the writers of the New Testament often show a correct acquaintance with the idioms of the Greek language. In many cases their language rises superior to the common dialect of the time, and approaches marvelously near to the precision of Attic Greek, while in other passages it seems to sink below the average standard, and to present to us the peculiarities of the later Greek, distorted and exaggerated by Aramaic forms of expression. Where, however, in a merely-literary point of view, the Sacred Volume may thus seem weakest, it is, considered from a higher point of view, incomparably strongest. It is this investiture of its doctrines with the peculiar richness and force of Hebraistic modes of expression, rather than with the diffluent garb of a corrupted and decayed Hellenism, that does truly reveal to us the overruling providence and manifold wisdom of God."

It is also to be borne in mind, that, while all the writers of the New Testament partook, to some extent, of the Hebraistic influence, some did so considerably more than others. The Hebraistic element differed even with the same writers in different parts of their writings, as in the Apocalypse of John, which is considerably more Hebraistic than either his Gospel or Epistles. The Gospel of Luke is decidedly less marked with Hebraisms than those of Matthew and Mark. While, therefore, there are peculiarities which distinguish the New Testament Greek, as a whole, from other Greek writings, there are also peculiarities distinguishing the Greek of one writer from that of another, words and phrases used by one and not used by the others, or used in a manner peculiar to himself. Thus there is an *individual*, as well as a *general*, impress on the language of the New Testament writers—another mark of their authenticity.

We have shown how fully the language of the Gospels accords with the personality and situation of those to whom they are ascribed. We may go still further and assert, that they could not have been written by any person or persons who lived in another age than that of the apostles. The conjunction of such Latinisms as *κεντυρίων*, (centurion,) *λεγεών*, (legion,) *πραιτώριον*, (prætorium, judgment-hall,) *κουστωδία*, (watch,) *κῆνσος*, (census, tribute,) *κοδράντης*, (quadrans, farthing,) *δηνάριον*, (denarius, penny,) *ἀσσάριον*, (assarius, farthing,) *σπεκουλάτωρ*, (speculator, executioner,) *φραγελλώσας*, (having scourged, a participle formed from the Latin verb flagellare,) and many other terms, referring to the military force, revenue, and offices of the Roman Government, with such Hebraisms as *κορβᾶν*, (Mark vii, 11,) *ραββουνί*, (my Lord,) *δύο δύο*, (literally, two, two, Mark vi, 7,) *πρασιαί πρασιαί*, (literally, onion-beds, onion-beds, that is, in squares, like a garden-plot, Mark vi, 40, a Hebraistic repetition, as in the previous instance,) *τὸ βδέλυγμα τῆς ἐρημώσεως*, (the abomination of desolation,) was natural only in Palestine during the period between Herod the Great and the destruction of Jerusalem, and marks the writers for Jews of that time and country. If we bear in mind that although the New Testament diction has much in common with the LXX and the Greek apocryphal literature of the Old Testament, yet it has also much that is peculiar to itself; that these conclusive peculiarities could possibly arise only in the apostolic age, in such a state of the Jewish polity, as characterized the time between the death of our Savior and the destruction of Jerusalem, and, finally, that the later Christian Greek literature necessarily presupposes the New Testament diction as its basis, we see at once how powerful a proof of the authenticity of our Gospels their peculiar idiom is. Apart from every other consideration, this circumstance alone exposes the absurdity of the theory which assigns the second century to the composition of the Gospels or of any one of them.

Before dismissing, however, the argument for the authenticity of the Gospel records drawn from the New Testament Greek, it is proper to notice an objection. It has been asked: Was the current language of the common Jewish people not the Aramaic dialect of the Hebrew language? Did our Savior and his apostles not usually speak in that language? How does it come, then, that the Evangelists, as well as the other writers of the New Testament, being Jews, should write in Greek? It is true that our Lord is represented on several occasions as speaking in Aramaic: as when he said to the daughter of the Jewish ruler, Jairus, "Talitha cumi," and to the blind man, "Ephphatha," or when he referred to the terms currently employed among the people, such as raka, rabbi, corban; when he applied to his disciples such epithets as Cephas, Barjona, Boanerges, or when, on the cross, he exclaimed, "Eli, Eli, lama sabachthani." There is, on the other hand, a very remarkable circumstance to which the Duke of Manchester—in his Essay on the Harmonizing of the Gospels—has called attention. If we compare the Old Testament passages in the synoptical Gospels, we find that those of them which occur *in the sermons or sayings of the Lord*, are always from the LXX, while those of them which are quoted by *the Evangelists themselves*, deviate from the LXX in favor generally of the Hebrew text. If Christ had generally spoken the Aramaic, it would be incomprehensible why the Evangelists should put quotations from the LXX *only upon his lips*, while *they themselves*, in *their own* quotations, do not restrict themselves to the LXX. The verbal harmony of the synoptical Evangelists is also best accounted for by the presumption that our Lord spoke usually in Greek with his disciples, and this presumption is confirmed by the fact that at the raising of Jairus's daughter, where Jesus spoke Aramaic with the ruler of the synagogue, the verbal harmony of the Synoptist's report of his saying is defective; so, also, in the history of his sufferings, the Old Testament is no longer quoted from the LXX, because at Jerusalem the Aramaic was spoken more generally than in Galilee.

Though Dr. Fairbairn contends that the Aramaic, or later Syro-Chaldaic orm of the Hebrew, was the vernacular language of the Jewish people in the age of our Lord, and, consequently, the medium of intercourse on all ordinary occasions, he admits, "that from a long and varied concatenation of circumstances, the Greek language must have been very commonly understood by the higher and more educated classes throughout Syria. It was the policy both of Alexander and his successors, in that part of the world, to extend the language and culture as well as ascendency of Greece. With this view cities were planted at convenient distances, which might be considered Grecian rather than Asiatic in their population and manners. The Syriac kings, by whom the Macedonian line of rulers was continued, kept up Greek as the court language, and were, doubtless, followed by their official representatives and the influential classes generally throughout the country. The army, too, though not entirely, nor perhaps even in the major part, yet certainly in very considerable proportions, was composed of persons of Grecian origin, who could not fail to make the Greek language in some sense familiar at the various military stations in the regions of Syria. Even after the Macedonian rule had terminated and all became subject to the sway of the Romans, it was still usually through the medium of the Greek tongue that official intercourse was maintained, and the decrees of government were made known. It is in the very nature of things impossible that so many Hellenizing influences should have continued in operation for two or three centuries without leading somewhat generally to a knowledge of Greek among the better classes in all parts of Syria. There were also circumstances more strictly peculiar to the Jewish people, which could not be without their effect in making them to some extent acquainted with the Greek language. Partly from special encouragements held out to them at the founding of Alexandria, a Grecian city, and partly, perhaps, from the mercantile spirit which began to take possession of them from the time of the Babylonish exile, Alexandria became one of their great centers, where, as we are told by Philo, they formed about two-fifths of the entire population. They abounded also, as is clear from the Acts of the Apostles, in the Greek-speaking cities of Asia Minor, and in those of Greece itself. From whatever causes, the dispersion seems, for some generations previous to the Christian era, to have taken very much a western, and especially a Grecian, direction; in every place of importance inhabited by Greeks, members of the stock of Israel had their homes and synagogues. It is only, too, what might have been expected in the circumstances, that the culture and enterprise, which distinguished the communities in those Grecian cities, would act with stimulating effect upon the Jewish mind, and bring its powers into more energetic play and freedom of action than was likely to be found among the Palestinian Jews, who were sealed up in their national bigotry and stagnant Pharisaism. Hence the only moral and religious productions which are known to have appeared among the Jews, between the closing of the Old Testament canon and the birth of Christ—those contained in the apocryphal writings—came chiefly, if not entirely, from the pen of the Hellenistic Jews, and exist only—most probably never did exist but—in the Greek language. Hence also the Greek translation of the Old Testament, which was completed several generations before the Christian era, and which, there is good reason to believe, was in extensive use, about that time, among the Jewish people. So that, looking to the numbers, the higher intelligence, and varied *resources* of the Hellenistic Jews, and taking into account their frequent personal visits to Palestine, at the ever-recurring festivals, we can not doubt that they materially contributed to a partial knowledge and use of the Greek tongue among their brethren in Palestine."

There is scarcely left any doubt, but our Lord and his disciples spoke generally in Greek, and even if this should not have been the case, the fact that the books of the New Testament, and especially those which contain our Lord's personal discourses, should have been originally composed in the Greek instead of in the Aramaic language, is easily accounted for. "It was," says Dr. Fairbairn, "comparatively but a small portion of the people resident in Jerusalem and Judea who embraced the Christian faith; and those who did, having, in the first instance, enjoyed many opportunities of becoming personally acquainted with the facts of Gospel history, and enjoying afterward the ministry of apostles and Evangelists, who were perfectly cognizant of the whole, were, in a manner, independent of any written records. Besides, the troubles which shortly after befell their native land, and which were distinctly foreseen by the founders of the Christian faith, destined, as they were, to scatter the power of the Jewish nation, and to render its land and people monuments of judgment, presented an anticipative reason against committing the sacred and permanent records of the Christian faith to the Hebrew language. That language itself, already corrupted and broken, was presently to become to all but the merest fragment of the Jews themselves, antiquated and obsolete. The real centers of Christianity—the places where it took firmest root, and from which it sent forth its regenerating power among the nations—from the time that authoritative records of its facts and expositions of its doctrines became necessary—were to be found in Greek-speaking communities—the communities scattered throughout the cities of Asia Minor, of Greece, at Rome, and the West—where also the first converts to the Christian faith consisted chiefly of those whose native tongue was Greek. Whether, therefore, respect were had to the immediate wants of the first Christian communities, or to the quarters in which the Gospel was to find its most active agents and representatives, and the direction which it was appointed to take in the world, the Greek was obviously the language in which its original and authoritative documents behooved to be written. Whatever reasons there were for the adherents of Judaism getting the Scriptures of the Old Testament into Greek; whatever reasons, also, Josephus could have for translating into Greek his Jewish histories, and the authors of the apocryphal writings for adopting that language in preference to the Aramaic, the same reasons existed, and in far greater force, for the inspired writings, which were to form, in earlier and later times, the fundamental records of the Christian faith, being composed in the Greek language, and in that language committed to the faithful keeping of the Church. Had they not been originally composed in Greek, the course of Providence would presently have required that they should be translated into Greek; and considering how much depended on the correct knowledge of them, and how many sources we have for illustrating Greek, as compared with Aramaic productions, it was unspeakably better that, from the first, they should have appeared in a Greek form."

§ 15. Some other Characteristics of the Style in which the Gospels are Written.

1. The style of the Gospels, apart from the peculiar dialect of Greek in which they were written, is totally devoid of ornament; it presents no beautiful

transitions from one subject to another; the ear is not charmed with the melody of harmonious periods; the imagination is not fired with grand epithets. In short, we find in the Gospels the simplicity of writers who were more intent upon things than upon words; we find men of plain education honestly relating what they knew, without attempting to adorn their narratives by any elegance of diction. And this is precisely the kind of writing which we should expect from the persons to whom those books are ascribed.

2. The Gospels are not proper histories; that is, they do not furnish a full and satisfactory account of the ministry of Jesus to one previously unacquainted with the essential facts concerning it. Either individually or collectively, they present only a brief narrative of some of the most striking events in our Lord's ministry, and these told by the writers, for the most part, nakedly and in a few words. No skill is shown by any one of the Evangelists in connecting the different parts so as to form a continuous history. No explanations are given, except a few, which are parenthetical and unimportant. With the exception of some passages in John's Gospel, there is no comment or intimation of surprise with regard to any thing told which discovers the writer's feelings or state of mind. This peculiarity of the Gospels furnishes another proof that they could not have been forged, no more than they could have been written by men whose imaginations had been strongly excited by some extraordinary delusion.

3. We discover in the Gospel narratives a striking consistency with that which the Evangelists do not state expressly. This striking consistency has been

presented by Mr. Norton in detail; it is sufficient to quote from him the leading features:

In the narratives of the Evangelists, the existence of many facts which are not expressly mentioned is implied. In order to understand fully what is told, and to perceive its bearing and application, we must take into view very much that is not told. There is to be found in almost every part of the Gospels a latent reference to some existing state of things which is not described. But when we attend to the character of those facts with which different portions of the narrative are thus connected, we find that they are all probable or certain; that we have distinct evidence of them from other sources, or that they are such as must or might have existed. The inferences from these histories, though many and various, are all consistent with the histories themselves, and whatever we can learn from other sources. In tracing out the necessary or probable bearing of those actions and discourses which are recorded, or in assigning their probable occasions or consequences, we detect no inconsistency with the history itself, and find no contradiction of known facts; but, on the contrary, we are continually perceiving new marks of probability and truth. This coincidence between what is told and what is implied does not appear here and there only, but discovers itself throughout the Gospels. But such a consistency of the narrative with itself can evidently not be the work of study or artifice. The Gospels are very inartificial compositions, and if the coincidences had been intended to give an air of probability to the narrative, the writer would have taken care that they should be noticed by the reader. The just and lively conception—which the writers of the Gospels evidently possessed of those numerous facts and circumstances that must or might have existed, if their history be true—admits of no other explanation, than that the narratives rest on the authority of those who were witnesses of what is related, and were themselves concerned in the transactions recorded. It follows, therefore, that these histories were committed to writing either by some of the immediate disciples of Christ, or by persons who derived, generally speaking, correct and particular information from such disciples. And if this conclusion is reached, there is no room left to doubt that they are the works of those particular individuals to whom they have always been ascribed.

We discover, therefore, in the characteristics of the Gospels which we have described, another mode in which it has pleased God to preserve to us in the very books themselves the evidence of their authenticity. Such is their incompleteness, that they are necessarily complicated with a great body of circumstantial evidence of the most unsuspicious kind. Thus, what we might consider as their defects, when regarded merely as literary compositions, contribute greatly to enhance their value.

§ 16. The Frequent Allusions of the Evangelists to the History of their Times.

"Whoever," says Michaelis, "undertakes to forge a set of writings, and ascribe them to persons who lived in a former period, exposes himself to the utmost danger of a discordancy with the history and manners of the age to which his accounts are referred; and this danger increases in proportion as they relate to points not mentioned in general history, but to such as belong only to a single city, sect, religion, or school. Of all books that ever were written, there is none, if the historical books of the New Testament are a forgery, so liable to detection; the scene of action is not confined to a single country, but displayed in the greatest cities of the Roman Empire; allusions are made to the various manners and principles of the Greeks, the Romans, and the Jews, which are carried so far with respect to this last nation, as to extend even to the trifles and follies of their schools. A Greek or Roman Christian, who lived in the second or third century, though ever so well versed in the writings of the ancients, would still have been wanting in Jewish literature; and a Jewish convert in those ages, even the most learned rabbi, would have been equally deficient in the knowledge of Greece and Rome. If, then, the historical books of the New Testament thus exposed to detection—had it been an imposture—are found after the severest researches to harmonize with the history, the manners, and the opinions of the first century; and since the more minutely we inquire, the more perfect we find the coincidence, we must conclude that they were written in the age in which they profess to have been written."

The numerous incidental allusions to the civil history of the times, which the Gospels and the Acts furnish, and which are most strikingly verified by profane writers, have been most carefully collated by Mr. George Rawlinson in his "Historical Evidences of the Truth of the Scripture Records." He groups them under two heads, considering, first, all such as bear upon the general condition of the countries, which were the scene of the history, and, secondly, such as have reference to the civil rulers, who are represented as exercising authority in the countries at the time of the narrative, as follows:

1. The political condition of Palestine at the time to which the New Testament narrative properly belongs, was one curiously complicated and anomalous; it underwent frequent changes, but retained through all of them certain peculiarities, which made the position of the country unique among the dependencies of Rome. Not having been conquered in the ordinary way, but having passed under the Roman dominion with the consent and by the assistance of a large party among the inhabitants, it was allowed to maintain, for a while, a species of semi-independence, not unlike that of various native States in India, which are really British dependencies. A mixture, and to some extent an alternation, of Roman with native power resulted from this arrangement, and a consequent complication in the political *status*, which must have made it very difficult to be thoroughly understood by any one who was not a native and a *cotemporary*. The chief representative of the Roman power in the East—the President of Syria, the local Governor, whether a Herod or a Roman procurator, and the high-priest, had each and all certain rights and a certain authority in the country. A double system of taxation, a double administration of justice, and even in some degree a double military command, were the natural consequence, while Jewish and Roman customs, Jewish and Roman words, were simultaneously in use, and a condition of things existed full of harsh contrasts, strange mixtures, and abrupt transitions. Within the space of fifty years Palestine was a single united kingdom under a native ruler, a

set of principalities under native ethnarchs and tetrarchs, a country in part containing such principalities, in part reduced to the condition of a Roman province, a kingdom reunited once more under a native sovereign, and a country reduced wholly under Rome, and governed by procurators dependent on the President of Syria, but still subject in certain respects to the Jewish monarch of a neighboring territory. These facts we know from Josephus, and other writers, who, though less accurate, on the whole confirm his statements; they render the civil history of Judea during this period one very difficult to master and remember; the frequent changes, supervening upon the original complication, are a fertile source of confusion, and seem to have bewildered even the sagacious and painstaking Tacitus. The New Testament narrative, however, falls into no error in treating of the period; it marks, incidentally and without effort or pretension, the various changes in the civil government—the sole kingdom of Herod the Great, (Matt. ii, 1; Luke i, 5;) the partition of his dominions among his sons, (Matt. ii, 22; xiv, 1; Luke iii, 1;) the reduction of Judea to the condition of a Roman province, while Galilee, Iturea, and Trachonitis continued under native princes, (Luke iii, 1;) the restoration of the old kingdom of Palestine, in the person of Agrippa the First, (Acts xii, 1, etc.,) and the final reduction of the whole under Roman rule, and reëstablishment of procurators, (Acts xxiii, 24; xxiv, 27, etc.,) as the civil heads, while a species of ecclesiastical superintendence was exercised by Agrippa the Second, (Acts xxv, 14, etc.) Again, the New Testament narrative exhibits in the most remarkable way the mixture in the government—the occasional power of the President of Syria, as shown in Cyrenius's "taxing," (Luke ii, 2; compare Acts v, 37;) the ordinary division of authority between the high-priest and the procurator, (Matt. xxvii, 1, 2; Acts xxii, 30; xxiii, 1–10;) the existence of two separate taxations—the civil and the ecclesiastical—the "census," (Matt. xvii, 17,) and the "didrachm," (Matt. xvii, 24;) of two tribunals, (John xviii, 28, 32, etc.,) two modes of capital punishment, two military forces, (Matt. xvii, 64, 65,) two methods of marking time, (Luke iii, 11;) at every turn it shows, even in such little matters as verbal expressions, the coexistence of Jewish with Roman ideas and practices in the country—*a coexistence which*, it must be remembered, *came to an end within forty years of our Lord's crucifixion.* The general tone and temper of the Jews at the time, their feelings toward the Romans, and toward their neighbors, their internal divisions and sects, their confident expectation of a deliverer, are represented by Josephus, and other writers, in a manner which very strikingly accords with the account incidentally given by the Evangelists. The extreme corruption and wickedness, not only of the mass of the people, but even of the rulers and chief men, is asserted by Josephus in the strongest terms;* while, at the same time, he testifies to the existence among them of a species of zeal for religion, a read-

*Joseph., De Bell. Jud., vii, 8, § 1: "For that time was fruitful among the Jews in all sorts of wickedness, so that they left no evil deed undone; nor was there any new form of wickedness which any one could invent if he wished to do so. Thus they were all corrupt both in their public and their private relations; and they vied with each other who should excel in impiety toward God and injustice to men. The more powerful oppressed the common people, and the common people eagerly sought to destroy the more powerful, for the former class were governed by the love of power, and the latter by the desire to seize and plunder the possessions of the wealthy." (Compare Ant. Jud., xx, 7, § 8; Bell. Jud., v, 13, § 6; and 10, § 5.)

iness to attend the feasts,* a regularity in the offering of sacrifice,† an almost superstitious regard for the Temple,‡ and fanatic abhorrence of all who sought to change the customs which Moses had delivered," (Acts vi, 14.) The conspiracy against Herod the Great, when ten men bound themselves by an oath to kill him, and, having armed themselves with short daggers, which they hid under their clothes, entered into the theater where they expected Herod to arrive, intending, if he came, to fall upon him and dispatch him with their weapons,§ breathes the identical spirit of that against Paul, which the promptness of the chief captain, Lysias, alone frustrated, (Acts xxiii, 12–41.) We find, from Josephus, that there was a warm controversy among the Jews themselves as to the lawfulness of "giving tribute to Cæsar,"‖ (Matt. xxii, 17;) that the Samaritans were hostile to such of the Galileans as had their "faces

*Joseph., Ant. Jud., xvii, 9, § 3; xx, 4, § 3; Bell. Jud., ii, 19, § 1, etc. On one occasion it appears that more than two and a half millions of persons had come up to Jerusalem to worship. (Bell. Jud., vi, 9, § 3.)

†Ant. Jud., xv, 7, § 8: "In Jerusalem there were two fortresses, one belonging to the city itself, and the other to the Temple. Whoever held these had the whole nation in their power; for without the command of these, it was not possible to offer the sacrifices; and no Jew could endure the thought that these should fail to be offered; they were even ready sooner to lay down their lives than omit the religious sacrifices which they were accustomed to offer to God.

‡Not only was Caligula's attempt to have his statue set up in the Temple resisted with determination, (Joseph., Ant. Jud., xviii, 8,) but when the younger Agrippa, by raising the hight of his house, obtained a view into the Temple courts, the greatest indignation was felt. The Jews immediately raised a wall to shut out his prospect, and when Festus commanded them to remove it, they positively refused, declaring that they would rather die than destroy any portion of the sacred fabric. (See Ant. Jud., xx, 8, § 11, and on the general subject compare Philo, De Legat. ad Caium. pp. 1022, 1023.)

§Ant. Jud., xv, 8, §§ 1–4.

‖Josephus tells us that when Cyrenius came to take the census of men's properties throughout Judea, a controversy arose among the Jews on the legality of submission to foreign taxation. Judas of Galilee (Acts v, 37) maintained that it was a surrender of the theocratic principle; while the bulk of the chief men, including some considerable number of the Pharisees, took the opposite view, and persuaded the people to submit themselves. (Ant. Jud., xviii, 1, § 1.)

set to go to Jerusalem," (Luke ix, 51;) that on one occasion, at least, they fell upon those who were journeying through their land to attend a feast, and murdered a large number,* that the Pharisees and Sadducees were noted sects, distinguished by the tenets which in Scripture are assigned to them;† that the Pharisees were the more popular, and persuaded the common people as they pleased, while the Sadducees were important chiefly as men of high rank and station;‡ and that a general expectation, founded upon the prophecies of the Old Testament, existed among the Jews during the Roman war, that a great king was about to rise up, in the East, of their own race and country.§ This last fact is confirmed by both Suetonius|| and Tacitus,¶ and is one

*Ant. Jud., xx, 6, § 1: "Now, there arose an enmity between the Samaritans and the Jews, from the following cause: The Galileans were accustomed, in going up to the feasts that were held in Jerusalem, to pass through the country of the Samaritans. At this time there was, on the road which they took, a village called Ginea, situated on the boundary between Samaria and the great plain. When the Galileans came to this place they were attacked, and many of them killed.

†Ant. Jud., xviii, 1, §§ 3, 4. Note especially the following: Of the Pharisees—"They believe that souls have immortal vigor, and that beyond the grave there are rewards and punishments, according as they follow a virtuous or a vicious course of life in this world." Of the Sadducees—"But the doctrine of the Sadducees is, that the soul is annihilated together with the body." (Compare Acts xxiii, 8.)

‡Ant. Jud., I, s. c. [The Pharisees] "are very influential with the people; and whatever prayers to God or sacrifices are performed, are performed at their dictation. The doctrine (of the Sadducees) is received by but few: but these are the men who are in the highest authority."

§Bell. Jud., vi, 5, § 4. "But that which most of all roused them to undertake this war, was an ambiguous article, . . . found in their sacred books, that, at that time, a man of their country should rule over the whole earth."

||Sueton., Vit. Vespasian, § 4: "An ancient and settled opinion had prevailed throughout the whole East, that fate had decreed that at that time persons proceeding from Judea should become masters of the world. This was foretold, as the event afterward proved, of the Roman emperor; but the Jews applied it to themselves, and this was the cause of their rebellion." (Compare Vit. Octav., § 94, and Virg. Eclog., iv.)

¶Tacit. Histor., v, 13: "These things [the prodigies that occurred just before the capture of Jerusalem by the Romans] were regarded by a few as alarming omens; but the greater number believed that it was written in the ancient books

which even Strauss does not venture to dispute. It would be easy to point out a further agreement between the Evangelical historians and profane writers with respect to the manners and customs of the Jews at this period. There is scarcely a matter of this kind noted in the New Testament, which may not be confirmed from Jewish sources, such as Josephus, Philo, and the Mishna. The points of agreement hitherto adduced have had reference to the Holy Land and its inhabitants. It is not, however, in this connection only that the accuracy of the Evangelical writers in their accounts of the general condition of those countries which are the scene of their history is observable. Their descriptions of the Greek and Roman world, so far as it comes under their cognizance, are most accurate. No where have the character of the Athenians and the general appearance of Athens been more truthfully and skillfully portrayed than in the few verses of the Acts which contain the account of Paul's visit. The people—"Athenians *and strangers* spending their time in nothing but hearing or telling of some new thing," (Acts xvii, 21;) philosophizing and disputing on Mars' Hill and in the market-place, (ibid., verse 17,) glad to discuss, though disinclined to believe, (Acts xvii, 32, 33,) and yet religious withal, standing in honorable contrast with the other Greeks in respect of their reverence for things divine, (ibid., verse 22,)—are put before us with all the vividness of life, just as they present themselves to our view in the pages of their own historians and orators.* Again,

of the priests, that at that very time the East should become very powerful, and that persons proceeding from Judea should become masters of the world."

* How attractive to *strangers* Athens was, even in her decline, may be seen from the examples of Cicero, Germanicus, Pausanias, and others. (See Conybeare and

how striking, and how thoroughly classical is the account of the tumult at Ephesus, (Acts xix, 23,) where almost every word receives illustration from ancient coins and inscriptions, as has been excellently shown in a recent work of great merit on the life of Paul.* Or, if we turn to Rome and the Roman system, how truly do we find depicted the great and terrible emperor, whom all feared to provoke—the provincial administration by proconsuls and others chiefly anxious that tumults should be prevented—the contemptuous religious tolerance—the noble principle of Roman law, professed, if not always acted on, whereby accusers and accused were brought "face to face," and the latter had free "license to answer for themselves concerning the crimes laid against them, (Acts xxv, 16)—the privileges of Roman citizenship, sometimes acquired by birth, sometimes by purchase—the right of appeal possessed and exercised

Howson's Life of St. Paul, vol. i, pp. 398, 399.) On the greediness of the Athenians after *novelty* see Demost. Philipp., i, p. 43, ("Or tell me, do you wish to go about asking each other in the market-place, What is the news? And can there be any thing newer than that the man of Macedon," etc.;) Philipp. Epist., pp. 156, 157; Ælian., Var. Hist., v, 13; Schol. ad Thucyd., iii, 38, etc. On their religiousness, compare Pausan., i, 24, § 3, (the Athenians are more zealous than others in the worship of gods;) Xen., Rep. Atheniens., iii, §§ 1, 8; Joseph., Contra Apion., ii, 11, ("All say that the Athenians are the most religious of the Greeks;") Strab., v, 3, § 18; Ælian., Var. Hist., v, 17; Philostrat., Vit. Appollon., vi, 3; Dionys. Hal. De Jud. Thucyd., § 40; and among later authors, see Mr. Grote's History of Greece, vol. iii, pp. 229–232.

* See the Life and Epistles of St. Paul by Messrs. Conybeare and Howson, vol. ii, pp. 66, etc. (1.) The "Great Goddess Diana" is found to have borne that title as her *usual title*, both from an inscription, (Bœckh, Corpus Inscript., 2,963,) and from Xenophon, (Ephes., i, p. 15,) "I invoke our ancestral God, the Great Diana of the Ephesians." (2.) The Asiarchs are mentioned on various coins and inscriptions. (3.) The town-clerk (γραμματεὺς) of Ephesus is likewise mentioned in inscriptions. (Bœckh, No. 2,963 C, No. 2,966, and No. 2,990.) (4.) The curious word νεωκόρος, (Acts xix, 35,) literally "sweeper" of the temple, is also found in inscriptions and on coins, as an epithet of the Ephesian people. (Bœckh, No. 2,966.) The "silver shrines of Diana," the "court-days," the "deputies" or "proconsuls," (ἀνθύπατοι,) might receive abundant classical illustration. The temple was the glory of the ancient world; enough still remains of the "theater" to give evidence of its former greatness.

by the provincials—the treatment of prisoners—the peculiar manner of chaining them—the employment of soldiers as their guards—the examination by torture—the punishment of condemned persons not being Roman citizens by scourging and crucifixion—the manner of this punishment—the practice of bearing the cross, of affixing a title or superscription, of placing soldiers under a centurion to watch the carrying into effect of this sentence, of giving the garments of the sufferer to these persons, of allowing the bodies after death to be buried by the friends—and the like! The sacred historians are as familiar not only with the general character, but even with some of the obscurer customs of Greece and Rome, as with those of their own country. Fairly observant and always faithful in their accounts, they continually bring before us little points which accord minutely with notices in profane writers nearly cotemporary with them, while occasionally they increase our knowledge of classic antiquity by touches harmonious with its spirit, but additional to the information which we derive from the native authorities.* Again,

*Among minute points of accordance may be especially noticed the following: 1. The geographical accuracy. (1.) Compare the divisions of Asia Minor mentioned in the Acts with those in Pliny. Phrygia, Galatia, Lycaonia, Cilicia, Pamphylia, Pisidia, Asia, Mysia, Bithynia, are all recognized as existing provinces by the Roman geographer writing probably within a few years of Luke. (Plin., H. N., v, 27, etc.) (2.) The division of European Greece into the two provinces of Macedonia and Achaia, (Acts xix, 24, etc.,) accords exactly with the arrangement of Augustus noticed in Strabo, (xvii, ad fin.) (3.) The various tracts in or about Palestine belong exactly to the geography of the time, *and of no other*. Judea, Samaria, Galilee, Trachonitis, Iturea, Abilene, Decapolis, are recognized as geographically distinct at this period by the Jewish and classical writers. (See Plin., H. N., v, 14, 18, 23; Strab., xvi, §§ 10, 34; Joseph., Ant. Jud., xix, 5, § 1, etc.) (4.) The routes mentioned are such as were in use at the time. The "ship of Alexandria," which, conveying Paul to Rome, lands him at Puteoli, follows the ordinary course of the Alexandrian corn-ships, as mentioned by Strabo, (xvii, 1, § 7,) Philo, (in Flacc., pp. 968-9,) and Seneca, (Epist. 77,) and touches at customary harbors. (See Sueton., Vit. Tit., § 25.) Paul's journey from Troas by Neapolis to Philippi presents an exact parallel to that of Igna-

it has been well remarked that the condition of the Jews beyond the limits of Palestine is represented by the Evangelical writers very agreeably to what may be gathered of it from Jewish and heathen sources. The wide dispersion of the chosen race is one of the facts most evident upon the surface of the New Testament history. "Parthians, and Medes, and Elamites, and dwellers in Mesopotamia, and Judea, and Cappadocia, Pontus, and Asia, Phrygia, and Pamphylia, in Egypt, and in the parts of Lybia about Cyrene, strangers of Rome, Cretes, and Arabians," (Acts ii, 9–11,) are said to have been witnesses, at Jerusalem, of the first outpourings of the Holy Ghost. In the travels of Paul through Asia

tius, sixty years later, (Martyr. Ignat., c. 5.) His passage through Amphipolis and Appollonia, on his road from Philippi to Thessalonica, is in accordance with the Itinerary of Antoine, which places those towns on the route between the two cities. (5.) The mention of Philippi as the first city of Macedonia to one approaching from the East, ("the chief city of that part of Macedonia," Acts xvi, 12,) is correct, since there was no other between it and Neapolis. The statement that it was a "colony" is also true, (Dio. Cass., li, 4, p. 445, D.; Plin., H. N., iv, 11; Strab., vii, Fr., 41.) 2. The minute political knowledge. (1.) We have already seen the intimate knowledge exhibited of the state of Ephesus, with its proconsul, town-clerks, Asiarchs, etc. A similar exactitude appears in the designation of the chief magistrates of Thessalonica as "the rulers of the city," (Acts xvii, 6,) their proper and peculiar appellation. (Bœckh, Corp. Inscr., No. 1,967.) (2.) So, too, the Roman Governors of Corinth and Cyprus are given their correct titles. (3.) Publius, the Roman Governor of Malta, has again his proper technical designation, ("the chief man of the island," Acts xxviii, 7,) as appears from inscriptions commemorating the chief of the Melitans, or "Melitensium primus." (See Alford ii, p. 282.) (4.) The delivery of the prisoners to the "captain of the [Prætorian] guard" at Rome is in strict accordance with the practice of the time. (Trajan. ap. Plin., Ep. x, 65: "He ought to be sent bound to the Prefects of my Prætorian guard." Compare Philostrat., Vit. Sophist., ii, 32.)

Among additions to our classical knowledge for which we are indebted to Scripture it may suffice to mention, 1. The existence of an Italian cohort, (the Italian band,) as early as the reign of Tiberius, (Acts x, 1.) 2. The application of the term Σεβαστὴ, (Augustan,) to another *cohort*, a little later, (Acts xxviii, 1.) 3. The existence of an altar at Athens with the inscription, "To the unknown God," (Acts xvii, 23,) which is not to be confounded with the well-known inscriptions to unknown gods. 4. The use of the title στρατηγοὶ (Prætors) by the Duumviri or chief magistrates of Philippi, (Acts xvi, 20.) We know from Cicero, (De Leg. Agrar., 34,) that the title was sometimes assumed in such cases, but we have no other proof that it was in use at Philippi.

Minor and Greece, there is scarcely a city to which he comes but has a large body of Jewish residents. Compare with these representations the statements of Agrippa the First, in his letter to Caligula, as reported by the Jewish writer, Philo. "The Holy City, the place of my nativity," he says, "is the metropolis, not of Judea only, but of most other countries, by means of the colonies which have been sent out of it from time to time; some to the neighboring countries of Egypt, Phœnicia, Syria, Cœlo-Syria—some to more distant regions, as Pamphylia, Cilicia, Asia as far as Bythnia, and the recesses of Pontus—and in Europe, Thessaly, Bœotia, Macedonia, Ætolia, Attica, Argos, Corinth, together with the most famous of the islands, Eubœa, Cyprus, and Crete, to say nothing of those who dwell beyond the Euphrates. For, excepting a small part of the Babylonian, and other satrapies, all the countries which have a fertile territory possess Jewish inhabitants; so that, if thou shalt show this kindness to my native place, thou wilt benefit not one city only, but thousands in every region of the world, in Europe, in Asia, in Africa—on the continents, and in the islands—on the shores of the sea, and in the interior." In a similar strain, Philo himself boasts, that "one region does not contain the Jewish people, since it is exceedingly numerous; but there are many of them in almost all the flourishing countries of Europe and Asia, both continental and insular." And the customs of these dispersed Jews are accurately represented in the New Testament. That they consisted in part of native Jews, in part of converts or proselytes, is evident from Josephus;* that they had

*Joseph., Ant. Jud., xx, 2; De Bell. Jud., vii, 3, § 3; Contr. Apion., ii, 36, etc.

places of worship, called Synagogues or oratories, in the towns where they lived, appears from Philo; that these were commonly by the seaside, as represented in the Acts, (Acts xvi, 13,) is plain from many authors;* that they had also—at least sometimes—a synagogue belonging to them at Jerusalem, whither they resorted at the time of the feasts, is certain from the Talmudical writers; that at Rome they consisted in great part of freed men, or "Libertines," whence the synagogue of the Libertines, (Acts vi, 9,) may be gathered from Philo and Tacitus. Their bearing toward the apostolic preachers is such as we should expect from persons whose close contact with those of a different religion made them all the more zealous for their own; and their tumultuous proceedings are in accordance with all that we learn from profane authors of the tone and temper of the Jews generally at this period.†

II. The civil governors and administrators distinctly mentioned by the New Testament historians are the following: the Roman Emperors Augustus, Tiberius, and Claudius; the Jewish Kings and Princes, Herod the Great, Archelaus, Herod the Tetrarch, (or as he is commonly called, Herod Antipas,) Philip the Tetrarch, Herod Agrippa the First, and Herod Agrippa the Second; the Roman Governors, Cyrenius, (or Quirinius,) Pontius Pilate, Sergius Paulus, Gallio, Festus, and Felix, and the Greek

*Philo frequently mentions the synagogue under the name of "places of prayer." (In Flacc., p. 972, A., B., E.; Legat. in Caium, p. 1,014, etc.) Their position by the seaside or by a riverside is indicated, among other places, in the Decree of the Halicarnassians reported by Josephus, (Ant. Jud., xiv, 10, § 23,) where the Jews are allowed to offer prayers by the seaside according to their national custom. See also Philo, Legat. in Caium, p. 982, D.; Tertull. ad Nat. i, 13; and Juv. Sat., iii, 13.

†For the tumultuous spirit of the foreign Jews, see Sueton., Vit. Claud., p. 25; Dio Cassius, lx, 6; Joseph., Ant. Jud., xviii, 8, § 1; 9, § 9; xx, 1, § 1, etc.

Tetrarch, Lysanias. It may be shown from profane sources, in almost every case, that these persons existed; that they lived at the time, and bore the offices assigned to them; that they were related to each other, when any relationship is stated, as Scripture declares; and that the actions ascribed to them are either actually such as they performed, or at least in perfect harmony with what profane history tells us of their characters.

The Jewish kings and princes, whose names occur in the New Testament narrative, occupy a far more prominent place in it than the Roman emperors. The Gospel narrative opens, "In the days of Herod the King," (Matt. ii, 1; Luke i, 5;) who, as the father of Archelaus, (Matt. ii, 22,) may be identified with the first monarch of the name, the son of Antipater the Idumean. This monarch is known to have reigned in Palestine cotemporaneously with Augustus, who confirmed him in his kingdom, and of whom he held the sovereignty till his decease. Cunning, suspicion, and cruelty are the chief traits of his character, as depicted in Scripture, and these are among his most marked characteristics in Josephus.* The consistency of the massacre at Bethlehem with his temper and disposition is now acknowledged;† skepticism

* The cruelties, deceptions, and suspicions of Herod the Great fill many chapters in Josephus. (Ant. Jud., xv, 1, 3, 6, 7, etc.; xvi, 4, 8, 10; xvii, 3, 6, 7, etc.) His character is thus summed up by that writer: "He was a man cruel to all alike, yielding to the impulse of passion, but regardless of the claims of justice; and yet no one was ever favored with a more propitious fortune." (Ant. Jud., xvii, 8, § 1. His arrest of the chief men throughout his dominion, and design that on his own demise they should all be executed, (Ibid., 6, § 5; Bell. Jud., i, 33, § 6,) shows a bloodier temper than even the massacre of the Innocents.

† Strauss grants the massacre to be "not inconsistent with the disposition of the aged tyrant to the extent that Schleiermacher supposed," but objects that "neither Josephus, who is very minute in his account of Herod, nor the rabbins, who were assiduous in blackening his memory, give the slightest hint

has nothing to urge against it, except the silence of the Jewish writers, which is a weak argument, if it is not outweighed by the testimony, albeit somewhat late and perhaps inaccurate, of Macrobius.*

At the death of Herod the Great his kingdom—according to Josephus—was divided, with the consent of Augustus, among three of his sons. Archelaus received Judea, Samaria, and Idumea, with the title of ethnarch; Philip and Antipas were made tetrarchs, and received, the latter Galilee and Perea, the former Trachonitis and the adjoining regions.† The notices of the Evangelists are confessedly in complete accordance with these statements. Matthew mentions the succession of Archelaus in Judea, and implies that he did not reign in Galilee, (Matt. ii, 22.) Luke records Philip's tetrarchy, (Luke iii, 1;) while the tetrarchy of Antipas, who is designated by his family

of this decree." He omits to observe, that they could scarcely narrate the circumstance without some mention of its reason—the birth of the supposed Messiah—a subject on which their prejudices necessarily kept them silent.

* Macrob. Saturnal., ii, 4: "When Augustus had heard that *among the children under two years of age whom Herod, the king of the Jews, had commanded to be slain in Syria*, there was also one of the king's own sons, he said it was better to be the sow than the son of Herod;" Strauss contends that "the passage loses all credit by *confounding the execution of Antipater*, who had gray hairs, with the murder of the infants renowned among the Christians;" but Macrobius says nothing of Antipater, and evidently does not refer to any of the known sons of Herod. He believes that among the children massacred was an *infant* son of the Jewish king. It is impossible to say whether he was right or wrong in this belief. It may have simply originated in the fact that a jealousy of a *royal* infant was known to have been the motive for the massacre. (See Olshausen, Biblic. Comment., vol. i, p. 72, note, p. 67, E. T.)

† Josephus says, "When Cæsar had heard these things he dissolved the assembly, and a few days after he appointed Archelaus, not indeed king, but ethnarch of half the country which had been subject to Herod, . . . and the other half he divided, and gave it to two other sons of Herod, Philip and Antipas, . . . to the latter of whom he made Perea and Galilee subject, . . . while Batanea with Trachonitis and Auranitis, with a certain part of what is called the House of Zenadorus, were subjected to Philip; but the parts subject to Archelaus were Idumea, and Judea, and Samaria." (Antiq. Jud., xvii, 11, § 4.) Compare the brief notice of Tacitus: "The country which had been subdued was governed, in three divisions, by the sons of Herod." (Hist., v, 9.)

name of Herod, is distinctly asserted by both Evangelists, (Matt. xiv, 1.) Moreover, Matthew implies that Archelaus bore a bad character at the time of his accession, or soon afterward, which is consistent with the account of Josephus, who tells us that he was hated by the other members of his own family; and that shortly after his father's death he slew three thousand Jews, on account of a tumult at Jerusalem. The first three Evangelists agree as to the character of Herod Antipas, which is weak, rather than cruel or bloodthirsty; and their portraiture is granted to be "not inconsistent with his character, as gathered from other sources." The facts of his adultery with Herodias, the wife of one of his brothers,* and of his execution of John the Baptist for no crime that could be alleged against him, are recorded by Josephus;† and though in the latter case there is some apparent diversity in the details, yet it is plain that

*Josephus says, "Herod the tetrarch had married the daughter of Aretas, and had now lived with her a long time. But having made a journey to Rome, he lodged in the house of Herod, his brother, but not by the same mother. For this Herod was the son of the daughter of Simon, the high-priest. Now, he fell in love with Herodias, this man's wife, who was the daughter of Aristobulus, their brother, and the sister of Agrippa the Great; and he had the boldness to propose marriage. She accepted the proposal, and it was agreed that she should go to live with him whenever he should return from Rome." (Ant. Jud., xviii, 5, § 1.) And again: "Herodias, their sister, was married to Herod, the son of Herod the Great, who was born of Mariamne, the daughter of Simon the high-priest, who had also a daughter Salome; after the birth of whom Herodias, in shameful violations of the customs of our nation, allowed herself to marry Herod, the brother of her former husband by the same father, separating from him while he was living. Now this man [whom she married] held the office of tetrarch of Galilee." (Ibid., § 4.)

†Ant. Jud., xviii, 5, § 2: "Now some of the Jews thought that the army of Herod had been destroyed by God, in most righteous vengeance for the punishment inflicted upon *John, surnamed the Baptist*. For he taught the Jews to cultivate virtue, and to practice righteousness toward each other and piety toward God, and so to come to baptism. For he declared that this dipping would be acceptable to Him, if they used it not with reference *to the renunciation of certain sins*, but to the purification of the body, the soul having been purified by righteousness. And when others thronged to him—for they were profoundly moved at the hearing of his words—Herod feared that his great influence over the

the different accounts may be reconciled.* The continuance of the tetrarchy of Philip beyond the fifteenth, and that of Antipas beyond the eighteenth of Tiberius, is confirmed by Josephus,† who also shows that the ethnarchy of Archelaus came speedily to an end, and that Judea was then reduced to the condition of a Roman province, and governed for a considerable space by procurators. However, after a while, the various dominions of Herod the Great were reunited in the person of his grandson, Agrippa, the son of Aristobulus and brother of Herodias, who was allowed the title of king, and was in favor with both Caligula and Claudius. It can not be doubted that this person is the "Herod the King" of the

men would lead them to some revolt, for they seemed ready to do any thing by his advice; he, therefore, thought it much better to anticipate the evil, by putting him to death, before he had attempted to make any innovation, than to allow himself to be brought into trouble and then repent after some revolutionary movement had commenced. And so John, in consequence of the suspicion of Herod, was sent as a prisoner to the aforementioned castle of Machærus, and was there put to death." The genuineness of this passage is admitted even by Strauss. (Leben Jesu, § 48; vol. 1, pp. 344–47, E. T.)

* This even Strauss admits. The chief points of apparent difference are the motive of the imprisonment and the scene of the execution. Josephus makes fear of a popular insurrection, the Evangelist's offense at a personal rebuke, the motive. But here, as Strauss observes, there is no contradiction, for Antipas might well fear that John, by his strong censure of the marriage and the whole course of the tetrarch's life, might stir up the people into rebellion against him. Again, from the Gospels we naturally imagine the prison to be near Tiberias, where Herod Antipas ordinarily resided; but Josephus says that prison was at Machærus in Perea, a day's journey from Tiberias. Here, however, an examination of the Gospels shows, that the place where Antipas made his feast and gave his promise is not mentioned. It only appears that it was near the prison. Now, as Herod was at this time engaged in a war with Aretas, the Arabian prince, between whose kingdom and his own lay the fortress of Machærus, it is a probable solution of the difficulty that he was residing with his court at Machærus at this period. (Strauss, § 48, ad fin.) This supposition is confirmed by the fact that Josephus connects the imprisonment and death of the Baptist with the defeat of Herod in battle by his father-in-law, Aretas—this defeat being regarded by many of the Jews as a just punishment sent by God upon Herod for this act of injustice and cruelty.

† Philip is said to have retained his tetrarchy till the twentieth year of Tiberius. (Ant. Jud., xviii, 5, § 6.) Herod Antipas lost his government in the first of Caligula. (Ibid., ch. 7.)

Acts, (Acts xii, 1,) whose persecution of the Church, whose impious pride, and whose miserable death, are related at length by the sacred historian. Josephus records, with less accuracy of detail than Luke, the striking circumstances of this monarch's decease—the "set day," the public assemblage, the "royal dress," the impious flattery, its complacent reception, the sudden judgment, the excruciating disease, the speedy death.* No where does profane history furnish a more striking testimony to the substantial truth of the sacred narrative, no where is the superior exactness of the latter over the former more conspicuous.

On the death of Herod Agrippa, Judea—as Josephus informs us—became once more a Roman prov-

*Josephus, Ant. Jud., xix, 8, § 2: "Now after he had reigned three full years over the whole of Judea, he *was at the city of Cæsarea*, which was formerly called Strato's Tower. And there he held public shows in honor of Cæsar, having learned that a certain festival was celebrated at that time to make vows for his safety. Now, at that festival, there were assembled a multitude of those who were first in office and authority in the province. On the second day of the shows, putting on a robe made entirely of silver, the texture of which was truly wonderful, he came into the theater early in the morning. When the first beams of the sun shone upon the silver, it glittered in a wonderful manner, flashing forth a brilliancy which amazed and awed those who gazed upon him. Whereupon his flatterers immediately cried out—though not for his good—one from one place, and one from another—addressing him as a god—'Be propitious unto us,' and adding, 'Although we have heretofore feared thee as a man, yet henceforth we acknowledge thee to be of more than mortal nature.' The king did not rebuke them, nor reject their impious flattery. A little after, therefore, looking up, he saw an owl sitting on a certain rope over his head; and he immediately understood that it was a messenger of evil, as it had formerly been of good; whereupon he was overcome with a profound sadness. There was also a severe pain in his bowels, which began with a sudden violence. Turning, therefore, to his friends he said: 'I, your god, am now commanded to end my life; and fate immediately reproves the false shouts that were just now addressed to me; and so I, whom you call immortal, am now snatched away by death. But we must accept the fate which God ordains! And, indeed, we have not lived ill, but in the most brilliant good fortune.' When he had said this he was overcome by the intensity of the pain. He was, therefore, quickly carried to the palace, and the report went abroad to all that he must inevitably soon die. . . Being consumed thus, for five days in succession, with the pain in his belly, he departed this life."

ince under procurators,* but the small kingdom of Chalcis was, a few years later, conferred by Claudius on this Herod's son, Agrippa the Second, who, afterward, received other territories.† This prince is evidently the "King Agrippa" before whom Paul pleaded his cause. (Acts xxv, 13, etc.) The Bernice, who is mentioned as accompanying him on his visit to Festus, was his sister, who lived with him, and commonly accompanied him upon his journeys.‡ Besides his separate sovereignty he had received from the emperor a species of ecclesiastical supremacy in Judea, where he had the superintendence of the Temple, the direction of the sacred treasury, and the right of nominating the high-priests.§ These circumstances account sufficiently for his visit to Judea, and explain the anxiety of Festus that he should hear Paul, and Paul's willingness to plead before him.

The Roman procurators, Pontius Pilate, Felix, and Festus, are prominent personages in the history of Josephus, where they occur in the proper chronolog-

* Ant. Jud., xix, 9, § 2: "[Claudius] therefore sent Caspius Fadus as a procurator over Judea and all the kingdom."

† Ant. Jud., xx, 5, § 2; vii, 1; and 8, § 4. Agrippa II bore the title of king, (De Bell. Jud., ii, 12, § 8.)

‡ Ant. Jud., xix, 9, § 1; xx, 7, § 3. The evil reports which arose from this constant companionship are noticed by Josephus in the latter of these passages. They are glanced at in the well-known passage of Juvenal, (Sat. vi, 155–169;) "That well-known diamond made even more precious by being worn on the finger of Bernice. This jewel the barbarian formerly gave to that unchaste woman, and Agrippa gave it to his sister, in that country where kings keep the Sabbath festival with naked feet, and an ancient indulgence allows the old men to eat pork." (Compare Tacit., Hist., ii, 2, 81.)

§ Joseph., Ant. Jud., xx, 8, § 8; 9, § 7: "The king had been intrusted by Claudius Cæsar with the care of the Temple." In one passage, (Ant. Jud., xx, 1, § 3,) Josephus says that these privileges continued to be exercised by the *descendants* of Herod, king of Chalcis, from his decease to the end of the war. But he here uses the term "descendants" very loosely, or he forgets that Agrippa II was the nephew, and not the son of this monarch. (See the note of Lardner. Credibility, vol. i, p. 18, note g.)

ical position,* and bear characters very agreeable to those which are assigned to them by the sacred writers. The vacillation of Pilate, his timidity, and, at the same time, his occasional violence,† the cruelty, injustice, and rapacity of Felix,‡ and the comparatively-equitable and mild character of Festus,§ are apparent in the Jewish historian, and have some sanction from other writers.

It only remains to notice an objection that has been made to the evidence presented in the many historical allusions of the Evangelists, and their verification by profane writers. It is said that there are remarkable facts in the Gospels, which we do not find alluded to by profane historians, though we

* The procuratorship of Pilate lasted from the twelfth year of Tiberius—A. D. 26—to the twenty-second—A. D. 36. (See Joseph., Ant. Jud., xviii, 3, § 2; 4, § 2.) Felix entered upon his office as *sole* procurator in the twelfth year of Claudius—A. D. 53—and was succeeded by Porcius Festus early in the reign of Nero, (Ant. Jud., xx, 7, § 1; 8, § 9.)

† The vacillation and timidity of Pilate appear in his attempt to establish the images of Tiberius in Jerusalem, followed almost immediately by their withdrawal. (Ant. Jud., xvii, 3, § 1.) His violence is shown in his conduct toward the Jews who opposed his application of the Temple money to the construction of an aqueduct at Jerusalem, (Ibid., § 2,) as well as in his treatment of the Samaritans on the occasion which led to his removal. (Ibid., iv, § 1.) Agrippa the elder speaks of the iniquity of his government in the strongest terms, (Ap. Philon., Leg. ad Caium, p. 1,034:) "He feared lest they should examine and expose the misdeeds of his former procuratorship, the taking of bribes, the acts of violence, the extortions, the tortures, the menaces, the repeated murders without any form of trial, the harsh and incessant cruelty."

‡ Tacitus says of Felix: "Antonius Felix exercised the royal authority in a manner agreeable to the baseness of his disposition, with all cruelty and wantonness." (Hist., v, 9.) And again: "But his father, whose surname was Felix, did not conduct himself with the same moderation. Having been a long time governor of Judea, he thought he could commit all crimes with impunity, relying on his great power." (Ann., xii, 54.) Josephus gives a similar account of his government. (Ant. Jud., xx, 8.) After he quitted office he was accused to the emperor, and only escaped a severe sentence by the influence which his brother Pallas possessed with Nero.

§ See Ant. Jud., xx, 8, §§ 10, 11; Bell. Jud., ii, 14, § 1. In the latter passage Josephus says: "Now Festus having succeeded this man in the office of procurator, relieved the country of its greatest scourge. For he captured a large number of the robbers, and destroyed not a few. But Albinus, who succeeded Festus, did not govern after the same manner. For it is not possible to mention any form of evil-doing which he omitted to practice."

might justly expect them to have attracted their attention. We shall speak of these in § 23.

Great stress is laid upon the difficulty with regard to the taxing of Cyrenius. A satisfactory solution of this and a few other minor difficulties, the reader will find in most of the Commentaries. Mr. Rawlinson closes his historical review with the following remarks: "We have found that the historical books of the New Testament contain a vast body of incidental allusions to the civil history of the times, capable of being tested by comparison with the works of profane historians. We have submitted the greater part of these incidental allusions to the test of such comparison; and we have found, in all but some three or four doubtful cases, an entire and striking harmony. In no case have we met with clear and certain disagreement; in such cases we must take into consideration that profane writers are not infallible; Josephus, our chief profane authority for the time, has been shown, even in matters where he does not come into any collision with the Christian Scriptures, to teem with inaccuracies. If, therefore, in any case it should be thought that we must choose between Josephus and an Evangelist, sound criticism requires that we should prefer the latter to the former. Josephus is not entirely honest; he has his Roman masters to please, and he is prejudiced in favor of his own sect, the Pharisees. He has been convicted of error, which is not the case with any Evangelist. His authority, therefore, is, in the eyes of a historical critic, inferior to that of the Gospel writers, and in any instance of contradiction, it would be necessary to disregard it. In fact, however, we are not reduced to this necessity. The Jewish writer no where actually contradicts the Gospel Records, and in hundreds of instances he confirms them. It is evident that the entire historical framework, in which the Gospel picture is set, is real; that the facts of the civil history, small and great, are true, and the personages correctly depicted." We have only to add that such correctness could not have been attained, *unless the Gospels were written by the men, to whom they are ascribed, who were living in the age in which the events described by them took place.*

§ 17. The Relation of the Four Gospels to Each Other and to the Acts of the Apostles.

In the case of three out of the five historical books of the New Testament, there is an internal testimony to their composition by cotemporaries, which is of no small importance. "*And he that saw it,*" says John, "bare record, and his record is true, and he knoweth that he says true, that ye may believe." (John xix, 35.) And again, still more explicitly, after speaking of himself, he says: "*This* is the disciple which testifieth of these things *and wrote these things;* and we know that his testimony is true." (John xxi, 24.) Either, therefore, John must be allowed to have been the writer of the fourth Gospel, or the writer must be deemed guilty of willful fraud.

That the Acts of the Apostles and the third Gospel have a "testimony of a particular kind," which seems to give them a special claim to be accepted as the works of a cotemporary, is admitted even by Strauss. The writer of the Acts, he allows, "by the use of the first person, identifies himself with the companion of Paul," and the prefaces of the two books make it plain that they "proceeded from the same author." Yet, while Strauss does not venture to deny that a companion of Paul *may have* written the two works, he finds it "difficult" to believe that this was actually the case, and "suspects" that the passages of the Acts, where the first person is used, "belong to a distinct memorial by another hand, which the author of the Acts has incorporated into his history"(!) But still he allows the alternative—that "it is possible the companion of Paul may have composed the two works"—only it must have been "at a time when he was no longer protected by apostolic influence from the tide of tradition,"(!) and so was induced to receive into his narrative, and join with what he had heard from the apostle, certain marvelous—and, therefore, incredible—stories which had no solid basis. A hypothesis like this is not worthy of a serious refutation. The Acts, as is clear from the fact of their terminating where they do, were composed at the close of Paul's first imprisonment at Rome, A. D. 58—or 63, according to some writers—and the Gospel, as being the "former treatise," must have been written earlier.

We may, therefore, independently of the general voice of antiquity on the authenticity of the third Gospel, allow it to have been composed by one who lived in the apostolic age and companied with the apostles. And a new argument is presented to us for the early date of the first and second, based upon their accordance with the third, their resemblance to it in style and general character, and their diversity from the productions of any other period. The first three Gospels belong so entirely to the same school of thought, and the same type and stage of language, that, on critical grounds, they must be regarded as the works of cotemporaries; while in their contents they are at once so closely accordant with one another, and so full of little differences, that we must assign to them an almost instantaneous origin. So peculiar is their relation to each other that the authenticity of one involves that of the others. If the evidence for either of the Gospels had been much weaker than that for the other three, its discrepancies from them, if there had been no other cause, would have decided its rejection. Moreover, if one of the gospels had been published much in advance of the others, it is not probable that a second account of the ministry of Christ, confirmatory to any great extent of the preceding one, would have been written. A supplementary gospel, like that of John, might of course have been added in any case; but had the Gospel of Matthew, for instance, been composed, as some have supposed, before the separation of the apostles and the formation of distinct Christian communities, it would have been carried, together with Christianity, into all parts of the world; and it is very unlikely that, in that case, the Gospels of Mark and Luke, which cover chiefly the same ground, would have been written. The need of written gospels was not felt at first, while the apostles and companions of Christ were in full vigor, and were continually moving from place to place, relating with all the fullness and variety of oral discourse the miracles which they had seen wrought, and the gracious words which they had heard uttered by their Master. But, as they grew old, and as the sphere of their labors enlarged, and personal superintendence of the whole Church by the apostolic body became difficult, the desire to possess a written gospel arose, and simultaneously, in different parts of the Church, for different portions of the Christian body, the three Gospels of Matthew, Mark, and Luke were published.

The peculiar relation of the synoptic Gospels to one another, and to the Gospel of John, and the points which modern criticism has made on this relation with reference to their inspiration, the reader will find fully discussed in Part IV. It is sufficient, here, to quote the following remarks of Dr. Lange on the bearing which the peculiar relation of the Gospels to each other have on their authenticity. He says: "The attempts that have been made, in modern times, to prove that the four Gospels weaken each other's authority have had the very opposite result. By their mutual relation to each other the Gospels gain the compactedness of a house hewn into a rock; for the relation of their differences and points of agreement is so peculiar that sound criticism finds in them, after every new investigation, four independent witnesses for one and the same fact, and accordingly, also, for each other. If, for instance, a critic wishes to disprove the authority of the Gospel of John, he recognizes that of three synoptic Gospels in order to gain a point of attack against the fourth Gospel. But the points of agreement between this and the three other Gospels prove so many and so strong, that, by recognizing the authority of the latter, the former is virtually, also, recognized. Or, the Gospel of John is taken for the authentic record of the Gospel history, and the differences between this and the three other Gospels are pointed out in order to shake thereby the authority of the latter. But in this case, also, the force of the agreement between the two sets of documents proves stronger than that of the differences, so that, if the fourth Gospel is true, the subject-matter of the three others must also be true. Again, Luke and Matthew are taken in hand to undermine the authority of Mark. But Mark has so much in common with the two others, that if he falls they must fall with him, while at the same time his peculiarities establish his independent authority. So, if the second Gospel is made the original Gospel at the expense of the first and third, Matthew and Luke have so much that is peculiar to them, that their own originality is placed beyond any and every reasonable doubt, while they have, at the same time, so much in common with Mark, that the recognition of the latter involves that of their own authority. In all these different directions the Gospels have been attacked by modern criticism, but all such attacks have proved futile. Their peculiar relation to one another is a fine net of truth, spread out to catch all impure criticism, and to entangle the critics in their own contradictions. Or we may compare the four Gospels to a wondrous grove, in which a magic influence makes the godless critics run to and fro in utter confusion, finding neither ingress nor egress. This magic influence proceeds from the circle of the four Gospels, because, from the fourfold refraction of the One Light of the world, there are issuing a thousand dazzling reflections for every oblique look, while the straightforward look sees in the fourfold refraction but the one Sun of the day. We may say that the relation of the four Gospels to each other, while it courts and challenges the spirit of criticism more than any single one for itself, becomes in turn the withering critique of every false criticism. Whenever criticism undertakes to undermine one Gospel through the other, it overlooks the mysterious links that bind them together, and thus digs its own grave. While the four Gospels testify to the Divine origin which they have in common, so completely and so mysteriously, that every impure critique is put to shame, they are in their outward form so purely human, that they thereby invite critical examination; and they rest on so firm a basis that every new examination can only bring them additional gain."

§ 18. The Authenticity of the Gospels—a Postulate of Reason, as it alone Accounts for the Existence of the Christian Church, and for some of Paul's Epistles, whose Authenticity is Universally Admitted.

The Christian Church is in the world, and has been in it a little more than eighteen centuries; that it can be traced back to the historically-attested death of Christ is placed beyond the possibility of a doubt by heathen and Jewish as well as Christian writers. Josephus, born 37 A. D., says, in a passage, of which we will include in brackets what has been justly declared to have been interpolated: "About this time Jesus appears, a wise man, [if it is right to call him a man, for he was] performing surprising deeds, [a teacher of men, who willingly received the truth,] and many Jews as well as heathen became his followers; [being the Messiah] on the accusations of our chief men, Pilate condemned him to the cross; nevertheless, those who had loved him before did not give up their faith in him; [for he appeared to them alive on the third day, as the prophets had predicted of him, besides many other marvelous things,] and the generation of Christians, that are named after him, is not extinct to this day." (Ant. Jud., XVIII, 3, § 3.) In another passage, which can not be justly suspected, Josephus, who grew up at Jerusalem till he was twenty-six years of age, and was thus a witness of the principal occurrences at Jerusalem, mentioned in the Acts, subsequently to the accession of Herod Agrippa, says: "Ananus . . . . called the council of judges, and bringing before them James, the brother of *Jesus, who was called Christ*, and certain others, he accused them of transgressing the laws, and delivered them up to be stoned." (Ant. Jud., XX, 9, § 1.) There existed, therefore, according to the testimony of Josephus, in the early part of the first century, a body of followers of Christ. Tacitus, the Roman historian, who wrote in the second half of the first century, says, (Ann., XV, 44,) speaking of the fire which consumed Rome in Nero's time, and of the general belief that he had caused it: "In order, therefore, to put a stop to the report, he laid the guilt, and inflicted the severest punishments upon a set of people who were holden in abhorrence for their crimes, and called by the vulgar, *Christians. The founder of that name was Christ, who suffered death in the reign of Tiberius, under his Procurator, Pontius Pilate.* This pernicious superstition, thus checked for a while, broke out again, and spread not only over *Judea, where the evil originated*, but *through Rome also*, whither all things that are horrible and shameful find their way, and are practiced. Accordingly, the first who were apprehended confessed, and then on their information *a vast multitude* were convicted, not so much of the crime of setting Rome on fire, as of hatred to mankind." Suetonius says briefly in reference to the same occasion: "*The Christians* were punished, a set of men of a *new* and mischievous superstition." (Vita Ner., § 16.) The younger Pliny, while he was Governor of Bithynia, says, in an official report to Trajan: "They [that is, those Christians who recanted] declared that the whole of their guilt, or their error, was, that they were accustomed to meet on a stated day, before it was light, and to sing in concert a hymn of praise to Christ, as God, and to bind themselves by an oath, not for the perpetration of any wickedness, but that they would not commit any theft, robbery, or adultery, nor violate their word, nor refuse, when called upon, to restore any thing committed to their trust. After this, they were accustomed to separate, and then to reassemble to eat in common a harmless meal. Even this, however, they ceased to do, after my edict, in which, agreeably to your commands, I forbade the meeting of secret assemblies. After hearing this, I thought it the more necessary to endeavor to find out the truth by putting to the torture two female slaves, who were called 'deaconesses.' But I could discover nothing but a perverse and extravagant superstition; and therefore I deferred all further proceedings till I should consult with you. For the matter appears to me worthy of such consultation, especially on *account of the number of those who are involved in peril.* For *many of every age, of every rank, and of either sex* are exposed, and will be exposed to danger. Nor has the contagion of this superstition been confined to the cities only, but *it has extended to the villages, and even to the country.* Nevertheless, it still seems possible to arrest the evil, and to apply a remedy. At least, it is very evident that *the temples, which had already been almost deserted*, begin to be frequented, and the sacred solemnities, so long interrupted, are again revived; and the victims, which heretofore could hardly find a purchaser, are now every-where in demand. From this it is easy to imagine *what a multitude of men* might be reclaimed, if pardon should be offered to those who repent." (Pliny, Ep. X, 97.) It is not necessary to quote any more testimonies concerning the existence of a great body of Christians before the close of the first century.

Now, to some of these Christians at various places the apostles addressed their Epistles, and there are no valid reasons for entertaining any doubt concerning their authorship, except, perhaps, in the case of that to the Hebrews, and of the two shorter Epistles which are assigned to John. All these Epistles are not only consistent with, but *imperatively demand*, our belief in the *authenticity* of such historical documents as our four Gospels are. It is indisputable that the writers, and those to whom they wrote, believed in the recent occurrence of a set of facts similar to, or identical with, those recorded in the Gospels and the Acts, especially those fundamental facts upon which the Christian faith rests. "Great is the mystery of godliness," says Paul. "God was manifest in the flesh, justified in the Spirit, seen of angels, preached unto the Gentiles, believed on in the world, received up into glory." (1 Tim. iii, 16.) "Christ," says Peter, "suffered once for sins, the just for the unjust, that he might bring us to God, being put to death in the flesh, but quickened in the Spirit." (1 Peter iii, 18.) "He received from God the Father honor and glory, when there came such a voice to him from the excellent glory: This is my beloved Son in whom I am well pleased; and this voice which came from heaven we heard, when we were with him in the holy mount." (2 Peter i, 17, 18.) "God raised up Christ from the dead, and gave him glory." (1 Peter i, 21.) "He is gone into heaven, and is on the right hand of God, angels and authorities and powers being made subject to him." (1 Peter iii, 22.) "Remember," says Paul, "that Jesus Christ of the seed of David was raised from the dead." (2 Tim. ii, 2, 8.) "If Christ be not risen, then is our preaching vain, and your faith also is vain." (1 Cor. xv, 14.) "I delivered unto you first of all that which I also received, how that Christ died for our sins according to the Scriptures; and that he was buried, and that he rose again the third day according to the Scriptures; and that he was seen of Cephas, then of the twelve, after that he was seen of James, then of all the apostles." (1 Cor. xv, 3–7.) These are only half a dozen texts out of hundreds which might be adduced to show that Paul represented the death of Christ on the cross, as necessary to procure the pardon of our sins, or to make that pardon consistent with God's justice and truth; he does not mention the charge on which he was condemned to this ignominious death, but that was necessarily implied. It was a Roman punishment, and Pilate could not condemn a public teacher, whose morals were spotless, on any other charge than that which the Evangelists state at large, and which no enemy of Christ gainsayed, to which He himself pleaded guilty in reply to the adjuration of Caiaphas; namely, "that he said, he was the Christ, the Son of God"—a declaration by which the Roman governor, interpreting it according to the well-known Jewish notions of the Messiah, understood Jesus to have proclaimed himself "the king of the Jews;" on which account he wrote that charge on the tablet over the cross. Paul tells us, (Gal. i, 12,) that he had received his Gospel by the revelation of Jesus Christ, and he proves it by preaching the same Christ, whom the four Evangelists delineate. Matthew records the last commission of Jesus, commanding his disciples to baptize all nations "in the name of the Father, and of the Son, and of the Holy Ghost." God is here called Father, Son, and Holy Ghost, and the same divinity is claimed for the Son and Holy Ghost as for the Father. John calls Jesus in his antemundane state "the Word, that was with God from the beginning, and that was God," and says: "the Word became flesh." Paul teaches Christ's divinity proper, and his incarnation not less distinctly and emphatically than John or Matthew. "To us there is but one God, the Father, of whom are all things, and we in him; and one Lord Jesus Christ, by whom are all things, and we by him." (1 Cor. viii, 6.) "Ye know the grace of our Lord Jesus Christ, that, though he was rich, yet for your sakes he became poor, that ye through his poverty might be rich." (2 Cor. viii, 9.) "Let this mind be in you, which was also in Christ Jesus; who, being in the form of God, thought it not robbery to be equal with God; but made himself of no reputation, and took upon him the form of a servant, and was made in the likeness of men." (Phil. ii, 6, 7.) "God sent his own Son in the likeness of sinful flesh." (Rom. viii, 3, 32.) These are only a few texts out of a hundred, which might be adduced to show that the writers of the Epistles entirely agree with the Evangelists, as to the facts on which Christianity is based, and as strongly assert their reality. If we find in Paul's Epistles some doctrines that are not in the Gospels, and if others are set forth more fully and distinctly, it is exactly what we have to expect according to John xvi, 12–14.

But we will go a step further and make the argument more direct and more pointed in giving it a strictly *historical* character. "Christianity or revealed religion is," as Rawlinson remarks in the opening of his Lectures on the "Historical Evidences," "in nothing more distinguished from the other religions of the world, than in its objective or historical character. The religions of Greece and Rome, of Egypt, India, Persia, and the East generally, were speculative systems, which did not even seriously postulate a historical basis. But it is otherwise with the religion of the Bible. There, whether we look to the Old or the New Testament, to the Jewish dispensation, or to the Christian, we find a scheme of doctrine which is bound up with facts; which depends absolutely upon them, and which is null and void without them." The truth of this remark we will illustrate and confirm by a consideration *of the incontestable facts implied in Paul's Epistle to the Romans, the Corinthians, and the Galatians*—Epistles *which, even by those critics* who have assailed the authenticity of every other portion of the New Testament Canon, *are admitted to be authentic*, that is, *to have been composed by the man whose name they bear, at the time and for the class of readers that are claimed for them.*

There was in the churches in Galatia and at Corinth a party which denied the apostolic authority of Paul, which saw in him, at best, an apostle's disciple. Paul, in vindicating his apostolic authority, appeals to his call by the risen Savior, and to his possessing the power to work miracles. He commences the

Epistle to the Galatians with these words: "Paul, an apostle, not of men, neither by man, but by Jesus Christ and God the Father, who raised him from the dead." The mention of the resurrection of Christ, in this connection, is evidently made to remind the Galatians that he had seen the risen Savior as well as the other apostles. It appears from verses 13–17, that they were well acquainted with his former enmity against Christ and his disciples, and with the miraculous event which resulted in his conversion. In 1 Cor. xv, 8, the apostle tells the Corinthians that the risen Savior was seen (*ὤφθη*) by him, as he had been seen by others, and, 1 Cor. ix, 1, he bases his apostleship upon his personal knowledge of Christ, obtained by actual sight (*ἑώρακα.*) From this sight, which took place with the natural eye, in a state of perfect self-consciousness, Paul distinguishes a vision, of which he himself does not know whether he had it in or out of the body. (2 Cor. xii, 1, 2.) Yet the personal manifestation of the risen Savior, narrated Acts ix, although it was the most important in point of its effects and differed also in its nature from subsequent manifestations of the Lord, was not an isolated fact in the life of the apostle, but only the grand opening act of his personal communion with the Lord. He appeals in different places to especial revelations of Christ on doctrinal points, in full accordance with what the Lord had told him at his conversion: "I have appeared unto thee for this purpose, to make thee a minister both of these things which thou hast seen, and of those things in the which I will appear unto thee."

Now, what deductions are we compelled to draw from what Paul writes to the Galatians and Corinthians respecting his having seen the risen Savior? If he has told the truth, if Christ appeared to him, then the truth of what the Evangelists have reported of the resurrection of Christ receives an incontestable confirmation, and the verity of that fact involves the *authenticity* of the Gospels. The latter has never been called in question by any who admit the resurrection of Jesus. It is attacked simply, as we shall show in the next Part, on the ground of the miraculous elements of the Gospel narratives. Whoever admits the miracle of Christ's resurrection can not object to the other miracles recorded in the Gospels.

But is Paul's testimony of having seen the risen Savior trustworthy? Was he a man of veracity, and of a sound mind? Has he told the truth? We answer: 1. If Christ did not appear to Paul, neither did he receive those miraculous powers to which he appealed in vindication of his apostolic authority, in letters whose authenticity, even those who assail every other portion of the New Testament Canon have felt themselves compelled to acknowledge. And how were, then, the Galatians and Corinthians brought to believe his Gospel of a risen Savior? 2. If Paul has not told the truth, we must set him down either as one of the most stupid victims of a disordered imagination, or as a willful impostor. For we must bear in mind that he did not become an apostle for the promulgation of mere theories or speculations, such as would admit of both intellect and candor. All he preached was based upon his testimony of the fact of the resurrection of the crucified Redeemer.

Can we conceive the author of such a composition as the Epistle to the Romans to have been the wretched dupe of an entirely unaccountable self-deception? That he was—far from being a weak-minded enthusiast or fanatic—a man of gigantic intellect, high culture, dialectic skill, inflexible purpose, and indomitable courage, the destructive criticism of modern infidelity must unwillingly admit, inasmuch as, in order to put the person of Christ out of the way, Paul is made the self-constituted founder of the Christian Church, and, consequently, the author of the whole modern civilization and culture.

Or was Paul a willful impostor? Is it conceivable that he should have blasted all his earthly prospects, and subjected himself to unceasing privations and sufferings, (2 Cor. xi, 23–27,) in order to make Jews and Gentiles believe what, in the case supposed, he must have known to be a lie? The thought is as great an outrage upon common-sense, and as black a libel upon humanity as it is a daring blasphemy against God. Hear how the apostle himself affirms his candor and soberness: "Yourselves, brethren, know our entrance in unto you, that it was not in vain. . . . . . For our exhortation was not of deceit, nor of uncleanness, nor in guile. But as we were allowed of God to be put in trust with the Gospel, even so we speak, not as pleasing men, but God, which trieth our hearts." (1 Thess. ii, 1, 3, 4.) "Therefore, seeing we have this ministry, as we have received mercy, we faint not; but have renounced the hidden things of dishonesty, not walking in craftiness, nor handling the Word of God deceitfully; but by manifestation of the truth commending ourselves to every man's conscience in the sight of God." (2 Cor. iv, 1, 2.) "If Christ be not risen, then is our preaching vain, and your faith is also vain. Yea, and we are found false witnesses of God, because we have testified of God that he raised up Christ. . . . . If in this life only we have hope in Christ, we are of all men most miserable." (1 Cor. xv, 14, 15, 19.)

So much with regard to Paul's testimony of having seen the risen Savior. Let us also consider what he says concerning the existence of miraculous powers in the primitive Churches. In the Epistle to the Corinthians (1 Cor. xii–xiv) the apostle speaks of certain extraordinary gifts, (*charismata*,) not for the purpose of proving their reality, or instructing his readers about their origin, but taking their existence for granted, he merely gives direction about their proper use. He mentions the gift of healing, prophecy, the discerning of spirits, and working of miracles. If the existence of these gifts had not been an incontestable fact, the apostle could not have written thus to a society of Christians, a part of whom did not recognize his apostolical authority, for it would have given his opponents the best means to destroy all confidence in him even as a man of veracity. In the Epistle to the Romans, (c. xii, 6,) these gifts are likewise referred to. In Galatians iii, 5, we meet again the working of miracles. Thus these *charismata* appear in all the Churches, however remote from each other they are. In the Epistle to the Galatians the apostle has a special object in appealing to them. The Galatians had been shaken in their Christian faith, and were in danger of apostatizing from the Gospel which Paul had preached to them. He reminds them that they had received, through his preaching of the Gospel, the Holy Spirit and the power to work miracles. Now, if they had not received these powers, how could the apostle have dared to argue thus? In vindicating his apostleship against his detractors at Corinth, he appeals to the miracles performed by himself before their eyes: "The signs of an apostle were wrought among you in all patience, in signs, wonders, and mighty deeds." According to Acts xviii, 11, 18, the apostle was at Corinth some eighteen months. From his miracles not being mentioned there, we see that the writers of the New Testament did not eagerly mention every miracle of which they had knowledge, but passed by many in silence for the reason given by John in his Gospel, (c. xx, 30; xxi, 25.)

Other epistles of Paul show a decline of these *charismata* in the Churches; in his pastoral letters the apostle finds it necessary to point out the proper qualifications of a minister of the Gospel, undoubtedly because the rich stream of miraculous gifts had comparatively ceased to flow, and they no longer pointed out to the Churches the proper persons for the various offices. The Epistle to the Hebrews, no matter by whom it was written, was certainly written before the close of the first century; Clement of Rome quotes from it largely, and internal evidences demonstrate that it was composed while the Temple worship was still in its full glory. The believing Jews, like the Galatians, came in danger of apostatizing from the faith; for this reason they are reminded, (Heb. ii, 4,) of the miracles performed among them and accompanying the preaching of the Gospel by those who had heard the Lord. These miraculous powers appear here in nearly the same order in which they stand, 2 Cor. xii, 12. We have thus the strongest evidence that there was no difference in this respect between the Jewish and heathen converts, that the one enjoyed these gifts as well as the other.

From this fact we have to infer that the Lord himself wrought such miracles as are recorded in the Gospels, for the Master was certainly not inferior to his disciples, and it is expressly so stated, Heb. ii, 4.

The Acts of the Apostles and the Epistles of Paul sustain the nearest relation to each other, and are wonderfully confirmed one by the other. The incidental allusions in the Epistles to facts related at length in the Acts, and *vice versa*, as well as the mention of facts in the one that are omitted in the other, complete each other. No less striking is the agreement between the Acts of the Apostles and the Gospels.

§ 19. The Absurdity of the Mythical Theory.

Unless all the arguments by which we have established the authenticity of the Gospel records are of no account, the mythical theory, laid down by Strauss in his "Life of Jesus," has no ground on which it can stand, and deserves no formal refutation. To state it is to refute it; and inasmuch as no English or German writer has stated this theory so clearly and fairly as Mr. Norton, we will give his statement, showing thereby how utterly futile this last effort of infidelity is to explain the origin of Christianity or any one essential fact connected with its origin.

The external testimonies for the authenticity Strauss sets aside by simply making the following assertions: "The most ancient testimonies tell us, firstly, that an apostle, or some other person who had been acquainted with an apostle, wrote a Gospel history; but not whether it was identical with that which afterward came to be circulated in the Church under his name; secondly, that writings similar to our

Gospels were in existence, but not that they were ascribed with certainty to any one apostle or companion of an apostle. Such is the uncertainty of these accounts, which, after all, do not reach further back than the third or fourth decade of the second century. According to all the rules of probability the apostles were all dead before the close of the first century, not excepting John, who is said to have lived till A. D. 100; concerning whose age and death, however, many fables were early invented. What an ample scope for attributing to the apostles manuscripts they never wrote!" (Strauss, Life of Jesus, i, 62.) In the following passage he asserts still more emphatically, that the apostles and their associates are not to be held responsible for the fables contained in the Gospels: "The fact that many such compilations—as the Gospels—of narratives concerning the life of Jesus were already in general circulation during the lifetime of the apostles, and more especially that any one of our Gospels was known to an apostle and acknowledged by him, can never be proved. With respect to isolated anecdotes, it is only necessary to form an accurate conception of Palestine and of the real position of the eye-witnesses referred to, in order to understand that the origination of legends, even at so early a period, is by no means incomprehensible. Who informs us that they must necessarily have taken root in that particular district of Palestine where Jesus tarried longest, and where his actual history was well known? And with respect to eye-witnesses, if by these we are to understand the apostles, it is to ascribe to them absolute ubiquity to represent them as present here and there weeding out all the unhistorical legends concerning

Jesus, in whatever places they had chanced to spring up and flourish." (Ibid., i, 63, 64.)

The internal evidences for the authenticity of the Gospels are entirely ignored by Strauss on account of the internal evidences which he sets up in opposition to them; namely, the contradictory statements which he charges upon the Evangelists, and the impossibility of miracles. As these two objections are directed against the historic verity or credibility of the Gospel records, we shall consider them in the next Part, and proceed now to the statement of the mythical theory itself in the words of Norton.

As there was among the Jews an eager expectation of their Messiah, Jesus, at least during a part of his ministry, regarded himself as the Messiah, as "the greatest and last of the prophetic race." He was, consequently, so regarded by his followers. The expectation, which the Jews entertained of their Messiah, was definite and "characterized by many important particulars." They had formed many imaginations concerning him connected with allegorical and typical misinterpretations of the Old Testament; and, after the appearance of Jesus, there were some among the Jews who converted their imaginations of what the Messiah was to be into fictions of what Jesus had been, and embodied those fictions in a history of his ministry. The Jewish people generally rejected him, as not their Messiah, and their leaders persecuted and crucified him as a religious impostor and blasphemer. Nor, according to Strauss, were the supposed fictions concerning him propagated by his immediate disciples, who had witnessed his deeds and listened to his words, his apostles, and their associates; nor, consequently, by those who knew and held the truth concerning him, as taught by them. To affirm that they were propagated by the apostles and their associates would be to maintain what the most reckless infidelity has shrunk from directly asserting; namely, that the received history of Jesus is a collection of enormous falsehoods, fabricated by his immediate disciples, and preached by them with ineffable effrontery in the very face of those who knew them to be false. From this simple solution of the origin of our religion, the "mythical" theory of Strauss essentially differs; for though he does not define the sense in which he uses the term "*mythus*," it is fundamental in his theory that *mythi*, and particularly the *mythi* or fables concerning Jesus, are not generally intentional falsehoods. It is this characteristic alone which distinguishes it from the more obvious and base solution of the origin of Christianity which has been adverted to. According to Strauss, the greater part of those fictions concerning Jesus, which are embodied in the Gospels, became connected with his history during the period of about thirty years which intervened between his death and the destruction of Jerusalem, (Strauss, i, 84,) that is, during the period throughout which many of his apostles and their associates—the first preachers of our religion—and the great body of those instructed by them were living. These fictions did not proceed from, nor were they countenanced by, them, nor were they received as true by those who relied on their authority. How, notwithstanding, they obtained such currency as almost immediately to obscure and obliterate his true history, is to be thus explained:

The age, it is true, was "a historical age," by which term Strauss, I suppose, must be understood as meaning an age in which facts would be recorded, and mythological fables would not find ready currency—but "the pure historic idea was never developed among the Hebrews." "Indeed, no just notion of the true nature of history is possible, without a perception of the inviolability of the chain of finite causes and of the impossibility of miracles. This perception, which is wanting to so many minds of our own day, was still more deficient in Palestine, and, indeed, throughout the Roman Empire. And to a mind still open to the reception of the marvelous, if it be once carried away by the tide of religious enthusiasm, all things will appear credible; and should this enthusiasm lay hold of a yet wider circle, it will awaken a new creative vigor even in a decayed people. To account for such an enthusiasm it is by no means necessary to presuppose the Gospel miracle as the existing cause. This may be found in the known religious dearth of that period, a dearth so great that the cravings of the mind after some religious belief excited a relish for the most extravagant forms of worship; secondly, in the deep religious satisfaction which was afforded by the belief in the resurrection of the deceased Messiah, and by the essential principles of the doctrine of Jesus." (Strauss, i, 64, 65.)

The theory of Strauss necessarily supposes that Jesus was a conspicuous individual who acted strongly on the minds of men. Before this theory can be received, it becomes requisite to explain the very rapid growth of those most extraordinary fictions concerning him, which sprung up and flourished while very many of his cotemporaries were still living; especially as by a great majority of those cotemporaries, his enemies, they would be at once indignantly spurned and trampled under foot, as being, what they were, monstrous falsehoods; while by another portion, the first adherents of Jesus, and the original witnesses of his ministry, their growth, to say the least, was not fostered—they did not rest on their testimony. Strauss has shown himself sensible that an explanation of this phenomenon is requisite; and the solution which he gives of the sudden development of such an array of fables concerning Jesus may be found in the following passage. It may be readily understood, if we bear in mind what has been before stated, that, according to his theory, the Jews had entertained many imaginations concerning their expected Messiah; and that the process in forming the history of Jesus which has come down to us, consisted in converting these imaginations of what was to be into fables concerning Jesus.

He says: "A frequently-raised objection still remains, . . . the objection, namely, that the space of about thirty years from the death of Jesus to the destruction of Jerusalem, during which the greater part of the narratives must have been formed—or even the interval extending to the beginning of the second century, the most distant period which can be allowed for the origin of even the latest of these Gospel narratives—is much too short to admit of the use of so rich a collection of *mythi*. But as we have shown, the greater part of these mythi did not arise during that period, for their first foundation was laid in the legends of the Old Testament before and after the Babylonish exile; and the transferrence of these legends, with suitable modifications, to the expected Messiah was made in the course of the centuries which elapsed between that exile and the time of Jesus. So that, for the period between the foundation of the first Christian community and the writing of the Gospels, there remains to be effected only the transferrence of Messianic legends, almost all ready formed, to Jesus, with some alterations to adapt them to Christian opinions and to the individual character and circumstances of Jesus; only a very small proportion of mythi having to be formed entirely new." (Strauss, i, 84, 85.) This is the only explanation he affords.

It appears, then, according to Strauss, that some time during the thirty or forty years after the death of our Lord, the small body of his followers among the Jews was divided into two parties of very different characters. One was composed of his personal friends and followers, the apostles and their associates, who knew his true history and doctrines, and who did not propagate those falsehoods concerning him on which the religion of Christians is founded. The other was composed of persons who did propagate those falsehoods. These had their origin, as Strauss suggests, in districts of Palestine where Jesus did not tarry long, and where his actual history was not well known, and it would, he says, be ascribing absolute ubiquity to the apostles to suppose them to have been capable of being present here and there to weed out all the unhistorical legends concerning him in whatever places they had chanced to spring up and flourish. (Strauss, i, 63, 64.) Those who propagated these fictions concerning him had no intention of deceiving. They were unconscious of falsehood; they believed that what they related had actually taken place. They had so little acquaintance with Jesus or with the eye-witnesses of his ministry, that they did not know that all which they affirmed concerning him was untrue. On the contrary, they were persuaded that it was true. But though, as Strauss suggests, their fictions may not originally "have taken root in that particular district of Palestine where Jesus tarried longest," (Strauss, i, 84,) yet, in order to make converts to the belief of them, it was necessary that they should be preached in parts of Palestine where our Lord had been well known, and where there could be no ignorance respecting the essential facts in his ministry. Here, on the one hand, they would be indignantly and vehemently contradicted by the great body of the unbelieving Jews, and on the other, they would be denied and discountenanced by the true followers of Christ. The innocent impostors, who, in their ignorance, propagated unconsciously such enormous falsehoods concerning him, must have been surprised to find all those acquainted with the facts in his history, whether friends or enemies, utterly confounded, to say the least, by their marvelous stories. One might think that their own confidence would have been shaken by the direct and authoritative evidence, which they must have encountered on every side, of the falsehood of their narrations. It might seem, moreover, that it would be impossible under such circumstances to procure converts to the belief of them. But such was not the case. Their own confidence was not shaken; they persisted in promulgating their stories, and they triumphed signally. They are the true authors of Christianity. It is to them we are indebted for the Gospels. Their fictions have supplanted the real history of Christ, the original testimony of eye-witnesses, and have become the foundation of Christian faith! Nor is this all. Keeping themselves out of view, they have had complete success in putting their stories before the world as resting on the authority of the apostles and their associates, in making them responsible for their marvelous tales. The whole Christian world has believed that these stories proceeded from apostles and their associates. But it was not so. They proceeded from another party among the followers of Jesus Christ, a party that does not appear in history, the existence of which is irreconcilable with all remaining records and memorials of the times when it is supposed to have flourished, utterly irreconcilable with all probability, and which, therefore, was unknown to the world before its discovery by Strauss.

It is to be borne in mind that the distinguishing characteristic of the theory of Strauss, the "mythical" theory of the origin of Christianity, consists in the supposition that the *mythi* or fictions in the history of Jesus were not intentional fabrications for the purpose of deception, but that they sprang up, as it were, spontaneously; those among whom they originated, and by whom they were propagated, being unconscious of falsehood. This fact is fully recognized by Strauss, though not clearly apprehended by him in its necessary relations. His reader should keep it in mind. We must not suffer ourselves to vacillate between two theories wholly inconsistent with each other. The apostles and their associates were, or were not, the most shameless of impostors. According to Strauss they were not impostors. It follows that the history of our Lord, which the Christian world has received, was not derived from them, though it grew to its present form principally while the most, or many, of them were living. It proceeded, therefore, from other individuals, of whom history has preserved no record, and who must have taught under the circumstances which have been described.

We may next observe, that, however difficult was the task of these teachers of our present religion in persuading the cotemporaries and countrymen of an individual as conspicuous as our Lord must have been, to give credit to a history of him full of marvels that were utterly devoid of truth, yet this was not the sole, nor the greatest, difficulty which they are supposed to have overcome. This teaching consisted, as we are informed by Strauss, in identifying the history of Jesus with the anticipations of the Jews concerning their expected Messiah. The *mythi* respecting this imaginary personage were ready made for their use, and they had only to turn them into historical fictions, and accommodate them to Jesus.

But every one knows what were the popular expectations of the Jews respecting their coming Messiah. Of him, David, the greatest of their kings, the founder of their monarchy, was, in their view, the especial type; though in all by which the favor of God had distinguished David, the Messiah was to be far more distinguished. He, too, was to be a monarch, the restorer of the kingdom of Israel, a warrior, a conqueror, the deliverer and exalter of his people. Establishing the seat of his empire at Jerusalem, he was to found a kingdom extending over the world, and enduring to the consummation of all things, over which he was to rule without a successor. This was the outline of their expectations, which, doubtless, before the coming of our Lord, was filled up, as it has been since, with many particular imaginations corresponding to its general character.

But according to Strauss, it was the purpose of those who propagated the fabulous history of Jesus, to evince that he was the Messiah through the correspondence of its fictions with the previous expectations of the Jews concerning the Messiah. This history actually shows one striking point of resemblance in representing Jesus as the last great messenger of God to the Jewish nation endowed with miraculous powers. But the whole representation of the purpose and effects of his mission, of his personal character, of his humble condition in this world, of his determined repression of all hope of worldly aggrandizement for himself, his followers, or his countrymen, of his annunciation to his immediate disciples that they must submit to poverty and suffering, and prepare themselves for the last outrage of persecution, together with the account of the apparent triumph of his enemies, and of his cruel death—this representation, if it were a fiction, might seem to have been devised in direct opposition to the expectations of the Jews respecting their Messiah.

But it may be said that the facts to which I have referred were so notorious that no other account could be given by the honest impostors, who, unconscious of falsehood, propagated the stories of his miracles. Certainly these facts were so notorious that no other account could be given but that which we have received. But such being the case, it follows that no attempt could be more hopeless or more foolish, than an attempt to persuade the Jews that the life and death, the character, acts, and teachings of Jesus corresponded to their previous expectations of the Messiah. So far, indeed, from their finding any such correspondence, we know that, during his ministry, and after his death, he was rejected by a very great majority of the nation, as disappointing all their hopes from a Messiah, and exasperating their strongest prejudices.

This theory of Strauss is, indeed, an outrage upon common-sense, if the preceding account of it be correct, and no one will pretend that it is not. But we have as yet viewed this theory only under one aspect; namely, in its relation to the Jewish nation. We will consider it in some other very important relations in which its author has not presented it, and in regard to which he has, of course, given no explanation.

The heathens believed the Gospel, and of the strength of their belief they gave sure proof by the marvelous change which it wrought in their hearts and lives, by the wide separation which it produced between them and the heathen world, by their readiness to submit to all the deprivations and evils which it brought upon them. Now, from whom did the heathens receive their knowledge of Christianity and of the Gospels? The theory of Strauss admits of but one answer. According to this theory, they must have received it not from the main body of the Jewish Christians, but from those few mistaken men among them who, having little or no acquaintance with Jesus, propagated, unconscious of falsehood, those *mythi* concerning him with which the Gospels are filled, and who thus established in the world not merely a fabulous history of him, the professed Messiah of whom they knew nothing correctly, but likewise a new religion, embracing the noblest principles of action, founded upon faith in one whose real history they had obliterated or rendered doubtful, and whose character they had essentially misrepresented. This is the only answer which the theory of Strauss admits. But the only answer admitted by authentic history and indisputable fact is that the heathens were instructed in Christianity by the immediate followers and companions of our Lord, and by their associates—by those who were perfectly aware whether their teaching was or was not true; that they received our religion from Barnabas, and Paul, and Luke, from Peter and Mark, from the apostle John, who resided so long among them, and from others associated with these early teachers. Above all, no degree of folly, certainly none to which a rational person can be required to give heed, will lead any one to pretend expressly that there is any evidence or any ground whatever for imagining that the Gospel was preached to the heathen world in two different forms; in one form by half-crazy fanatics, who filled the history of our Lord with stories of fictitious miracles, and in another, by his immediate followers and friends, who told the truth concerning him, whatsoever that was. But turning from unquestionable truths, we will enter the regions of mere hypothesis. We will clear the ground, as far as possible, of those facts that stand in our way. The Epistles of Paul we will regard as forgeries, and the whole history of the propagation of Christianity, which may be gathered from the New Testament, as a fabrication. We will suppose that these Christians received their instruction in Christianity from the fanatical and ignorant portion of Christ's disciples. Every one knows what these teachers effected. Let us consider their means and the obstacles which they had to encounter.

They were men very deficient in good sense. They had taken no pains to inform themselves correctly concerning the character, acts, and teaching of him whose disciples they professed to be, and whom they were so zealous in exhorting others to obey. They had, on the contrary, fallen into the grossest mistakes concerning them. God did not "bear them witness with signs, and wonders, and divers miracles, and gifts of the Holy Ghost." The pretense that he did so is merely one of those fables which are put forward throughout the New Testament. It was not only morally, but physically, impossible that they should produce any miraculous evidence of the truth of their fictions. Nor were they distinguished for eloquence or ability of any sort, since, though they effected such an astonishing work, history has not even preserved their names, but has falsely substituted for them those of other individuals—apostles of Christ and the associates of apostles. Such were the character and the facilities for accomplishing their purpose, possessed by these zealous missionaries of falsehood. What obstacles, then, had they to encounter?

According to Strauss their main purpose in their mythical history of Christ, which we now find in the Gospels, was to evince that a Messiah—named Jesus—had appeared among the Jews. This was the story which they propagated in the heathen world. But the heathen world would have regarded only with indifference or ridicule such a story from such preachers—a story that a Messiah had appeared among the Jews, a people toward whom the prevalent feelings of the heathens had been those of dislike and contempt; and in whose supposed good or ill fortune in the advent of their Messiah it must have been very hard to persuade them that they had any concern.

Admitting, however, that it were possible to excite their attention to the subject, with what ineffable scorn must they have regarded the sort of evidence thus laid before them! How would they have listened to proofs founded on a pretended correspondence between a body of incredible fictions and certain passages of a book called the Old Testament—a book for which they had no respect, which even many of them had never heard of, and which, it may be safely presumed, no one of them had read—which passages were represented to them as expressing typically or mystically what the Jews had expected concerning the Messiah? With how much patience would they have listened to these Jewish proselyting missionaries who had come among them, when these missionaries themselves told them that the person, whom they called on them to receive as the Jewish Messiah, had been rejected by his own nation as an impostor and blasphemer, and had, in consequence of his pretensions, suffered a public execution, as ignominious as it was cruel? What must they have thought of this Jewish Messiah, the deliverer of his people, when he was preached to them after the destruction of Jerusalem and the dispersion of the Jewish nation? Is it possible, an intelligent reader may ask, that any one can have been so bewildered and confounded by irreligion and mysticism, as to imagine that the most astonishing moral revolution in the history of mankind, the establishment of Christianity in the heathen world, was effected by such agents, under such circumstances?

We add to Mr. Norton's critique of Strauss a few remarks:

1. The mythical theory is a tissue of self-contradictory statements. One Gospel is rejected as spurious, and then, again, treated as authentic, in order to prove from it the spuriousness of another. In one place we are told that the people, among whom these myths originated, were in a state of childish ignorance and credulity, under the influence of an untutored, extravagant imagination; in another place we are called upon to admire the deep philosophy, lying at the bottom of these evangelical myths, the expansive views, thorough analysis, and far-seeing sagacity of those ignorant and superstitious persons who propagated them!

2. What we are called upon to believe by the mythical theory, is, in short, that Jesus—if he wrought no miracles, and was the subject of no miracles—contradicted, in every circumstance of his birth, and education, and teaching, and life, and death, the best established and most cherished notions of all around him, concerning the promised Messiah, and was, nevertheless, believed to be that Messiah. We are called upon to believe that miracles were ascribed to him, because the Messiah *ought* to have wrought miracles; that he was believed to have risen again, because it suddenly occurred to somebody that he *ought* to have risen again; and that, *by such a process as this*, a creed of fables was transmuted into a creed of facts, and, toward the close of the second century, stamped indelibly, and with one impression, upon the faith and institutions of the great Christian communities

throughout the world, so that the consentient tradition of all these Churches ascribes their foundation to the first disciples of Jesus Christ, and our Gospels to those whose names they bear; and this tradition is confirmed by the universal observance of the sacraments, of the weekly Lord's day, and of Easter, the special festival in remembrance of Christ's resurrection.

3. That no speculative system, based upon the myth of an incarnate God, could have started such a revolution in the moral world, as has been produced by Christianity for over eighteen centuries, with the manifest destiny to leaven and change the whole world, is evident, from the fact, that all the philosophical elements, to which the mythical theory attributes the propagation of Christianity, are found in the lofty speculations of Plato, in the logology of Philo, and a host of Oriental myths, concerning incarnations of Deity; but though they were in the world for centuries, they never exerted a world-renewing influence.

4. "With this last effort," says Dr. Schaff, "infidelity seems to have exhausted its scientific resources. It can only repeat itself hereafter. Its different theories have all been tried and found wanting. One has in turn transplanted and refuted the other, even during the lifetime of their champions. They explain nothing in the end; on the contrary, they only substitute an unnatural for a supernatural miracle, an inextricable enigma for a revealed mystery. They equally tend to undermine all faith in God's providence, in history, and ultimately in every principle of truth and virtue, and they deprive a poor and fallen humanity, in a world of sin, temptation, and

sorrow, of its only hope and comfort in life and in death.—The same negative criticism which Strauss applied to the Gospels, would, with equal plausibility, destroy the strongest chain of evidence before a court of justice, and resolve the life of Socrates, or Charlemagne, or Luther, or Napoleon, into a mythical dream. The secret of the mythical hypothesis is the pantheistic denial of a personal, living God, and the *a priori* assumption of the impossibility of a miracle. In its details it is so complicated and artificial, that it can not be made generally intelligible, and in proportion as it is popularized, it reverts to the vulgar hypothesis of intentional fraud, from which it professed, at the start, to shrink back in horror and contempt."

PART III.

THE HISTORIC VERITY OF THE GOSPEL RECORDS.

PART III.

THE HISTORIC VERITY OF THE GOSPEL RECORDS.

---

§ 20. INTRODUCTORY REMARKS.

IN the preceding Part, the authenticity of the Gospels has been established by the most conclusive evidences. A book, however, may be authentic; that is, it may have been written by the author by whom it claims to have been written, and yet have no claims upon our confidence; that is, it may not be credible. Though this is rarely the case with historical books, and, in the nature of the case, inapplicable to such records as the Gospels, yet, we will consider them for the present, without any reference to their containing a divine revelation, and subject them to the same laws of historical criticism as may be applied to any historical record.

CHAPTER I.

A CONSIDERATION OF THE OBJECTIONS THAT HAVE BEEN RAISED AGAINST THE CREDIBILITY OF THE EVANGELISTS.

§ 21. THE ALLEGED DISCREPANCIES OR CONTRADICTIONS IN THE FOUR GOSPELS.

IT has been asserted that the Evangelists differ in some of their statements from each other to such a degree as to contradict each other. That we find their records as different as we should expect them, from independent writers, is admitted; but it can be satisfactorily shown, that they are not of such a nature as to impair their character as faithful and trustworthy reporters. The charge of alleged contradictions will be refuted in detail, in the interpretation of the respective passages to which the charge refers; such, for instance, as the difference with regard to the hour of the crucifixion of our Lord. Here we confine ourselves to general remarks:

1. The differences adduced, consist mostly of omissions by one Evangelist of what is mentioned by another, such omissions being regarded by Strauss as equivalent to direct negatives.* Throughout his

*With regard to the Annunciation, for instance, Mr. Rawlinson observes, we find the following enumeration of discrepancies: "1. The individual who appears is called, in Matthew, *an angel of the Lord;* in Luke, *the angel Gabriel.* 2. The person to whom the angel appears is, according to Matthew, Joseph; according to Luke, Mary. 3. In Matthew, the apparition is seen in a dream; in Luke, while awake. 4. There is a disagreement with respect to the time at which the apparition took place. 5. Both, the purpose of the apparition and the effect, are

"Life of Jesus," he conceives himself at liberty to discard facts recorded by one Evangelist only, on the mere ground of silence on the part of the others. Whatever an Evangelist does not record, he is argued not to have known; and his want of knowledge is taken as a proof that the event could not have happened. The sophistry of such an argument is apparent. Who will deny that eye-witnesses of one and the same event notice a different portion of the attendant circumstances, and that, moreover, those who record an event which they have witnessed, omit, ordinarily, by far the greater portion of the attendant circumstances, though they have noticed them at the

different." In this way five discrepancies are created out of the single fact that Matthew does not relate the Annunciation to the Virgin, while Luke gives no account of the angelic appearance to Joseph. Similarly, in the section where the calling of the first apostles is examined, discrepancies are seen between the fourth and the first two Evangelists, in the following respects: "1. James is absent, according to John's Gospel, and, instead of his vocation, we have that of Philip and Nathanael. 2. In Matthew and Mark, the scene is the coast of the Galilean Sea; in John, it is the vicinity of the Jordan. 3. In each representation there are two pairs of brothers; but, in the one, they are Andrew and Peter, James and John; in the other, Andrew and Peter, Philip and Nathanael. And, 4. In Matthew and Mark, all are called by Jesus; in John, Philip only, the others being directed to him by the Baptist." Here, again, we have four discrepancies made out of the circumstance, that the first two Evangelists relate only the actual call of certain disciples, while John informs us what previous acquaintance they had of Jesus. So, from the mere silence of Matthew, Strauss concludes, positively, that he opposes Luke, in not considering Nazareth, but Bethlehem, to have been the original residence of our Lord's parents; from the omission, by the three earlier writers, of the journeys into Judea, during our Lord's ministry, he pronounces that they contradict John, who speaks of such journeys; he finds a discrepancy between this Evangelist's account of the relations between the Baptist and our Lord, and the account of the others, since he gives, and they do not give, the testimony borne by the former to our Lord's character; he concludes, from Luke's *not saying* that John the Baptist was in prison when he sent his two disciples to our Lord, that he considered him as not yet cast into prison; he finds Luke's and Matthew's accounts of the death of Judas "irreconcilable," because Luke *says nothing* of remorse, or of suicide, but relates what has the appearance of a death by accident; he regards the presence of Nicodemus at our Lord's interment, as a "fabrication of the fourth Evangelist," simply because it is unnoticed by the others; he concludes, from their silence as to the raising of Lazarus, that "it can not have been known to them," and, therefore, that it can not be true; and, in other instances, too numerous to mention, he makes similar use of the mere fact of omission.

time! Strauss's cavils could only have been precluded by the mere repetition, on the part of each Evangelist, of the exact circumstances mentioned by every other—a repetition which would have been considered to mark collusion, and which would thus have destroyed their value as distinct and independent witnesses. The deviations, therefore, with regard to particular circumstances attending an event, are so far from lessening the credibility of the Gospel history, that they rather increase it. They are deviations, such as are most sure to appear, wherever there is the highest degree of harmlessness, the calmest consciousness of entire truthfulness, and an entire absence of collusion. And, suppose we should have to acknowledge the existence of a deviation, for which—from a want of a full knowledge of all the attending circumstances—we could not offer a satisfactory explanation; as, for instance, with regard to the cure of the blind at Jericho, (Matt. xx, 29, 34; Mark x, 46, 52; Luke xviii, 35, 19)—such a concession would still leave the credibility of the Gospel history untouched. It would only conflict with the verbal inspiration of the Evangelists, but they would remain historical authorities of the first order, witnesses as fully to be trusted for the circumstances of our Lord's life, as Xenophon for the sayings and doings of Socrates. Even Lessing, that severe critic, while he pointed out apparent discrepancies in the accounts of Christ's resurrection, did not feel himself justified to reject the fact itself on the ground of these discrepancies. "Who," he says, "has ever drawn such an inference in profane history? If Livy, Polybius, and Tacitus record the same event, but with such a difference, as regards the attending circumstances, that the details of the one seem irreconcilable to that of the other, is, therefore, the event itself put in question? Now, if we deal so trustfully with profane writers, why should we torture the Evangelists for every syllable?" To which Tholuck adds: "It will not be easy to find two historians in classic antiquity, who, though equally trustworthy, do not differ from, or even contradict, each other, when they relate the same event, be it from the imperfections of man's faculties of observation and description, or because the writers could not anticipate our circumstances and meet our wants. How insoluble are often the difficulties which arise from the conflicting testimonies of trustworthy witnesses at court! He that would make shipwreck of faith on account of some few insignificant discrepancies in the Gospel narratives, would be no greater loss to the Church than *he* would be a gain, who is induced to embrace the faith of the Gospel by no weightier argument, than the proof that the Evangelists stated alike every particular of each event, and wrote down the words of our Lord *verbatim* and *literatim*, like stenographers."

2. By far the greatest number of the so-called discrepancies in the Gospels are of a chronological character, and some of them—as, for instance, the journey of Jesus into the country of the Gadarenes, which, according to Matthew, was preceded by a number of events that followed it according to Mark and Luke—might, indeed, be called contradictory, if it could be shown that any of the Evangelists designed to furnish us with a complete, consecutive account of the ministry of Christ. The very contrary of this assumption is an undeniable fact. They evidently do not intend, or pretend, to give us more than a selec-

tion from the rich materials of the life and labors of their Master. All that the Synoptists report of the earlier half of his ministry is confined to a few fragments. From Matt. xi, 21, it appears that Christ had endeavored by mighty works to call Chorazin to repentance; but neither Matthew nor the other Evangelists say any thing of the works of Christ performed there. It has, however, been contended, that Luke, in the preface to his Gospel, does claim to give a history of Christ in chronological order. But this is not so. Compared with the sketches, which some Christians had made in an unauthorized manner, Luke could very properly call his work "perfect" and "in order," even though he did not pursue the life of Christ from day to day, and week to week, but gave what appeared to him most important, in some systematic order. Each of the Evangelists had a plan of his own, according to which he arranged and grouped the events, and, therefore, the sequence—called *akolouthia*—of the events and sermons differs in each of the Synoptists. But if this difference in the selection and arrangement of the material in each of the Synoptists has its ground in the special plan which each followed, it is evident that this variety implies no incongruity or disharmony. The question, whether and how the chronological order of the events, recorded by the Evangelists, can be established, belongs to the subject of the Harmony of the Gospels, which we shall treat in Part V. It is sufficient to remark here, with regard to such sayings and discourses of the Lord as are placed by the Evangelists in connection with different occasions, that we are fully justified to assume, that similar sayings and discourses were delivered by our Savior more than once, at different times and under different circumstances, as appears, for instance, clearly from those denunciations of the scribes and Pharisees which were first uttered by our Lord on his journey to Jerusalem, (Luke xi, 37,) afterward solemnly repeated in the Temple at the close of his public ministry. (Matt. xxiii.)

§ 22. The Assumption that Miracles are Impossible and Unsusceptible of Proof.

While German rationalism has vainly tried to disprove the verity of the miracles recorded in the Gospels, that is, to explain away the miraculous nature of these occurrences by means of an interpretation, admitted now on all hands to be entirely unauthorized and absurd—pantheistic and atheistic philosophy denies the miracles on the plea of their *impossibility*. This stupendous assumption is the basis upon which the criticism of Strauss, in his "Life of Jesus," rests. Miracles are to be declared impossible, and, therefore, a narrative of which supernatural occurrences form an essential part, is, just so far, said to be devoid of historic character. The thesis that miracles are impossible, implies, of course, that the word "miracle" is not used in the sense of the Latin "*mirabile*," meaning something wonderful arising from *natural* causes not known at the time of its taking place, or yet unknown. With this is conceded the proper definition of a miracle. It is a Divine interposition to accomplish, by special agency, an effect not to be reached in the natural course and order of events. But the denial of the possibility of such an interposition—from whatever stand-point the argument is attempted, whether with reference to philosophical conceptions of God's nature and attributes, or with reference to experience and the empirical laws of Nature, which are said to preclude the possibility of a sufficient evidence of the miracle—can be shown to be a mere begging of the question. Let us examine this axiom of modern infidelity in its chameleon-like phases, which all may be summed up under two general heads.

I. Spinoza, the father of modern pantheism, to whom God and nature are one, says in substance: "A miracle is inconsistent with the perfections of the Deity, for it is conceivable only upon the supposition that the self-manifestation of God in nature proved defective, but such a supposition would be irreconcilable with a belief in God's perfection." In this syllogism Spinoza takes for granted: 1. That there is in the universe no self-conscious, personal Intelligence, independent of matter, for he defines a miracle, at another place, "as something which we can not explain by a natural law, but which has always a natural cause," admitting evidently of no other Divinity *than what nature manifests. Matter is* to him *the only image of his God.* 2. That the world is still in its original, normal state, its harmony not having been disturbed by sin, the act of free moral agents, and that, therefore, there is no need of a Divine interposition for moral purposes, that is, for the sake of the moral beings in the physical universe. On the contrary, it is assumed, that the universe is governed only by physical laws, not by moral laws, and that a miracle would be an alteration of the established machinery of nature. 3. That, because nature is an expression of God's will, there can be no other expression. It is assumed that, because God acts after a particular mode in certain circumstances, he can never have reasons for acting after a different manner in other circumstances. It is assumed that an addition is an inconsistency, that to superinduce any thing further upon something previously existing is to declare that which thus existed to have been wrong or bad. It is evident that, unless these premises can be proved, the pantheistic argument against miracles falls to the ground. "The simple question," says Dr. J. Haven, in an article on miracles, (Bibl. Sacra, 1862,) "is this: *Is there a Deity at all?* Or is all power to be resolved into this great system of universal, inevitable, eternal law—this grand machinery of 'eternally-impressed consequences,' that goes grinding and clanking on from eternity to eternity? If the latter, then we grant that miracles are out of question. But *if there be a God*, as some of us in our simplicity have supposed; if we may crave the indulgence of this highly-cultivated age so far as to be permitted to retain the antiquated notion of a Deity at the head of affairs; and if we place this Deity where he belongs, behind all those laws, and above them all, as their source and spring, then why may not the power that usually works in and by such and such methods or laws, if occasion requires, act in some other way, without or above those laws? Nay, why may he not, if necessary to the accomplishment of his purposes, even reverse, or wholly set aside for the time, those usual methods of procedure which we call laws of nature?" We call an event natural, when it is produced by natural means or agencies. But God, who created these agencies and set them in operation, is himself supernatural, and when he operates in nature otherwise than through those so-called natural causes, we call the work supernatural. The work of creation is supernatural; it is a work in nature, proceeding from a power above nature. The raising of the dead would be supernatural, for there is no physical or physiological law capable of producing such a result. To contend that every event or phenomenon must be referred as an effect to a physical law, is simply to deny both the existence of a Supreme Intelligence as the original cause or creator, and that of the power of self-determination of the human will, either of which being denied, neither the possibility of miracles nor any other question of relation or morality is worth speaking about. "Admit, on the other hand, the existence of a free will in man, and we have the experience of a power analogous, however inferior, to that which is supposed to operate in the production of a miracle, and forming the basis of a legitimate argument from the less to the greater— as Twesten shows in his 'Vorlesungen über die Dogmatik.' In the will of man we have the solitary instance of an efficient cause, in the highest sense of the term, acting among and along with the physical causes of the material world, and producing results which would not have been brought about by any invariable sequence of physical causes left to their own action. We have evidence also of an *elasticity*, so to speak, in the constitution of nature, which permits the influence of human powers on the phenomena of the world to be exercised or superseded at will, without affecting the stability of the whole. We have thus a precedent for allowing the possibility of a similar interference by a higher will on a grander scale, provided for by a similar elasticity of the matter subjected to its influence. Such interferences, whether produced by human or by superhuman will, are not contrary to the laws of matter; but neither are they the result of those laws. They are the work of an agent who is independent of the laws, and who, therefore, neither obeys them nor disobeys them. (See Rothe in Studien und Kritiken, 1858, p. 33.) If a man, of his own free will, throws a stone into the air, the motion of the stone, as soon as it has left his hand, is indeed determined by a combination of purely-material laws. But by what *law* came it to be thrown at all? What law brought about the circumstances through which the aforesaid combination of material laws came into operation on this particular occasion and in this particular manner? The law of gravitation, no doubt, remains constant and unbroken, whether the stone is lying on the ground or moving through the air; but neither the law of gravitation nor all the laws of matter put together could have brought about this particular result, without the interposition of the free will of the man who throws the stone. *Substitute the will of God for the will of man;* and the argument, which in the above instance is limited to the narrow sphere within which man's powers can be exercised, becomes applicable to the whole extent of creation and to all the phenomena which it embraces." (Mansell on Miracles, p. 28.) As this argument ought to be apprehended with the utmost clearness, we will give it as stated by another late English writer, Dr. Heurtley, in his refutation of Baden Powell: "The human will is the element, the action of whose disturbing force upon the material system around us comes most frequently or most strikingly under our notice.

Man, in the exercise of his ordinary faculties, is perpetually interfering with, or molding, or controlling the operation of those ordinary laws of matter which are in exercise around him. He does so, if he does but disturb one pebble in a state of rest, or stay the fall of another before it reaches the ground. He does so to a vastly-greater extent when, by means of the appliances with which art, instructed by science, has furnished him, he projects a ball to the distance of four or five miles, or constrains steam, or light, or electricity, or chloroform to do his bidding. Still his doings are not miracles, because they do not extend beyond the range of his unassisted powers. But what is there in the reason of things to make it incredible or even improbable, that God, on special occasions, and for special ends, may have endowed some men with *superhuman* powers, by which the laws of the material world may be controlled to an extent beyond what could have been done by *unassisted* nature? or that he may have directed or permitted beings superior in might to man to exercise such powers? That he has done so Scripture affirms. To say that it is contrary to experience is to beg the whole question at issue. The fact is, once admit that there is a God, and that he may, for special reasons, endow man with higher powers, and you grant that there are *agents* who have it in their power to interfere with or control the laws ordinarily in operation in the material world, so as to work miracles. Admit, further, that there may be an *occasion* calling for superhuman interference—and such surely is the authentication of a revelation containing truths which it was of the utmost consequence for man to know, but of which, except by revelation, he could know nothing—and the possibility is advanced to the highest probability."

We have shown, then, that "a miracle is *not* a violation of the laws of nature, in any sense in which such a violation is impossible or inconceivable. It is simply the introduction of a new agent, possessing new powers, and therefore not included under the rules generalized from a previous experience. Its miraculous character, distinguishing it from mere new discoveries in nature, consists in the fact that the powers in question are supposed to be introduced for a special purpose, and to be withdrawn again when that purpose is accomplished, and thus to be excluded from the field of future observation and investigation. But the supposition of such powers needs not imply any violation of the present laws observed by present natural agents. The *laws of nature* are simply general statements concerning the powers and properties of certain classes of objects which have come under our observation. They say nothing about the powers and properties of other objects or classes of objects which have not been observed, or which have been observed with a different result. There are laws, for instance, of one class of material agents which do not apply to another; and there are laws of matter in general which are not applicable to mind; and so there may be other orders of beings of which we have no knowledge, the laws of whose action may be different from all that we know of mind or body. *A violation*, in the proper sense of the word, *of the laws of nature would only take place*, *if*, *in two cases in which the cause or antecedent fact were exactly the same*, *the effect or consequent fact were different.* But no such irregularity is asserted by the believer in miracles.

He does not assert that miracles are produced by the abnormal action of natural and known causes—on the contrary, he expressly maintains that they are produced by a special interposition of Divine power; and that such an interposition, constituting in itself a different cause, may reasonably be expected to be followed by a different effect. So far, then, as a miracle is regarded as the operation of a special cause producing a special effect, it offers no antagonism to that general uniformity of nature, according to which the same effects will always follow from the same causes. The opposition between science and miracle, if any exist, must be sought in another quarter; namely, in the assumption that the introduction of a special cause is itself incredible. The ground of such an assumption appears to lie in the hypothesis that the existing forces of nature are so mutually related to each other that no new power can be introduced without either disturbing the whole equilibrium of the universe, or involving a series of miracles, coextensive with the universe, to counteract such disturbance." (Mansel, pp. 24, 25.) To the last-named assumption it is sufficient to reply: 1. If we admit the personality and, as implied in the personality, the moral nature of God, without which admission no religion, no feeling of a spiritual relation between God and man, and no conception of a mind superior to nature can have any existence, we may doubtless believe that God from the beginning so ordered the constitution of the world as to leave room for the exercise of those miraculous powers which he foresaw would, at a certain time, be exercised; just as he has left similar room for the exercise, within narrower limits, of the human will.

2. That God should interpose in the uniformities which exist among natural phenomena, by introducing a new (miraculous) power, is the less surprising, as he has permitted man, as a free moral agent, to act contrary to the design for which he was created, and thus, by sinning, to violate the originally-established order of nature, and the miraculous interposition of God has really for its object to restore the order of things which has been disturbed by the fall.

II. It is asserted that "even supposing a miracle were wrought, it would be impossible to establish the fact by evidence." On what grounds is this assertion made? Hume says: "A miracle is contrary to human experience, and, therefore, incredible." To state this argument is to refute it. Neither the major nor the minor premise is true. To assert that miracles are contrary to all human experience is an assumption which begs the whole question in dispute. That miracles are contrary to general experience is very true, else they would not be miracles. That they are contrary to *all* human experience is not true. So far from this, they have become actually the objects of human experience in connection with the promulgation both of the Jewish and, afterward, of the Christian systems of religion. The facts are well attested, the statements clear, full, explicit. The instances, though rare, yet, in the aggregate, are numerous. The witnesses are many, men of good character and good sense. They testify to plain facts, about which there could well be no mistake. They appeal to their cotemporaries for the truth of their statements; and that testimony goes uncontradicted, nay, is confirmed, by their enemies. Now, it is a sheer begging of the question for any man to assert that miracles are contrary to human experience, when so many witnesses testify positively to the occurrences under their own observation of events, which, if they really did occur as stated, must be admitted to be miraculous. The fact that Mr. Hume, or any number of men, did not see a miracle, does not prove that nobody has ever seen one. Mere negative testimony can not outweigh positive. Nor is the major premise of Mr. Hume's argument more tenable. An event is not necessarily incredible, because not known to have occurred before. Is it quite certain that nothing can take place in the world which has not already taken place? Even if it were conceded, then, as it is not, that miracles are contrary to human experience, it by no means follows that they are, on that account, necessarily incredible. If in ten thousand millions of occurrences we have found nothing but natural occurrences—this will never entitle us, by any logical rule, to declare that in no other occurrence can there be supernatural agency.

Again, it is said: "You can not prove a miracle, as it is beyond the capacity of a man to tell what powers are in nature. You may show us a phenomenon inexplicable in our present state of knowledge, but this does not prove it to be beyond agencies of nature as yet undiscovered by man." It is sufficient to reply to this, that, though we do not know the full extent of the powers of nature, there are some things—just such things as the works actually recorded as having been done by Christ and his apostles—of which we are quite certain that they are not within the range of natural agency. Moreover, "in proportion as the science of to-day surpasses that of former generations, so is the improbability that any man could have wrought in past times, by natural means, works which no skill of the present age is able to imitate. The effect, therefore, of scientific progress, as regards Scriptural miracles, is gradually to eliminate the hypothesis which refers them to unknown natural causes, and to reduce the question to the following alternative: Either the recorded acts were not performed at all, or they were performed, as their authors themselves declare, by virtue of a supernatural power consciously exercised for that very purpose. The theory which attempts to explain them as distorted statements of events reducible to *known natural causes*, has been tried by the rationalists of Germany, and has failed so utterly as to preclude all expectation of its revival, even in the land of its birth. There remains only the choice between accepting the sacred narrative as a true account of miracles actually performed, and rejecting it as wholly fictitious and incredible; whether the fiction be attributed to the gradual accretion of mythical elements, or—for a later criticism has come back again to the older and more intelligible theory—to the conscious fabrication of a willful impostor." (Mansel, pp. 22, 23.) Again, it is said by Strauss, and repeated by a writer in the late "Essays and Reviews:" "No testimony can reach to the supernatural; testimony can apply only to apparent, sensible facts; testimony can only prove an extraordinary and perhaps inexplicable occurrence or phenomenon: that it is due to *supernatural* causes is entirely dependent on the previous belief and assumptions of the parties." To this Mansel (pp. 14, 15) makes the pertinent and weighty reply: "It may, with certain exceptions, be applicable to a case in which the assertion of a supernatural cause rests solely on the testimony of the *spectator* of the fact; but it is not applicable to those in which the caúse is declared by the *performer.* Let us accept, if we please, merely as a narrative of 'apparent, sensible facts,' the history of the cure of the blind and dumb demoniac, or of the lame man at the Beautiful Gate; but we can not place the same restriction upon the words of our Lord, and of Peter, *which expressly assign the supernatural cause:* 'If I cast out devils by the Spirit of God, then the kingdom of God is come unto you,' (Matt. xii, 28,) and, 'By the name of Jesus Christ of Nazareth doth this man stand here before you whole,' (Acts iv, 10.) We have here, at least, a testimony reaching to the supernatural; and if that testimony be admitted in these cases, it may be extended to the whole series of wonderful works performed by the same persons. For if a given cause can be assigned as the true explanation of any single occurrence of the series, it becomes at once the most reasonable and probable explanation of the remainder. . . . One miracle is enough to show that the series of events with which it is connected is one which the Almighty has seen fit to mark by exceptions to the ordinary course of his providence; and, if this be once granted, we have no *a priori* grounds on which we can determine how many of such exceptions are to be expected. If a single miracle recorded in the Gospels be once admitted, the remainder cease to have any special antecedent improbability, and may be established by the same evidence, which is sufficient for ordinary events." Again, we are told: "In nature, and from nature, by science and by reason, we neither have, nor can possibly have, any evidence of a *Deity working miracles;* for that we must go out of nature and beyond reason. If we could have any such evidence *from nature*, it could only prove extraordinary natural effects, which would not be *miracles* in the old theological sense, as isolated, unrelated, and uncaused; whereas, no *physical* fact can be conceived as unique, or without analogy and relation to others, and to the whole system of natural causes." To this Dr. J. Haven, quoted above, replies: "True, that which is *from* nature, that is, produced by natural causes, can not be supernatural; but it is not true that *in* nature, that is, within the limits and domain of nature, there can be no occurrence of the supernatural. Nor is it true that whatever is beyond the power of natural causes to produce is, therefore, beyond the domain of reason to investigate, and must be received, if at all, only by a blind and unquestioning faith. That is not for a moment to be conceded. That which is extra-natural is not of necessity incapable of proof. The question whether a dead man was, on a certain occasion, restored to life, is a question to be settled wholly by evidence and investigation of reason. If the event *did* occur, clearly it was supernatural; the laws and forces of nature are not adequate to produce such a result. But *did* it occur? That is the real question; and it is a question which falls as clearly and fully within the range of rational investigation, and the laws of evidence, as any question in physical science." One word more with reference to a phrase which Strauss and a writer in the "Essays and Reviews" use in place of an argument, "that miracles are inconceivable by reason." This phrase can certainly not mean that we can not have an idea of a miracle, for we can easily form the idea or notion of an event in nature—for instance, of a person rising from the dead, with a cause beyond nature. Those who use it no doubt mean by it, that a miracle is contrary to intuitive reason, that is, to a fundamental law or constitutional principle of the mind; such, for instance, as the law of causation. If this were the case, we grant that it would be impossible to establish a miracle. But what constitutional law of the mind is contradicted by a miracle? None has been named. It is certainly not the law of causation; for a supernatural event is not declared to be an effect without a cause; it is merely an effect not resulting from the agencies working in that system which we call nature. The principle of cause and effect must not be confounded with the principle of the uniformity of nature. While the former is universal, the latter is only partial; it declares, for instance, that fire left to itself will burn, but it does not say that fire may not be counteracted by a higher and Divine agency. Upon a disregarding of this distinction rests the assertion that a miracle is contrary to experience. Inductive philosophy has shown that there is a set of agencies working in nature, and that there is uniformity in their operations. All this is freely granted; but when it is said that there can be nothing else, we demand the proof that every occurrence must have a physical or mundane cause. To this demand infidelity has never given a response.

We have now met the assumption of the impossibility of miracles in all its various phases. The verity of the miracles recorded in the Gospel history rests upon the credibility of the Evangelists, and upon the divine seal which the subject of their narrative, Jesus Christ, stamps upon the whole Gospel history.

§ 23. The Alleged Lack of Sufficient Testimony by Profane Writers.

The verification by profane writers of the many incidental allusions to the civil history of the times, which the writings of the Evangelists furnish, has been set forth in § 16. In § 18 of the same chapter we have seen that the existence, at this time, of one called by his followers Christ, the place of his teaching, his execution by Pontius Pilate, Procurator of Judea under Tiberius, the rapid spread of his doctrine through the Roman world, the vast number of converts made in a short time, the persecutions which they underwent, the innocency of their lives, their worship of Christ as God, are witnessed to by heathen writers of eminence, and would be certain and indisputable facts, had the New Testament never been written. To expect from profane sources a testimony concerning the supernatural facts recorded by the Evangelists would be absurd, since those who believed them naturally and almost necessarily became Christians.

It has, however, been urged that, assuming the historical truth of the New Testament narrative, we might have expected far more frequent and fuller notices of the Christian religion and its Founder than the remains of antiquity furnish. It has, for instance, been said that Josephus ought to have said more of Christ; and Seneca, the brother of Gallio, the observant Pausanias, the voluminous Plutarch, the copious Dio, the exact Arian, should have made frequent mention of Christianity in their writings, instead of almost wholly ignoring it. To this objection Mr. Rawlinson makes the following reply:

"Let it be considered, in the first place, whether the very silence of these writers is not a proof of the importance which in their hearts they assigned to Christianity, and the difficulty which they felt in dealing with it—whether, in fact, it is not a *forced* and *studied* reticence—a reticence so far from being indicative of ignorance that it implies only too much knowledge, having its origin in a feeling that it was best to ignore what it was unpleasant to confess and impossible to meet satisfactorily. Pausanias must certainly have been aware that the shrines of his beloved gods were in many places deserted, and that their temples were falling into decay, owing to the conversion of the mass of the people to the new religion; we may be sure he inwardly mourned over this sad spirit of disaffection—this madness, as he must have thought it, of a degenerate age; but no word is suffered to escape him on the painful subject; he is too jealous of his gods' honor to allow that there are any who dare to insult them. Like the faithful retainer of a fallen house, he covers up the shame of his masters, and bears his head so much the more proudly, because of their depressed condition. Again, it is impossible that Epictetus could have been ignorant of the wonderful patience and constancy of the Christian martyrs, of their marked contempt of death, and general indifference to worldly things; he must, one would think, as a Stoic, have been moved with a secret admiration of those great models of fortitude, and if he had allowed himself to speak freely, could not but have made frequent reference to them. The one contemptuous notice, which is all that Arian reports, sufficiently indicates his knowledge; the entire silence, except in this passage, upon what it so nearly concerned a Stoical philosopher to bring forward, can only be viewed as the studied avoidance of a topic which would have been unpalatable to his hearers, and to himself perhaps not wholly agreeable. The philosopher who regarded himself as raised by study and reflection to an exalted hight above the level of ordinary humanity, would not be altogether pleased to find that his elevation was attained through the power of religion, which he looked on as mere fanaticism. Thus, from different motives—from pride, from policy, from fear of offending the chief of the State, from real attachment to the old heathenism, and tenderness for it—the heathen writers who witnessed the birth and growth of Christianity united in a reticence which causes their notices of the religion to be a very insufficient measure of the place which it really held in their thoughts and apprehensions. A large allowance is to be made for this studied silence in estimating the value of the actual testimonies to the truth of the New Testament narrative adducible from heathen writers of the first and second centuries.

"And the silence of Josephus is, more plainly still, willful and affected. It is quite impossible that the Jewish historian should have been ignorant of the events which had drawn the eyes of so many to Judea but a few years before his own birth, and which a large and increasing sect believed to possess a supernatural character. Jesus of Nazareth was, humanly speaking, at least as considerable a personage as John the Baptist, and the circumstances of his life and death must have attracted at least as much attention. There was no good reason why Josephus, if he had been an honest historian, should have mentioned the latter and omitted the former. He had grown to manhood during the time that Christianity was being spread over the world; he had probably witnessed the tumults excited against Paul by his enemies at Jerusalem (Acts xxi, 27, etc.; xxii, 22, 23; xxiii, 10;) he knew of the irregular proceedings against 'James, the Lord's brother,' (Gal. i, 9;) he must have been well acquainted with the persecutions which the Christians had undergone at the hands of both Jews and heathen; at any rate he could not fail to be at least as well informed as Tacitus on the subject of transactions of which his own country had been the scene, and which had fallen partly within his own lifetime. When, therefore, we find that he is almost entirely silent concerning the Christian religion, and, if he mentions Christ at all, mentions him only incidentally in a single passage, as, 'Jesus, who was called Christ;' when we find this, we can not but conclude that, for some reason or other, the Jewish historian practices an intentional reserve, and *will* not enter upon a subject which excites his fears or offends his prejudices. No conclusions inimical to the historic accuracy of the New Testament can reasonably be drawn from the silence of a writer who determinedly avoids the subject.

"Further, in estimating the value of that direct evidence of adversaries to the main facts of Christianity which remains to us, we must not overlook the probability that much evidence of this kind has perished. The books of the early opponents of Christianity, which might have been of the greatest use to us for the confirmation of the Gospel history, were, with an unwise zeal, destroyed by the first Christian Emperors. Other testimony of the greatest importance has perished by the ravages of time. It seems certain that Pilate remitted to Tiberius an account of the execution of our Lord, and the grounds of it; and that this document, to which Justin Martyr more than once alludes, was deposited in the archives of the empire. The 'Acts of Pilate,' as they were called, seem to have contained an account, not only of the circumstances of the crucifixion, and the grounds upon which the Roman Governor regarded himself as justified in passing sentence of death upon the accused, but also of the miracles of Christ."

Dr. Kurtz remarks, in his Church History:

"Among the *genuine non-Biblical* testimonies about Christ, probably the most ancient is a Syriac letter of Mara, addressed to his son Serapion, written about the year 73. Mara, a man thoroughly versed in Greek philosophy, but not satisfied with the consolations it offered, writes from his place of exile a letter of comfort and instruction to his son, in which he ranks Christ along with Socrates and Pythagoras; he honors him as a wise king; he charges the Jews with his murder, declares that thereby they had brought upon themselves the destruction of their commonwealth, but that Christ continued to live in the new law which he had given."

CHAPTER II.

THE CREDIBILITY OF THE EVANGELISTS.*

§ 24. THE EVANGELISTS WERE IN A CONDITION TO INFORM THEMSELVES ACCURATELY AND THOROUGHLY CONCERNING THE THINGS WHICH THEY RECORD.

Two of them were the chosen and almost constant companions of the wonderful person whose life they describe; they listened to his public discourses, they enjoyed his familiar intercourse and private instruction, they were eye-witnesses of his miracles, and consequently received them on the testimony of their own senses. Certainly no other biographer ever enjoyed such opportunities of informing himself thoroughly concerning the subject of his narrative. Even cotemporary historians rarely *see* the facts which

* The argument to be presented in this chapter has been stated at large in all the English works on the "Evidences of Christianity." We follow substantially Horne's Introduction, deviating, however, from that author in the order of the argumentation, and basing the personal credibility of the Evangelists upon the preceding proofs of the authenticity of the writings ascribed to them. If the Gospel Records have been written by the persons whose names they bear, it can not be denied that they were written by men who were possessed of a full knowledge of all they relate, and who had no conceivable motive to deviate from the truth. The credibility of a historian is established when there is sufficient evidence, 1. That he has had ample means of knowing the truth of the facts he relates, either by being himself an eye-witness, or by deriving his knowledge from an eye-witness; 2. That he is a man of sound mind, free from any mental bias to self-deception; 3. That he is above the suspicion of having any motive or design to mislead his readers. Though historical works are generally accepted without a special inquiry into these criteria of credibility, being rejected only where there is positive proof that the historian is destitute either of the ability or of the willingness to report correctly, the Gospel history can challenge its being subjected to the severest tests of historical criticism.

they relate; they are often in a distant country from that in which the event happened, and are informed of it only by public reports, which are seldom faithful in all points. If it happens that an author be at the same time both historian and witness—that he has accompanied the general whose actions he relates, as, for instance, Polybius accompanied Scipio—that he has been his particular confident—we set a high value upon his memoirs, and should consider it an act of injustice to call them in question *without solid proofs.* If Plato has been deemed a competent witness, and in every respect qualified to compose the biographical account of his master, Socrates, surely the Evangelists were equally-competent witnesses of the facts which they have related.

It is true, two of them were not eye-witnesses; but they received their information from eye-witnesses, and their accounts agree in every essential point with those of the eye-witnesses; though it is evident, at the same time, that they did not know, or paid no regard to what others had before written on the same subject. (See more on this subject, § 32.)

§ 25. The Evangelists Exhibit in their Narratives no Symptom of Mental Derangement, which might have made them Victims of Self-Delusion.

To every candid reader of the Gospels the certainty of the assertion made in the heading is self-evident, and a contrary supposition seems unworthy of an answer. Yet, as there are so many who condemn the Gospels without having subjected them to a candid examination, we will show how unreasonable it is to suspect the Evangelists of being the victims of self-delusion. In the first place, let it be borne in mind that their testimony did not relate to certain abstract doctrinal points, concerning which they might have erred through some mental defect. It respected facts concerning the reality of which they could not be misled. They became the disciples of Jesus Christ upon rational conviction, not upon internal persuasion alone, but on the irrefragable evidence of clear and stupendous miracles, proofs submitted to their senses, and approved by their reason—such proofs as enthusiasm could not have counterfeited, and never would have required; and at every step of their progress, as their faith was called to signalize itself by new exertions, or to sustain new trials, it was fortified by new proofs. The slowness and caution with which the apostles received the fact of their Lord's resurrection from the dead fully exempt them from all suspicion of being the dupes of delusion and credulity. In the second place, the style of enthusiasts is always obscure, arrogant, and violent; the style of the Evangelists is the very reverse of this, plain, calm, and unexaggerated, detailing the facts which establish the unparalleled perfection of their divine Lord with the particularity and consistency of Truth. Moreover, they do that which enthusiasts *never* do; they record their own mistakes, follies, and faults, and those of very serious magnitude, acknowledged to be such by themselves, and severely censured by their Master. Nor do we discover in the Gospels any effusion of passion and imagination, such as we find invariably in the writings of enthusiasts.

§ 26. The Evangelists can not be charged with having had any Motive or Design to impose upon the World what, if it did not take place, they must have known to be false.

No man of sense or candor ever dared to make such a charge. It is self-evident that, if the first disciples of Jesus had any disposition to commit such a fraud, it would have been impossible for them to succeed in it with their cotemporaries; and that, even if they could have done it, they would not have had a conceivable motive for it. No man will propagate a deliberate falsehood without having some advantage in view, either immediate or remote. Now, the first teachers of Christianity could have no prospect whatever of any advantage. They could expect none from him in whom they professed to believe. Jesus Christ, indeed, had warned them to expect persecution, ignominy, and death in this world, if they continued to be his disciples. They could not expect any honors or emoluments from the hands of the Jews and heathens, who persecuted them with unrelenting severity. They could not expect to acquire wealth, for their profession of the Christian faith subjected them to the loss of all things. Moreover, according to their own principles, either as Jews or Christians, they involved themselves in eternal misery if they made themselves guilty of propagating a deliberate falsehood. Again, how incredible that the sublimest precepts of piety and virtue should have been delivered by men of such abandoned principles, as they must have been, if they had really been impostors! How incredible that the first disciples should have been willing to die for the cause of Christ, who, if he had not risen again from the dead, would have miserably deceived them! Lastly, if the apostles and Evangelists had designed to impose upon mankind, they would have accommodated themselves to the opinions and inclinations of the people whom they addressed; they would carefully have avoided saying any thing that might offend them; but, instead of this, they did not spare the prejudices and corruptions of their cotemporaries.

That the Evangelists were, on the contrary, men of the strictest integrity and sincerity is, as has been already remarked from another stand-point, manifest from the style and manner of their writings. There are no artful transitions or connections, no effort to set off a doubtful action and reconcile it to some other, or to the character of the person that did it. They do not dissemble certain circumstances in the life and sufferings of their Master which have no tendency to enhance his glory in the eyes of the world: such as the low circumstances of his parents, the mean accommodations of his birth—that, when he appeared publicly to the world, his townsmen and near relations despised and rejected him—that few among his followers were men conspicuous for wealth, dignity, or knowledge—that the rulers, the scribes and Pharisees disowned his pretensions and opposed him continually—that some, who for a time followed him, afterward deserted him—that he was betrayed into the hands of high-priests and rulers by one of those who had been selected for his constant companions. Impostors would certainly have acted differently.

The same integrity and fidelity we find in what they record concerning themselves. They honestly acknowledge not only the lowness of their station, but also the inveteracy of their national prejudices, the slowness of their apprehension, the weakness of their faith, the ambition of some of the disciples, the intolerant temper of others, and the worldly views of all. They even tell us of their cowardice in deserting their Master when he was seized by his enemies; and that, after his crucifixion, they had for a while given up their hopes in their Master, notwithstanding all the proof that had been exhibited, and the conviction which they had before entertained that he was the Messiah, and his religion was from God. They mention, with many affecting circumstances, the incredulity of one of their number, who was convinced of the reality of their Lord's resurrection only by ocular and sensible demonstration. They might have concealed their mental and moral deficiencies, or, at least, they might have alleged some reasons to extenuate them. But they did no such thing. They related, without disguise, events and facts just as they happened, and left them to speak for themselves.

In short, it does not appear that it ever entered the minds of these writers to consider how this or the other action would appear to mankind, or what objections might be raised against it. Greater marks of sincerity than those which the Evangelists bear it is impossible to find in any historical compositions that are extant; they convince their readers, in all they have written, that they published nothing to the world but what they believed themselves. When they relate any of the miracles of Jesus Christ, or the exercise of the miraculous powers with which they were endowed, they relate these astonishing facts, without any ornaments of language, in the most concise and simple manner; saying nothing previously to raise expectation, nor after the recital of them breaking out into exclamations, but they leave the reader to draw his own conclusion. When they narrate the resurrection and ascension of Christ they afford no explanation of any difficulties; they never offer a single argument to enforce their credit; they leave the bare facts with their readers, who may receive or reject them. In perusing the simple and unadorned narratives of the Evangelists it is impossible not to feel that the purport of their writing was *to bear witness of the truth.*

Finally, the same striking integrity characterizes the Evangelists when speaking of their enemies. Of all who were concerned in the persecution and death of Christ, they mention by name only the high-priest Caiaphas and his coadjutor Annas, the Roman Procurator Pilate, and the treacherous disciple Judas. The suppression of their names would have impaired the evidence of their history to posterity; but not the slightest tincture of resentment is observable in the notice of these persons. The epithet attached to Judas by all the Evangelists—ὁ παραδοὺς, who delivered him up—is expressive of the simple fact rather than of its criminality, which latter would more aptly be signified by προδότης, traitor, as he is styled on one solitary occasion.

CHAPTER III.

THE DIVINE SEAL STAMPED UPON THE GOSPEL HISTORY BY ITS SUBJECT, THE PERSON OF JESUS CHRIST.

§ 27. The Verity of the Gospel History best accredited by the Personality of Jesus Christ.

After having proved that the canonical Gospels were written in the apostolic age, and having found no testimony contrary to the consentient tradition of Christian antiquity in regard to their having been written by the persons whose names they bear, we placed them on no higher ground than other ancient productions. We have, thus far, considered them merely as human productions, and subjected them, as such, to the common laws of historical criticism. The result of this critical investigation has been, that we found them to bear the highest marks of human credibility—such as no other historical work of antiquity has. The assumption that miracles are impossible, and that, therefore, credibility can not be claimed for a record of miracles, we have met by showing, on metaphysical grounds, that, and why, miracles are not impossible, and that, therefore, the miraculous elements of the Gospel history are not incompatible with its credibility. But we have now to go a step further, and produce the *positive* proofs of the historic verity of the miracles recorded in the Gospels.

Instead of basing the truth of Gospel history and the Divinity of Christ upon the miracles recorded by the Evangelists, we may prove the historic verity of the miracles and the Divinity of Christ by the unparalleled perfectness of the moral and intellectual character of *the man Jesus of Nazareth*, as he is presented to us by the plain and honest fishermen of Galilee. "Demanding nothing more," says Mr. Young, in his *Christ of History*, "than the *simple humanity* of Jesus of Nazareth, we shall venture from this platform to assert and expound *his true Divinity*. Dismissing all preconceptions, however fondly cherished, and however long adopted into the faith of the Churches, assuming nothing which is not virtually and even formally admitted by enemies as well as friends, we hope to show that the *manhood* of Christ, as it appealed to the senses and the minds of the men of his own times, supplies and sustains the proof of his *Godhood*. Behold only *the man Jesus*—*he* shall indicate and demonstrate his union with absolute Godhead. Such a *humanity* as his is utterly inexplicable, except on the ground of true Divinity."*

* Mr. Norton, though not admitting the perfect exhibition of moral excellence in the teachings and actions of Christ, *as an intrinsic proof of his Divinity proper*, nevertheless argues from it *the truthfulness of the Gospel Records*. His argument is this: "The Gospels contain an exhibition of character incomparably more wonderful than is to be found in any other writings. It is the character of a messenger from God, assuming in his name the highest authority, constantly exercising supernatural powers, and appearing among men for the purpose of making them acquainted with God, with their own immortal nature, with their duty, and with those ennobling and awful sanctions by which it is enforced. He is represented as discovering to men a perfect system of religion. He always appears, whether teaching, or acting, or suffering, as displaying the highest excellence. His character is every-where consistent with itself and with the supernatural dignity of his office, though he is represented as passing through scenes the most trying and humiliating. We have, then, in these writings a just conception of a perfect system of religion, as taught by a Divine teacher, assuming the highest authority and exercising the most extraordinary powers, and displaying throughout a character in which we discover nothing but what is excellent and sublime. Now, the writers of the Gospels derived those conceptions which we find in their works either from reality or from their own imaginations. If it be contended that these writers did not draw from reality, but from imagination—the answer to this supposition is,

From this stand-point it is our object to show that the character and life of Jesus could not possibly have been the natural product of the times and country in which the Gospel Records incontestably originated—nor, indeed, of any other age or country; that the moral and intellectual perfectness of the character of Jesus, and the wonderful harmony and consistency of his doctrines and works, could not possibly have been conceived and delineated by the Evangelists, unless they had been actually witnessed by them; that the moral and intellectual perfectness of Jesus imparts to the testimony he gives of himself, as well as to the miracles which the Evangelists ascribe to him, a verity absolutely unassailable; and, finally, that the unparalleled *human* perfection of Jesus—which by almost universal consent, even of unbelievers, rises far above every human greatness known before or since—can not be rationally explained, except on the ground of such an essential union with the Godhead as he claimed himself, and

that the conceptions of moral excellence and sublimity which we find displayed and embodied in their writings would imply a transcendent genius and force of mind to which there is no parallel, which it is impossible should have existed in four anonymous, unknown authors, and which are irreconcilable with the actual want of extraordinary talents, and of skill in composition, that is discovered in their works. These conceptions likewise would imply a correctness of moral principle, and a purity and sublimity of moral feeling, which could not exist in union with intentional falsehood. The argument, therefore, is briefly this, that the religion and morality of the Gospels, as exhibited in the doctrines, precepts, and life of Christ, are such as could not have been conceived and represented by the writers of the Gospels if they had not had a living archetype before them; and that, without such an archetype, the power of conceiving and representing what we find in the Gospels, if it ever existed in any human being, would necessarily imply that that extraordinary being had a character which entitled him to perfect confidence. It was wholly out of the power of the writers of the Gospels to deceive us, as they must have done, supposing their representations false; and the very existence of such a power, in any case, would in itself imply the absence of all will to deceive. The intrinsic character of these writings, therefore, affords positive evidence of their historic verity as to all essential facts."

as the Evangelists ascribed to him. Thus, as the eye of a traveler at the foot of a mountain may slowly travel up the majestic slope till it is lost in the clouds or dazzling glories of the summit, so the mind may contemplate Christ from his lowliest and most human traits, where he is one with the humblest human being, up beyond the highest reach and limit of humanity, "far above all principalities, and powers, and every name that is named," to that dazzling summit of glory where he is one with God.

From whatever point of view we examine the human character and earthly life of Jesus, whether we contemplate the circumstances, times, and country in which he lived, or his moral and intellectual grandeur, or the testimony he gives of his own person, or the nature of the miracles ascribed to him, we shall be compelled, *by a strictly-historical process*, to acknowledge the justness of the deductions named above. This new homage to the Savior was first paid by the modern Evangelical theology of Germany. Dr. C. Ullmann opened the way by his work on "*The Sinlessness of Jesus an Evidence of Christianity;*" and, ever since the appearance of that classical work, greater prominence has been given by English, as well as German theologians, to the ethical element and human perfection of Christ. This branch of apologetical literature, in the English language, has been also enriched by Dr. John Young in his "Christ of History," by Dr. Horace Bushnell in his "Nature and the Supernatural," and by the theological tract of Dr. Schaff, entitled, "The Moral Character of Christ, or the Perfection of Christ's Humanity, a Proof of his Divinity."

§ 28. The admitted outer Conditions of the Life of Jesus—Leaving its Astounding Results, as well as the unlimited Scope of the Mind of Jesus and the Perfect Symmetry of his Character, utterly Inexplicable without the Admission of a Supernatural and Divine Element.

The most destructive criticism finds itself compelled to admit that Jesus of Nazareth is a historical personage, that he was a resident in the obscure village of Nazareth till about thirty years old, a carpenter's son, poor, unlearned, unbefriended, and that he was put to an ignominious death by the Jewish hierarchy a few years after he had appeared in public.

It is utterly inconceivable that such circumstances and conditions would have been made by any Jewish writer the substratum of the miraculous life of the Messiah. And it is equally inconceivable that a mere man, under such circumstances and conditions, could have become the turning-point of the world's history, accomplishing what neither the wisdom of the wisest, nor the power of the mightiest, neither philosophers nor emperors could accomplish. This Mr. Young, the author of "The Christ of History," has set forth in a very minute and complete argumentation, of which we will give the main points: Ordinarily the early life and social position of a man are the true key to the proper understanding of his future character and career. To this rule the life of Jesus makes an unqualified exception. In his early training and position there is nothing that but distantly accounts for his subsequent relation to the world. His life stands out a mysterious exception from all laws which generally govern the destiny of men; what he became and accomplished could not possibly be the natural development of earlier impressions received through favorable circumstances. He grew up among a people seldom and only contemptuously named by the ancient classics, and subjected at the time to the yoke of a foreign oppressor; in a remote and conquered province of the Roman Empire; in the darkest district of Palestine; in a little country town of proverbial insignificance; in poverty and manual labor, in the obscurity of a carpenter's shop; without the help of literary culture, as is testified by the surprise of the Jews, who knew all his human relations and antecedents. "How knoweth this man letters," they asked, when they heard Jesus teach, "having never learned?" (John vii, 15.) This question is unavoidable and unanswerable, if Christ be regarded as a mere man. For each effect presupposes a corresponding cause. The difficulty here presented can by no means be solved by a reference to the fact that many, perhaps the majority of great men, especially in the Church, have risen by their own industry and perseverance from the lower walks of life, and from a severe contest with poverty and obstacles of every kind. The fact itself is readily conceded; but in every one of these cases, schools, or books, or patrons and friends, or peculiar events and influences, can be pointed out, as auxiliary aids in the development of intellectual or moral greatness. There is always some human or natural cause, or combination of causes, which accounts for the final result. In the case of Christ no such natural explanation can be given. All the attempts to bring him into contact with Egyptian wisdom, or the

Essenic theosophy, or other sources of learning, are without a shadow of proof; and, even if he had been in connection with some sources of learning, the phenomenon he presents would remain unexplained, for, as we shall show, he taught the world as one who had learned nothing from it, and was under no obligation to it.

Another fact in the life of Jesus which leaves its astounding results unexplained on natural grounds, is his *early death*. On this point we will quote Mr. Young in full: "He, whom Christians recognize as the Redeemer of the world, was only a youth. Whether his religion be regarded as a system of doctrines, or as a body of laws, or as a source of extraordinary influence, it is passing strange that *he* should have died in early life. His brief period of existence afforded no opportunity for maturing any thing. In point of fact, while he lived he *did* very little in the *common* sense of *doing*. He originated no series of well-concerted plans, he neither contrived nor put in motion any extended machinery, he entered into no correspondence with parties in his own country and in other regions of the world, in order to spread his influence and obtain coöperation. Even the few who were his constant companions, and were warmly attached to his person, were not, in his lifetime, imbued with his sentiments, and were not prepared to take up his work in his spirit after he was gone. He constituted no society with its name, design, and laws all definitely fixed and formally established. He had no time to construct and to organize, his life was too short; and almost all that he did was to *speak*. He spoke in familiar conversation with his friends, or at the wayside to passers-by, or to those who chose to consult him, or to large assemblies, as opportunity offered. He left behind him a few spoken truths—not a line or word of writing—and a certain spirit incarnated in his principles, and breathed out from his life, and then he died. In the ordinary course of events the memory of a mere youth, however distinguished, would soon have utterly perished from among men. But Jesus lives in the world at this moment, and has influenced the world from his death till now. This is an unquestioned fact. There have been multitudes in all the ages since his death, and at this moment, after nearly two thousand years, there are multitudes to whom he is dearer than life. History tells of warriors who reached the summit of their fame in comparative youth; it tells of men of science also, and of scholars, and of statesmen, who in youth rose to great and envied distinction. But the difference is obvious, and it is wide between the conquest of territory and the conquest of minds—between scientific, literary, or political renown and moral, spiritual influence and excellence. Is there an instance of a man who died in youth, gaining vast influence of a purely-spiritual kind, not by force of arms, and not by secular aid in any form, but simply and only by his principles and his life—of such a man transmitting that influence through successive generations, and after two thousand years retaining it in all its freshness, and continuing, at that distance of time, to establish himself, and to reign almightily in the minds and hearts of myriads of human beings? If there be, or any thing approaching to it, where is it? There is not such an example in the whole history of the world, except Jesus Christ."

"There is," says Dr. Schaff, "another striking distinction of a general character between Christ and the heroes of history. We should naturally suppose that such an uncommon personage, setting up the most astounding claims and proposing the most extraordinary work, would surround himself with extraordinary circumstances, and maintain a position far above the vulgar and degraded multitude around him. We should expect something uncommon and striking in his look, his dress, his manner, his mode of speech, his outward life, and the train of his attendants. But the very reverse is the case. His greatness is singularly unostentatious, modest and quiet, and, far from repelling the beholder, it attracts and invites him to familiar approach. His public life never moved on the imposing arena of secular heroism, but within the humble circle of every-day life, and the simple relations of a son, a brother, a citizen, a teacher, and a friend. He had no army to command, no kingdom to rule, no prominent station to fill, no worldly favors and rewards to dispense. He was a humble individual, without friends and patrons in the Sanhedrim, or at the court of Herod. He never mingled in familiar intercourse with the religious or social leaders of the nation, whom he had startled in his twelfth year by his questions and answers. He selected his disciples from among the illiterate fishermen of Galilee, and promised them no reward in this world but a part in the bitter cup of his sufferings. He dined with publicans and sinners, and mingled with the common people without ever condescending to their low manners and habits. He was so poor that he had no place on which to rest his head. He depended for the supply of his modest wants on voluntary contributions of a few pious females, and the purse was in the hands of a thief and a traitor. Nor had he learning, art, or eloquence, in the usual sense of the term, nor any other kind of power by which great men arrest the attention and secure the admiration of the world. The writers of Greece and Rome were ignorant even of his existence till, several years after the crucifixion, the effects of his mission in the steady growth of the sect of his followers forced from them some contemptuous notice, and then roused them to opposition. And yet this Jesus of Nazareth, without money and arms, conquered more millions than Alexander, Cæsar, Mohammed, and Napoleon; without science and learning, he shed more light on things human and divine than all scholars and philosophers combined; without the eloquence of schools, he spoke words of life as were never spoken before or since, and produced effects which lie beyond the reach of orator or poet; without writing a single line, he has set more pens in motion, and furnished themes for more sermons, orations, discussions, learned volumes, works of art, and sweet songs of praise, than the whole army of great men of ancient and modern times. Born in a manger, and crucified as a malefactor, he now controls the destinies of the civilized world, and rules a spiritual empire which embraces one-third of the inhabitants of the globe. There never was in this world a life so unpretending, modest, and lowly in its outward form and condition, and yet producing such extraordinary effects upon all ages, nations, and classes of men. The annals of history produce no other example of such complete and astounding success in spite of the absence of those material, literary, and artistic influences which are indispensable to success for a mere man."

We have seen that the outer conditions of the life of Jesus make its astounding results utterly inexplicable on the basis of ordinary history, experience, and psychology. The same is true with regard to the unlimited scope of his mind and the perfect symmetry of his character. Let us first consider the one great central idea of his mission, that of the establishment of a new spiritual kingdom: "Contrary to every religious prejudice of his nation, and even of his time," says Horace Bushnell, "contrary to the comparatively-narrow and exclusive religion of Moses itself, and to all his training under it,* he undertakes to organize a kingdom of God, or a kingdom of heaven on earth. His purpose includes a new moral creation of the race—not of the Jews only, but of the whole human race. He declared thus, at an early date in his ministry, that many shall come from the east and the west and sit down with Abraham, and Isaac, and Jacob in the kingdom of God; that the field is the world; and that God so loveth the world as to give for it his only-begotten Son. He also declared that his Gospel shall be published to all nations, and gave his apostles their commission to go into all the world and publish his Gospel to every creature. Here, then, we have the grand idea of his mission—it is to new-create the human race, and

* And yet it has been asserted that Jesus' conception of his Messianic mission was nothing more than a reflection of the popular opinions of his day, more or less modified by his own individuality! Of all the attempts to account for the work and character of Christ on natural grounds, denying the Divine element, this is the most unscrupulous and absurd. For nothing can be proved more irrefutably than this, that Jesus' conception of his Messianic mission was diametrically opposed to the Messianic ideas which prevailed among the Jewish people.

restore it to God in the unity of a spiritual kingdom. And, upon this single fact, Reinhard erects a complete argument for his extra-human character, going into a formal review of all the great founders of States, and most celebrated law-givers, all the philosophers, all the prophet-founders of religions, and discovering as a fact that no such thought as this, or nearly proximate to this, had ever before been taken up by any living character in history; showing, also, how it had happened to every other great character, however liberalized by culture, to be limited in some way to the interests of his own people or empire, and set in opposition or antagonism more or less decidedly to the rest of the world. But to Jesus alone, the simple Galilean carpenter, it happens otherwise; that, having never seen a map of the world, or heard the name of half the great nations on it, he undertakes, coming out of his shop, a scheme as much vaster and more difficult than that of Alexander, as it proposes more, and what is more divinely benevolent! This thought of a universal kingdom, cemented in God—why, the immense Roman Empire of his day, constructed by so many ages of war and conquest, is a bauble in comparison, both as regards the extent and the cost! And yet the rustic tradesman of Galilee propounds even this for his errand, and that in a way of assurance as simple and quiet as if the immense reach of his plan were, in fact, a matter to him of no consideration. Nor is this all: there is included in his plan, what, to any mere man, would be yet more remote from the possible confidence of his frailty; it is a plan as universal in time as it is in the scope of its objects. It does not expect to be realized in a lifetime, or even in many centuries to come. He calls it, understandingly, his grain of mustard-seed; which, however, is to grow, he declares, and overshadow the whole earth. But the courage of Jesus, counting a thousand years to be only a single day, is equal to the run of his work. He sees a rock of stability where men see only frailty and weakness. Peter himself, the impulsive and rather-unreliable Peter, turns into a rock and becomes a good foundation, as he looks upon him. 'On this rock,' he says, 'I will build my Church, and the gates of hell shall not prevail against it.' His expectation, too, reaches boldly out beyond his own death; that, in fact, is to be the seed of his great empire; 'Except a corn of wheat fall into the ground and die, it abideth,' he says, 'alone.' And if we will see with what confidence and courage he adheres to his plan, when the time of his death approaches—how far he is from giving it up as lost, or as an exploded vision of his youthful enthusiasm—we have only to observe his last interview with the two sisters of Bethany, in whose hospitality he was so often comforted. When the box of precious ointment is broken upon his head, he justifies her against the murmuring disciples, and says, 'Let her alone. She has done what she could. She has come aforehand to anoint my body to the burying. Verily, I say unto you, wheresoever this Gospel shall be preached throughout the whole world, this also that this woman has done shall be told for a memorial of her.' Such was the sublime confidence he had in a plan that was to run through all future ages, and would scarcely begin to show its fruit during his own lifetime. Is this great idea, then, which no man ever before conceived—the raising of the whole human race to God, a plan sustained with such evenness of courage and a confidence of the world's future so far transcending any human example—is this a *merely-human development?* Regard the benevolence of it, the universality of it, the religious grandeur of it, as a work readjusting the relations of God and his government with men—the cost, the length of time it will cover, and the far-off date of its completion. For a Nazarene carpenter, a poor, uneducated villager, to lay out a project which can not be completed in many thousands of years, and transcends all human ability, doing it in all the airs of sobriety, entering on the performance without parade, and yielding life to it firmly as the inaugural of its triumph, is, we may safely affirm, more than human."

The unparalleled universality of the mind of Jesus, and the perfect symmetry of his character, are comprehensively set forth by Dr. Schaff in the following remarks: "History exhibits to us many examples of commanding geniuses, who stand at the head of their age and nation, and furnish material for the intellectual activity of whole generations and periods, till they are succeeded by other heroes at a new epoch of development. As rivers generally spring from high mountains, so knowledge and moral power rises and is continually nourished from the hights of humanity. . . . . But they never represent universal, but only sectional humanity; they are identified with a particular people or age, and partake of its errors, superstitions, and failings almost in the same proportion in which they exhibit their virtues. Moses, though revered by the followers of three religions, was a Jew in views, feelings, habits, and position, as well as by parentage; Socrates never rose above the Greek type of character; Luther was a German throughout, and can only be properly understood as a German; Calvin, though an exile from his native land, remained a Frenchman; and Washington, the purest and noblest type of the American character, can be to no nation on earth what he is to the American. Their influence may and does extend far beyond their respective national horizon, yet they can never furnish a universal model for imitation. . . . . What these representative men are to particular ages, or nations, or sects, or particular schools of science and art, Christ was to the human family at large in its relation to God. He, and he alone, is the universal type for universal imitation. Hence he could, without the least impropriety or suspicion of vanity, call upon all men to follow him. He stands above the limitations of age, school, sect, nation, and race. Although a Jew according to the flesh, there is nothing Jewish about him which is not at the same time of general significance. The particular and national in him is always duly subordinated to the general and human. Still less was he ever identified with a party or sect. He was equally removed from the stiff formalism of the Pharisees, the loose liberalism of the Sadducees, and the inactive mysticism of the Essenes. He rose above all the prejudices, bigotries, and superstitions of his age and people, which exert their power even upon the strongest and otherwise most liberal minds. Witness his freedom in the observance of the Sabbath, by which he offended the scrupulous literalists, while he fulfilled the true spirit of the law in its universal and abiding significance; his reply to the disciples, when they traced the misfortune of the blind man to a particular sin of the subject, or his parents; his liberal conduct toward the Samaritans as contrasted with the inveterate hatred and prejudice of the Jews, including his own disciples, at the time; and his charitable judgment of the slaughtered Galileans, whose blood Pilate had mingled with their sacrifices, and the eighteen upon whom the tower in Siloam fell and slew them. All the words and all the actions of Christ, while they were fully adapted to the occasions which called them forth, retain their force and applicability undiminished to all ages and nations. . . . . He was free from all one-sidedness, which constitutes the weakness as well as the strength of the most eminent men. He was not a man of one idea, nor of one virtue, towering above all the rest. The mental and moral forces were so well tempered and moderated by each other that none were unduly prominent, none carried to excess, none alloyed by the kindred failing; each was checked and completed by the opposite grace. His character never lost its even balance and happy equilibrium, never needed modification or readjustment. It was thoroughly sound and uniformly consistent from the beginning to the end. We can not properly attribute to him any one temperament. He was neither sanguine like Peter, nor choleric like Paul, nor melancholy like John, nor phlegmatic as James is sometimes represented to have been; but he combined the vivacity without the levity of the sanguine, the vigor without the violence of the choleric, the seriousness without the austerity of the melancholic, the calmness without the apathy of the phlegmatic temperaments. He was equally far removed from the excesses of the legalist, the pietist, the ascetic, and the enthusiast.

With the strictest obedience to the law, he moved in the element of freedom; with all the fervor of the enthusiast, he was always calm, sober, and self-possessed; notwithstanding his complete and uniform elevation above the affairs of this world, he freely mingled with society, male and female, dined with publicans and sinners, sat at the wedding feast, shed tears at the sepulcher, delighted in God's nature, admired the beauties of the lilies, and used the occupations of the husbandman for the illustration of the sublimest truths of the kingdom of heaven. His zeal never degenerated into rashness, nor his constancy into obstinacy, nor his tenderness into sentimentality. His unworldliness was free from indifference and unsociability, his dignity from pride, his affability from undue familiarity, his self-denial from moroseness, his temperance from austerity. He combined childlike innocence with manly strength, all-absorbing devotion to God with untiring interest in the welfare of man, tender love to the sinner with uncompromising severity against sin, commanding dignity with winning humility, fearless courage with wise caution, unyielding firmness with sweet gentleness. He is justly compared with the lion in strength, and with the lamb in meekness. He equally possessed the wisdom of the serpent and the simplicity of the dove. He brought both the sword against every form of wickedness, and the peace which the world can not give. He was the most effective, and yet the least noisy, the most radical, and yet the most conservative, calm, and patient of all reformers. He came to fulfill every letter of the law, and yet he made all things new. The same hand which drove the profane traffickers from the

Temple, blessed little children, healed the lepers, and resuscitated the sinking disciple; the same ear which heard the approbation from heaven, was open to the cries of women in travail; the same mouth which pronounced the terrible woe on the hypocrites, and condemned the impure desire and unkind feeling as well as the open crime, blessed the poor in spirit, announced pardon to the adulteress, and prayed for his murderers; the same eye which beheld the mysteries of God and penetrated the heart of man, shed tears of compassion over ungrateful Jerusalem, and tears of friendship at the grave of Lazarus. These are indeed opposite, yet not contradictory traits of character—as little as the different manifestations of God's power and goodness in the tempest and the sunshine, in the towering Alps and the lily of the valley, in the boundless ocean and dew-drops of the morning. They are separated in imperfect men, indeed, but united in Christ, the universal model for all."

Though the above sketch comprises all the elements which constitute mental and moral perfection,* we can not refrain from adding a few lineaments drawn by Bushnell, when he considers him as a teacher, his method and manner, and other characteristics, apart from his doctrine which does not come into consideration in our present investigation:

"First of all, we notice the perfect originality and independence of his teaching. We have a great many men who are original within a certain boundary of educated thought. But the originality of Christ is

*We are aware that we anticipate in part the subject-matter of the subsequent section on the moral perfection of Christ; but it is impossible to consider mental entirely apart from moral perfection. Besides, the moral perfection of Christ will be viewed for itself, as *sinlessness*. Here we consider only his moral as well as mental *greatness*.

uneducated. That he draws nothing from the stores of learning can be seen at a glance. The impression we have in reading his instructions justifies to the letter the language of his cotemporaries, when they say, 'This man hath never learned.' There is nothing in any of his allusions, or forms of speech, that indicates learning. Indeed, there is nothing in him that belongs to his age or country—no one opinion, or taste, or prejudice. If he is simply a man, he is most certainly a new and singular kind of man, never before heard of, one who is quite as great a miracle in the world as if he were not a man.

"Neither does he teach by the human methods. He does not speculate about God, as a school-professor, drawing out conclusions by a practice on words, and deeming that the way of proof; he does not build up a frame of evidence from below, by some constructive process, such as the philosophers delight in; but he simply speaks of God and spiritual things as one who has come out from him to tell us what he knows. And his simple telling brings us the reality; proves it to us in its own sublime self-evidence; awakens even the consciousness of it in our own bosom, so that formal arguments or dialectic proofs offend us by their coldness. Indeed, he makes even the world luminous by his words—fills it with an immediate and new sense of God, which nothing has ever been able to expel.

"At the same time, he never reveals the infirmity so commonly shown by human teachers, when they veer a little from their point, or turn their doctrine off by shades of variation, to catch the assent of multitudes. He never conforms to an expectation, even of his friends. When they look to find a great prophet in him, he offers nothing in the modes of the prophets. When they ask for places of distinction in his kingdom, he rebukes their folly, and tells them he has nothing to give but a share in his reproaches and his poverty. When they look to see him take the sword as the Great Messiah of their nation, calling the people to his standard, he tells them he is no warrior and no king, but only a messenger of love to lost men; one that has come to minister and die, but not to set up or restore the kingdom. Every expectation that rises up to greet him is repulsed; and yet, so great is the power of his manner, that multitudes are held fast, and can not yield their confidence.

"Again, the singular balance of character displayed in the teachings of Jesus, indicates an exemption from the standing infirmity of human nature. Human opinions are formed under a law that seems to be universal. First, two opposite extremes are thrown up in two opposite leaders or parties; then a third party enters, trying to find what truth they both are endeavoring to vindicate, and settle thus a view of the subject that includes the truth and clears the one-sided extremes. It results, in this manner, that no man, even the broadest in his apprehensions, is ever at the point of equilibrium as regards all subjects. Even the ripest of us are continually falling into some extreme and losing our balance, afterward to be corrected by some others who discover our error, or that of our school.* But Christ was of no school or

*It is worthy of note, that, while all other teachers have been refuted in something, no errors in science, theology, or morals, or no inconsistency with his own system has ever been, even plausibly, charged upon Jesus, though his sayings anticipate the sanction or condemnation of all religious thought, civilization, and philosophy.

party, and never went to any extreme—words could never turn him to a one-sided view of any thing. This is the remarkable fact that distinguishes him from any other teacher of the world. Having nothing to work out in a world-process, but every thing clear in the simple intuition of his superhuman intelligence, he never pushes himself to any human eccentricity. It does not even appear that he is trying, as we do, to balance opposites and clear extravagances, but he does it as one who can not imagine a one-sided view of any thing. He will not allow his disciples to deny him before kings and governors; he will not let them renounce their allegiance to Cæsar. He exposes the oppressions of the Pharisees in Moses' seat, but, encouraging no factious resistance, says, 'Do as they command you.' His position as a reformer was universal—according to his principles almost nothing, whether in Church, or State, or in social life, was right—and yet he is thrown into no antagonism against the world. With all the world upon his hands, and a reform to be carried in almost every thing, he is yet as quiet and cordial, and as little in the attitude of bitterness or impatience, as if all hearts were with him, or the work already done; so perfect is the balance of his feeling, so intuitively moderated is it by wisdom not human. . . . .
'Judge not,' he says, in holy charity, 'that ye be not judged;' and, in holy exactness, 'Whosoever shall break, or teach to break one of these least commandments, shall be least in the kingdom of God;' in the same way, 'He that is not with us is against us;' and, 'he that is not against us is for us;' 'Ye tithe mint, anise, and cummin;' and, 'These things ought ye to have done, and not to leave the other undone.'

So magnificent and sublime, so plainly Divine is the balance of Jesus! Nothing throws him off the center on which truth rests; no prejudice, no opposition, no attempt to right a mistake, or rectify a delusion, or reform a practice. If this be human, I do not know, for one, what it is to be human.

"Again, it is a remarkable and even superhuman distinction of Jesus, that, while he is advancing doctrines so far transcending all deductions of philosophy, and opening mysteries that defy all human power of explication, he is yet able to set his teachings in a form of simplicity that accommodates all classes of minds; and this for the reason that he speaks directly to men's convictions themselves, without and apart from any learned and curious elaboration, such as the uncultivated can not follow. No one of the great writers of antiquity had even propounded, as yet, a doctrine of virtue which the multitude could understand. But Jesus tells them directly, in a manner level to their understanding, what they want, what they must do and be, to inherit eternal life, and their inmost convictions answer to his words.

"Call him then, who will, a mere man; what human teacher ever came down thus upon the soul of the race as a beam of light from the skies—pure light, shining directly into the visual orb of the mind, a light for all that live, a full, transparent day, in which truth bathes the spirit as an element? Others talk and speculate about truth, and those who can may follow; but Jesus is the truth, and he lives it; and if he is a mere human teacher, he is the first who was ever able to find a form for truth at all adequate to the world's uses. And yet the truths he teaches outreach all the doctrines of all the philosophers of the world. He excels them, a hundredfold more, in the scope and grandeur of his doctrine, than he does in his simplicity itself. Is this human, or is it Divine?

"Once more, it is a high distinction of Christ's character, as seen in his teachings, that he is never anxious for the success of his doctrine. Fully conscious of the fact that the world is against him, scoffed at, despised, hated, alone too in his cause, and without partisans that have any public influence, no man has ever been able to detect in him the least anxiety for the final success of his doctrine. The consciousness of Truth, we are not about to deny, has an effect of this nature in every truly-great mind. But when has it had an effect so complete? What human teacher, what great philosopher has not shown some traces of anxiety for his school that indicated his weakness? But here is a lone man, a humble, uneducated man, finding all the world against him, and yet the world does not rest on its axle more firmly than he upon his doctrine. Questioned by Pilate what he means by truth, it is enough to answer, 'He that is of the truth heareth my voice.' If this be not more than human, no other man of the race, we are sure, has ever dignified humanity by a like example.

"Such is Christ as a teacher. When has the world seen a phenomenon like this? A lonely, uninstructed youth, coming forth amid the moral darkness of Galilee, even more distinct from his age, and from every thing around him, than a Plato would be rising up alone in some wild tribe in Oregon, assuming thus a position at the head of the world, and maintaining it for eighteen centuries by the pure self-evidence of his life and doctrine! Does he this by the force of mere human talent or genius? If so, it is time that we begin to look to genius for miracles; for there is really no greater miracle."

We close this section with some remarks of Dr. Ullman in regard to the hypothesis, that the wonderful character of Christ was not drawn from actual life, but from the mind of those who record his life: "Modern criticism holds the opinion, that the picture of the personality of Jesus was the work of the fancy of the earliest Christian Church, who invented, after his death, this description of the founder of their religion. But this runs counter to all historical analogy. The great revolutions of history have not been effected by fictitious personages, but by living men; and those men must have possessed within themselves a real power corresponding to, and accounting for, the influence they possessed. Then, it is not conceivable that a community—that is, a number of individuals differently constituted—should have succeeded in producing so harmonious a character. Or, is it imagined that one man was the author of this image? In that case, we are at a loss to understand how that individual could produce so rare a work. We must, moreover, have to rank him higher than the object which called forth his inventive power; to him we must accord the meed of wonder and praise which we withhold from Jesus. But we should not thus find an explanation of the problem, which has indeed only become more difficult and involved. For in this case, as well as in the former, the first question which we put is still this, How is it, that an ideal of so perfect a kind ever came into the mind of man, whether of many men or of one individual? . . . . How could a form of a sublime majesty, such as mankind had till then no conception of, and would not have at this day if it had not been here presented to us; how could that appear upon the bounded horizon of a Jewish mind? Or could the idea of him who was the first to embrace, in his boundless love, the whole human race, arise within the narrow consciousness of an Israelite? Further, the incredulity of all this will be fully apparent, if we take into consideration the education and mental training of the first disciples. They were plain, simple men; untrained as authors; the large proportion of them were any thing but men of fancy and imagination. They were, moreover, men of sincerity and simplicity in their religious belief; hence they would not have invented had they been able. And even if they would, it is certain that they could never have succeeded in achieving, with the means at their disposal—humanly speaking, so insignificant—what the masters of thought and of discourse, a Plato and a Xenophon, had, in their account of Socrates, failed to accomplish. Let criticism show us that any thing similar occurs elsewhere in the page of history! Till it does so—and it never will be able to do so—we shall continue to maintain—what seems so abundantly evident to every healthy mind—that the reason why the disciples have been able to place before our eye in such vivid reality so great a majesty of moral character, is, that they themselves had seen in real life one who manifested those qualities. The inimitable nature of the Gospel picture must ever remain one of its leading characteristics. But the fact that it can not be imitated is a pledge of its truth."

§ 29. THE SINLESSNESS OF JESUS, THE IDEA OF WHICH COULD NOT HAVE BEEN CONCEIVED BY THE EVANGELISTS, IF THEY HAD NOT SEEN IT ACTUALIZED IN THE LIFE OF JESUS—INCONTESTABLY PROVING THAT HE WAS NOT A MERE MAN.

Before we proceed to apply sinlessness to the person of Jesus, it is proper to define the term, and to make some remarks on the scope and importance of the investigation before us, in doing which we give a condensation of the elaborate argumentation of Ullmann. The idea of sinlessness is, in the first instance, a negative one. It is the absence of antagonism to the moral law, and to the Divine will, of which that law is the expression; and this not only in relation to separate acts of will and outward actions, but also in relation to the tendency of the whole moral nature, and to its most deep-seated disposition. Doubtless this conception is in itself of great importance, inasmuch as it marks off, more distinctly than any other, the line of demarkation between moral purity and any trace of moral pollution. Yet it is not sufficient to regard sinlessness as the absence of all opposition to the moral law. For the conception of sinlessness is one which, like that of sin, can be applied only to natures such as have been appointed to will and to do in the capacity of moral agents; in the case of which, therefore, the omission of such willing and doing is itself a deviation from the divine law of life. Sinlessness must, therefore, imply positive goodness—goodness of nature, and goodness in action. It is in this sense of the word, not as negative merely, but as essentially positive, that we apply the epithet "sinless" to Jesus. By this epithet he is characterized as not only free from all sin, but as holy. By it is meant that he was filled at every moment of his life with the spirit of obedience, and with a love to God which surrendered itself unconditionally to his will, and with those powers which flow from an uninterrupted communion with God. Such sinlessness can be predicated only of an individual in whose case, on the one hand, the impossibility of sinning does not follow at once from a necessity of his nature, who, in other words, is susceptible of being tempted,* and whom, on the other hand, we may believe endowed with an integrity of moral nature, by the right use of which the possibility of not sinning becomes an impossibility of sinning. In a case where both these conditions are fulfilled, the development of a life altogether pure and holy is conceivable; a life it would be which we should have to regard as at once typically perfect—raised far above every thing which history tells us of, and, at the same time, as truly human; and this is what we hold the moral character and life of Jesus to have been.

* The question, how far it can be affirmed, from a dogmatical or speculative stand-point, that sinfulness or actual transgression in Christ is *a priori* inconceivable, is out of the scope of our present investigation. It will be fully considered in our comments on the temptation of Christ, (Matt. iv.) It is sufficient here to remark, that we must be careful to distinguish the possibility of sinning from a leaning or bent toward sin. Sin may be possible where it has not existed in the faintest degree; but a *penchant* toward sin is inconsistent with sinlessness, for it involves a germ, a minimum of sin. The possibility of sin must be presupposed in Jesus, ere we can conceive that Jesus could be tempted. A liability to be tempted does not in itself imply the existence of any evil; for even the purest virtue, *if it dwells in a finite nature*, is liable to be tempted. The impossibility of sinning, in the abstract, can be ascribed to the infinite God alone; of him it is true in the absolute necessity of his nature—a necessity which is identical with the highest liberty. Had Jesus been endowed with an absolute impossibility of sin, he could not have been a true man; his temptation is, therefore, presented to us in the Scriptures as one of the most marked features of his history, and as the indispensable condition of his typical character, while, at the same time, the possibility of sin in him never became actual fact.

Hitherto the doctrine of the sinless character of Christ has been almost invariably contemplated in the light of an immediate postulate of faith, as a necessary consequence of the incarnation, or as an indispensable condition of the work of Christ as Redeemer; and those who have thus treated it, have not proceeded from this stand-point to a more detailed investigation and proof of the fact itself. We, on the contrary, will leave out of account this immediate conviction of the truth of the doctrine—without, at the same time, calling it in question, or denying that it may be right and valid in its own place—and begin by seeking to establish and vindicate our belief in the sinlessness of Christ. In the mode of proof that we shall adopt in so doing, our arguments will be drawn from the historical appearance of Christ. We do not say: Because Christ was the Son of God, he could not be subject to sin; or, because he was the Redeemer, he must have been free from sin. What we say is: Because he *was* free from sin, and showed himself in all respects perfectly pure and holy, we are warranted in believing that he was the Son of God, the deliverer from all sin, the author of true redemption, and the revealer of redeeming truth. Now, while we follow this historical and apologetical course, we do not mean to assert that the dogmatical or philosophical course is valueless. We are persuaded that, if both methods are rightly pursued, they must lead to the same result. Doctrinally to maintain the sinlessness of Christ were to believe an empty form, if that doctrine had no basis of historical reality; and the historical reality would lie on something fragmentary and detached, were it not organically united with the sum total of the Christian system. But while the two methods mutually presuppose and require one another, still, in their practical treatment, they must be carefully distinguished.

The apologetical mode of presenting the sinlessness of Jesus has a very peculiar import, in that it appeals to the moral consciousness of men. The truly-convincing evidences for Christianity are those which are at once theoretical and practical; for the object is not only by the use of argument to convince the understanding, but at the same time to touch the conscience, to move the will, and to give a decided impulse to the spirit, and a new direction to the whole life. The entrance into the domain of Christianity is not to be gained by a mere process of thought, but can only be attained by undergoing a new process of life, a radical change of the moral nature. Now, the subject which we have here to consider speaks directly to the conscience. The image of Jesus rises up before the soul as a thing that has really been, in all its clear and stainless purity. True, it can never be reproduced as a living reality in us, without shivering and shattering all our virtuous conceits, without casting us, as sinful men, prostrate in the dust before the Holy One. But while it thus humbles us, it exalts us too, and draws us with an inwardly-overpowering might into the communion of holy and compassionate Divine love, shining forth on us from him as the brightest mirror. If Jesus is holy, free from sin, and true to the exclusion of all error, and thus stands upon a platform elevated high above the common fate of mortals, all of whom, without exception, are subject to error and to sin—then we are both entitled and enjoined to reverence in him—in his whole manifestation upon earth, in all that he did and all that he taught—the exponent of the will of God concerning man; then we have every warrant to look to him, the Sinless One, as the author of our deliverance from sin, to him, being one with the Father, as the restorer of true union with God. It is thus that the apologetical mode of presenting the sinlessness of Jesus, while it vindicates belief, is at the same time fitted to call forth and increase the same.

After these preliminary remarks, let us contemplate the portrait of the moral perfection of Christ. We find it most comprehensively drawn by Dr. Schaff, and give it—detached from other traits of his character which we have dwelt upon in the preceding section, and from considerations to which we shall draw the attention afterward. He says:

"The first impression which we receive from the life of Jesus, is that of its perfect *innocency* in the midst of a sinful world. He, and he alone, carried the innocency of a pure childhood untarnished through his youth and manhood. . . . . Of the boyhood of Jesus we know only one fact, recorded by Luke; but it is in perfect keeping with the peculiar charm of his childhood, and foreshadows at the same time the glory of his public life, as one uninterrupted service of his Heavenly Father. When twelve years old we find him in the Temple, in the midst of the Jewish doctors, not teaching and offending them, as in the apocryphal Gospels, by any immodesty or forwardness, but hearing and asking questions, thus actually learning from them; and yet filling them with astonishment at his understanding and answers. There is nothing premature, forced, or unbecoming his age, and yet a degree of wisdom and an intensity of interest in religion which rises far above a purely-human youth. 'He increased,' we are told, 'in wisdom and stature, and in favor with God and man; he was subject to his parents, and practiced all the virtues of an obedient son; and yet he filled them with a sacred awe as they saw him absorbed 'in the things of his Father,' and heard him utter words which they were unable to understand at the time, but which Mary treasured up in her heart as a holy secret. Such an idea of a harmless and faultless, heavenly childhood, of a growing, learning, and yet surprisingly-wise boyhood, as it meets us in living reality at the portal of the Gospel history, never entered the imagination of biographer, poet, or philosopher before. On the contrary, as has been justly observed by Horace Bushnell, 'in all the higher ranges of character, the excellence portrayed is never the simple unfolding of a harmonious and perfect beauty contained in the germ of childhood, but it is a character formed by a process of rectification in which many follies are mended and distempers removed, in which confidence is checked by defeat, passion moderated by reason, smartness sobered by experience. Commonly a certain pleasure is taken in showing how the many wayward sallies of the boy are, at length, reduced by discipline to the character of wisdom, justice, and public heroism so much admired. Besides, if any writer, of almost any age, will undertake to describe, not merely a spotless, but a superhuman or celestial childhood, not having the reality before him, he must be somewhat more than human himself if he does not pile together a mass of clumsy exaggerations, and draw and overdraw, till neither heaven nor earth can find any verisimilitude in the picture.' This unnatural exaggeration, into which the mythical fancy of man, in its endeavor to produce a superhuman childhood and boyhood, will inevitably fall, is strikingly exhibited in the apocryphal Gospels, which are related to the canonical Gospels as the counterfeit to the genuine coin, or as a revolting caricature to the inimitable original, but which, by the very contrast, tend, negatively, to corroborate the truth of Evangelical history. While the Evangelists expressly reserve the performance of miracles to the age of maturity and public life, and observe a significant silence concerning the parents of Jesus, the pseudo-evangelists fill the infancy and early years of the Savior with the strangest prodigies.

"In vain we look through the entire biography of Christ for a single stain, or the slightest shadow on his moral character. There never lived a more harmless being on earth. He injured nobody, he took advantage of nobody, he never spoke an improper word, he never committed a wrong action.* The manner of expelling the profane traffickers from the Temple is the only instance which modern criticism has dared to quote against his freedom from the faults of humanity. But the very effect which it produced shows that, far from being the outburst of passion, the expulsion was a judicial act of a religious reformer, vindicating in just and holy zeal the honor of the Lord of the Temple, and that with a dignity

* "No vice that has a name can be thought of in connection with Jesus Christ. Ingenious malignity looks in vain for the faintest trace of self-seeking in his motives; sensuality shrinks abashed from his celestial purity; falsehood can leave no stain on him who is incarnate truth; injustice is forgotten beside his errorless equity; the very possibility of avarice is swallowed up in his benignity and love; the very idea of ambition is lost in his Divine wisdom and Divine self-abnegation." (*Bayne.*)

and majesty which at once silenced the offenders, though superior in number and physical strength, and made them submit to their well-deserved punishment without a murmur, and in awe of the presence of a superhuman power. The cursing of the unfruitful fig-tree can still less be urged, as it evidently was a significant symbolical act, foreshadowing the fearful doom of the impenitent Jews in the destruction of Jerusalem.* . . . But this freedom from the common sin and guilt is, after all, only the negative side of his character, which rises in magnitude as we contemplate the positive side, namely, his moral and religious perfection. It is universally admitted, even by Deists and rationalists, that Christ taught the purest and sublimest system of ethics, which throws all the moral precepts and maxims of the wisest men of antiquity far into the shade. The Sermon on the Mount alone is worth infinitely more than all that Confucius, Socrates, and Seneca ever said or wrote on duty and virtue. But the difference is still greater if we come to the more difficult task of practice. While the wisest and best of men never live up even to their own imperfect standard of excellency, Christ fully carried out his perfect doctrine in his life and conduct. He is the living incarnation of the ideal standard of virtue

* These and a few other instances in the life of Jesus—namely, the charge of disobedience toward his parents for remaining behind in the Temple, of interference with the rights of property in permitting the demons to rush among the herd of swine, his selection of Judas to the apostleship, the appearance of untruth in John vii, 8–10—though frivolous and scarcely worthy of notice in connection with a nature so elevated as that of Jesus, are fully considered in the exegesis of the respective passages. They certainly leave not the minutest stain on the purity of Jesus. The argument against the sinlessness of Jesus, drawn from a pretended impossibility of sinlessness in a finite nature, is a mere *petitio principii*, and can not fall within the scope of this investigation, which proposes to deal only with facts.

and holiness, and universally acknowledged to be the highest model for all that is pure, and good, and noble in the sight of God and man. We find him moving in all the ordinary and essential relations of life, as a son, a friend, a citizen, a teacher, at home and in public; we find him among all classes of society, with sinners and saints, with the poor and the wealthy, with the sick and the healthy, with little children, grown men and women, with plain fishermen and learned scribes, with despised publicans and honored members of the Sanhedrim, with friends and foes, with admiring disciples and bitter persecutors, now with an individual, as Nicodemus or the woman of Samaria, now in the familiar circle of the twelve, now in the crowds of the people; we find him in all situations, in the synagogue and the Temple, at home and on journeys, in villages and the city of Jerusalem, in the desert and on the mountain, at the wedding feast and the grave, in Gethsemane, in the judgment-hall and on Calvary. In all these various relations, conditions, and situations, as they are now crowded within the few years of his public ministry, he sustains the same consistent character throughout, without ever exposing himself to censure. He fulfills every duty to God, to man, and to himself, without a single violation of duty, and exhibits an entire conformity to the law, in the spirit as well as the letter. His life is one unbroken service of God in active and passive obedience to his holy will, one grand act of absolute love to God and love to man, of personal self-consecration to the glory of the Heavenly Father and the salvation of a fallen race. In the language of the people who were 'beyond measure astonished at his works,' we must say, the more we study his life: 'He did all things well.' In a solemn appeal to his Heavenly Father, in the parting hour, he could proclaim to the world that he had glorified him in the earth and finished the work he gave him to do.

"The first feature in this singular perfection of Christ's character which strikes our attention, is the perfect harmony of virtue and piety, of morality and religion, or of love to God and love to man. The ground-work of his character was the most intimate and uninterrupted union and communion with his Heavenly Father, from whom he derived, to whom he referred every thing. Already, in his twelfth year, he found his life-element and delight in the things of his Father. It was his daily food to do the will of Him that sent him, and to finish his work. To him he looked in prayer before every important act, and taught his disciples that model prayer, which, for simplicity, brevity, comprehensiveness, and suitableness can never be surpassed. He often retired to a mountain or solitary place for prayer, and spent days and nights in the blessed privilege. But so constant and uniform was his habit of communion with the great Jehovah, that he kept it up amid the multitude, and converted the crowded city into a religious retreat. But the piety of Christ was no inactive contemplation, or retiring mysticism and selfish enjoyment, but thoroughly practical, ever active in works of charity, and tending to regenerate and transform the world into the kingdom of God. 'He went about doing good.' His life is an unbroken series of good words and virtues in active exercise, all proceeding from the same union with God, animated by the same love, and tending to the same end, the glory of God and the happiness of man.

"Finally, as all the active virtues meet in him, so he unites the passive. No character can become complete without trial and suffering. The ancient Greeks and Romans admired a good man struggling with misfortune as a sight worthy of the gods. Plato describes the righteous man as one who, without doing any injustice, yet has the appearance of the greatest injustice, and proves his own justice by perseverance against all calumny unto death; yea, he predicts that, if such a righteous man should ever appear, he would be 'scourged, tortured, bound, deprived of his sight, and after having suffered all possible injury, nailed on a post.' (Politicus, p. 74, ss. ed., Ast., p. 361, E. ed. Bip.) No wonder that the ancient Fathers saw in this remarkable passage an unconscious prophecy of Christ. But how far is this ideal of the great philosopher from the actual reality, as it appeared three hundred years afterward! The highest form of passive virtue attained by ancient heathenism or modern secular heroism is that stoicism which meets and overcomes the trials and misfortunes of life in the spirit of haughty contempt and unfeeling indifference, which destroys the sensibilities, and is but another exhibition of selfishness and pride. Christ has set up a far higher standard by his teaching and example, never known before. . . . His passive virtue is not confined to the closing scenes of his ministry. As human life is beset at every step by trials, vexations, and hinderances, which should serve the educational purpose of developing its resources and proving its strength, so was Christ's. During the whole state of his humiliation he was 'a man of sorrows, and acquainted with grief,' and had to endure 'the contradictions of sinners.' He was poor, and suffered hunger and fatigue. He was tempted by the devil. His path was obstructed with apparently-unsurmountable difficulties from the outset. His words and miracles called forth the bitter hatred of the world, which resulted at last in the bloody counsel of death. The Pharisees and Sadducees forgot their jealousies and quarrels in opposing him. They rejected and perverted his testimony; they laid snares to him by insidious questions; they called him a glutton and wine-bibber for eating and drinking like other men, a friend of publicans and sinners for his condescending love and mercy, a Sabbath-breaker for doing good on the Sabbath day; they charged him with madness and blasphemy for asserting his unity with the Father, and derived his miracles from Beelzebub, the prince of devils. The common people, though astonished at his wisdom and mighty works, pointed sneeringly at his origin; his own country and native town refused him the honor of a prophet. Even his brothers, we are told, did not believe in him, and, in their impatient zeal for a temporal kingdom, they found fault with his unostentatious proceeding. His apostles and disciples, with all their profound reverence for his character, and their faith in his Divine origin and mission as the Messiah of God, yet, by their ignorance, their carnal, Jewish notions, and their almost habitual misunderstanding of his spiritual discourses, must have constituted a severe trial of patience to a teacher of far less superiority to his pupils.

"But how shall we describe his *passion*, more properly so called, with which no other suffering can be compared for a moment! Never did any man suffer more innocently, more unjustly, more intensely than Jesus of Nazareth. Within the narrow limits of a few hours we have here a tragedy of universal significance, exhibiting every form of human weakness and infernal wickedness, of ingratitude, desertion, injury, and insult, of bodily and mental pain and anguish, culminating in the most ignominious death then known among the Jews and Gentiles. The Government and the people combined against him who came to save them. His own disciples forsook him; Judas, under the inspiration of the devil, betrayed him. The rulers of the nation condemned him, the furious mob cried, 'Crucify him,' and rude soldiers mocked him. He was seized in the night, hurried from tribunal to tribunal, arrayed in a crown of thorns, insulted, smitten, scourged, spit upon and hung like a criminal and a slave between two robbers and murderers!

"How did Christ bear all these little and great trials of life, and the death on the cross? Let us remember first, that, unlike the icy stoics in their unnatural and repulsive pseudo-virtue, he showed the keenest sensibility in the agony of the garden, and the deepest sympathy with human grief in shedding tears at the grave of a friend, and providing a refuge for his mother in the last dying hour. But with this truly-human tenderness and delicacy of feeling he ever combined an unutterable dignity and majesty, a sublime self-control and imperturbable calmness of mind. There is a grandeur in his deepest sufferings, which forbids a feeling of pity and compassion on our side as incompatible with the admiration and reverence for his character. We feel the force of his words to the women of Jerusalem, when they bewailed him on the way to Calvary: 'Weep not for me, but weep for yourselves and your children.' We never hear him break out in angry passion and violence, although he was at war with the whole ungodly world. He never murmured, never uttered discontent, displeasure, or resentment. He was never disheartened, discouraged, ruffled, or fretted, but full of unbounded confidence that all was well ordered in the providence of his Heavenly Father. He moved serenely, like the sun above the clouds as they sailed under him. He was ever surrounded by the element of peace, and said in his parting hour: 'Peace I leave with you; my peace I give unto you; not as the world giveth give I unto you. Let not your heart be troubled, neither let it be afraid.' He was never what we call unhappy, but full of inward joy, which he bequeathed to his disciples in that sublimest of all prayers, 'that they might have his joy fulfilled in themselves.' With all his severe rebukes to the Pharisees, he never indulged in personalities. He ever returned good for evil. He forgave Peter for his denial; and would have forgiven Judas, if, in the exercise of sincere repentance, he had sought his pardon. Even while hanging on the cross, he had only the language of pity for the wretches who were driving the nails into his hands and feet, and prayed in their behalf, 'Father forgive them, for they know not what they do.' He did not seek or hasten his martyrdom in morbid enthusiasm or ambitious humility, but quietly and patiently waited for the hour appointed by the will of his Heavenly Father. But when it came, with what self-possession and calmness, with what strength and meekness, with what majesty and gentleness did he pass through its dark and trying scenes!* Here every word and act are unutterably significant, from the agony in Gethsemane, when overwhelmed with the sympathetic sense of the entire guilt of mankind, and in full view of the terrible

* On this point Dr. Bushnell makes the following profound remarks: "It will be observed that his agony, the scene in which his suffering is bitterest and most evident, is, on human principles, wholly misplaced. It comes before the time, when as yet there is no arrest, and no human prospect that there will be any. He is at large to go where he pleases, and in perfect outward safety. His disciples have just been gathered round him in a scene of more than family tenderness and affection. Indeed, it is but a few days since that he was coming into the city, at the head of a vast procession, followed by loud acclamations, and attended by such honors as may fitly celebrate the inaugural of a king. Yet here, with no bad sign apparent, we see him plunged into a scene of deepest distress, and racked in his feeling with a more than mortal agony. Coming out of this, assured and comforted, he is shortly arrested, brought to trial, and crucified; where, if there be any thing questionable in his manner, it is the fact that he is even more composed than some would have him to be, not even stooping to defend himself or vindicate his innocence. . . . . By the misplacing of his agony thus, and the strange silence he observes when the real hour of agony is come, we are put entirely at fault on natural principles. But it was not for him to wait. . . . . He that was before Abraham, must also be before his occasions. In a time of safety, in a cool hour of retirement, unaccountably to his friends, he falls into a dreadful contest and struggle of mind. . . . . Why now this so great intensity of sorrow? Why this agony? Was there not something unmanly in it, something unworthy of a really-great soul? Take him to be only a man, and there probably was. But this one thing is clear, that no one of mankind ever had the sensibility to suffer so intensely; even showing the body, for the mere struggle and pain of the mind, exuding and dripping with blood. Evidently there is something mysterious here. What, we begin to ask, should be the power of a superhuman sensibility? And how far should the human vehicle shake under such power? How, too, should an innocent and pure spirit be exercised, when about to suffer in his own person the greatest wrong ever committed! Besides, there is a vicarious spirit in love; all love inserts itself vicariously into the sufferings, and woes, and, in a certain sense, the sins of others, taking them on itself as a burden. How, then, if perchance Jesus should be Divine, an embodiment of God's love in the world—how should he feel, and by what signs of feeling manifest his sensibility, when a fallen race are just about to do the damning sin that crowns their guilty history; to crucify the only perfect being that ever came into the world; to crucify even him, the messenger and representative to them of the love of God, the deliverer who has taken their case and cause upon him? Whosoever duly ponders these questions, will more and more distinctly see that what he looks upon to be the pathology of a superhuman anguish. It stands, he will perceive, in no mortal key. It will be to him the anguish, not of any pusillanimous feeling, but of holy character itself; nay, of a mysteriously-transcendent, or, somehow, Divine character."

scenes before him—the only guiltless being in the world—he prayed that the cup might pass from him, but immediately added, 'Not my, but thy will be done,' to the triumphant exclamation on the cross, 'It is finished!' Even his dignified silence before the tribunal of his enemies and the furious mob, when, 'as a lamb dumb before his shearers, he opened not his mouth,' is more eloquent than any apology, and made Pilate tremble. Who will venture to bring a parallel from the annals of ancient or modern sages, when even a Rousseau confessed, 'If Socrates suffered and died like a philosopher, Jesus Christ suffered and died like a God!' The passion and crucifixion of Jesus, like his whole character, stands without a parallel, solitary and alone in its glory."

In the portraiture of the character and life of Jesus which we have been contemplating, we find all the different lineaments which lie scattered up and down the pages of the Gospel narrative in the most artless simplicity, without any trace of forethought and design, gathered together into one whole. It is evident that the picture of Jesus which the Gospels present to us, and which the apostles every-where describe, is such that, even if it had not been expressly stated in Scripture that Jesus was without sin, we could never have conceived of sin, of separation from God, of moral obliquity, as forming a feature in that picture, without being sensible that we should thus materially disfigure and deface it, nay, destroy it altogether. Nevertheless, it has been called in question on the ground that, in order to pronounce concerning any one that he is absolutely free from sin, a perfect knowledge of his heart is above all things requisite; and the apostles could not see into the heart of Jesus even in the time of their intercourse with him, while of the earlier part of his life they had no personal knowledge. In meeting this question, Ullman proves the verity of the picture which the New Testament presents of the sinlessness of Jesus, by the following unanswerable arguments, which we will give in his own language, though not in the order in which he discusses the subject:

1. It is unquestionably true that the disciples of Jesus could not look immediately into his heart like the omniscient Searcher of Hearts; but what is a man's life but the index and revelation of his spirit; and is it possible to account for a perfectly-moral life otherwise than on the supposition of a perfectly-moral soul which it represents? Can we explain purity of action otherwise than as flowing from purity of heart? What circumstance is there in the life of Jesus to favor the idea that he ever acted in a manner merely legal and external, while in heart he was not truly good, or that his inmost disposition was in conflict with his actions? The principle on which the objection is based would, if applied generally, abolish all faith in human virtue and spiritual greatness.

2. If Jesus had not unfolded before the eyes of those with whom he was surrounded a character of perfect purity and sinless holiness, his apostles could not have made a representation of such a character; for the idea of sinlessness in a human nature had never been thought of previous to the appearing of Christ; or, where the thought occurs, we find inseparably connected with it the conviction that it could not be realized in actual life, that a perfectly-sinless human being never did or could exist on earth. Plato, it is true, draws a sketch of a right-

eous man, in which he represents perfect virtue as necessarily conjoined with suffering; but the idea of the virtue he describes is entirely restricted to uprightness; no reference is made to that inward religiousness by which virtue rises into holiness, and, what is a still more important consideration, the sketch of Plato is only a conception of his mind, without any intimation that it was ever realized in actual life. Perhaps there is no man of antiquity with whom men would have associated the idea of moral perfection more readily than Socrates; and yet, although we possess such glorious descriptions of that great man, drawn by his revering disciples, neither they nor any one else, least of all Socrates himself, have ventured to maintain that he was entirely free from moral blemishes, a perfect man. The prevalent conviction in the heathen world, that moral perfection is a thing which it is impossible for man to attain, is clearly expressed by Epictetus, who, after setting forth the idea of moral stainlessness with more clearness than any preceding philosopher, asks the question, whether it be possible that it should ever be realized, and answers: "No, it is impossible; all that is possible is constantly to strive after a state of not sinning." The same sentiment we find in Judaism; its ruling principle was a consciousness of sin produced by a law given by a God of holiness; for although the Jew had, along with this consciousness of sin, also the belief in grace—still he felt himself under the curse of sin, which the law was incapable of removing. Neither the founder of the Old Testament dispensation laid any claim to the possession of spotless righteousness, nor that greatest prophet of the ante-Christian age, who had, indeed, an anticipation that the idea of moral purity would be realized, but not till it should be seen in him whom he announced. But, behold! here stand the plain, simple-minded apostles, themselves reckoned neither among the poets nor the philosophers, in whom we find only the idea of sinless holiness most clearly defined, and whose faith in its actual realization in the person of Jesus has become such a certainty that they could sacrifice for its sake all that men usually hold dear; further, we find that they have given a description of the pure and holy life of Jesus, in which the subsequent moral development of nineteen centuries has discovered no fault or blemish, in which men of the present day still recognize a picture of the most perfect character in the domain of religion and morality that can any where be found. From all this we certainly can not draw any other conclusion than this: If an idea arose in all its clearness in the minds of the apostles, which the great thinkers and poets of antiquity were entirely ignorant of, or saw but dimly, this can be accounted for only by the manifestation of a real life; and if those who till then had regarded faultlessness as a thing unattainable by man, had now the strongest belief in the reality of a sinless life, the cause for the change could only lie in the overpowering impression produced by that life itself, seen unfolding itself before their eyes.

3. The testimony of the apostles receives its full confirmation and its proper validity from the testimony of Jesus himself. The two must be taken together, for only together do they form a satisfactory proof. He, whom others regarded as a spotless and holy being, must be fully conscious in himself of per-

fect freedom from sin; and again, this consciousness of his must be corroborated by the impression which he produces upon others; thus united, alone, can either testimony receive its full import. In considering the testimony of Jesus concerning himself, let us first contemplate its negative aspect. He who had so keen an eye for the sins of others must, if we will not suppose him to have been self-blinded, have seen as clearly sin in himself, if it was there. But we find no where in his history, as we do in the case of the best of men, even the most occasional expression of consciousness of sin; there is no humbling of himself before God on account of sin, there is no prayer for the forgiveness of sin. Does not this inevitably lead to the conclusion, that the source from whence those feelings, which we find precisely in the men of highest moral character, proceed, had in him no existence whatever? It follows, likewise, from what he said on the occasion of his baptism, that he felt conscious that he needed for himself no repentance or regeneration. But more than this. So far was Jesus from standing in need of forgiveness for himself, that the position he held with reference to sinful men was that of a pardoner of sin. He came not only to preach forgiveness, he came to bestow it; and could this have been done by one who felt guilt and sin in himself? To forgive sin belongs to God only; hence, Jesus could claim that right only on the ground of a deep consciousness of oneness with God, a consciousness based upon a feeling of perfect freedom from sin.

But the positive testimonies are much stronger. Here we have, first of all, to notice that most conclusive saying of Jesus, which we find in John's Gospel:

"Which of you convinceth me of sin?"* When we read this question, the feeling forces itself upon us, that its author must have been a personality of a moral character most peculiar; a feeling greatly strengthened by the recollection that he who spoke these words was one who in his whole life presents to us a picture at once of purest truthfulness and most divine humility. Every man, too, must at once be fully convinced, that to apply these words to himself would only prove him a vain fool or a miserable hypocrite. Last of all could this happen in a community from the midst of which we hear that same apostle, who has preserved us the saying of Jesus, exclaim: "If we say that we have no sin we deceive ourselves, and the truth is not in us." It is certainly a fact of the highest significance, that, in opposition to this attestation of universal sinfulness, which every

*This passage has by some commentators been translated: "Which of you convinceth me of error?" Supposing this translation were correct, even in that case these words of Jesus would be of great importance for our purpose, for they would at least contain an *indirect* testimony to the religious and moral purity of Jesus. For if he claims exemption from error in that province which alone comes under consideration in this passage—namely, the domain of morality and religion—this must imply that he lays claim to purity of inward nature and of outward conduct. For freedom from sin presupposes freedom from error, and *vice versa;* the two act and react upon each other. The human mind, whatever divisions psychology may make of its powers, is not in reality separated into different departments. It is absolutely one and undivided, manifesting itself, however, in various ways, and exerting itself in different directions. The threads of our whole intellectual life are so subtilely and finely interwoven, that to touch one is to move the whole; that every impression affects in some way the whole spirit, and every action is the result of the complicated coöperation of the most different energies of the mind. The man as thinking can not be sundered from the man as feeling; nor the man as willing from the man as knowing. In consequence of this undivided unity of the soul, it is inconceivable that a person should be perfect in regard to volitions and acts, and yet be defective and imperfect in moral and religious knowledge. When our knowledge has the purity of truth, it acts with a purifying power on the life; and purity of life tends to enlighten, and to preserve the enlightenment of the intellect. From this it follows, that the necessary presupposition and result of the sinlessness of Jesus was the entire absence of error in respect of things religious and moral.

one without exception must indorse, there is One who steps forth from the ranks of humanity and exclaims: "Who convinceth me of sin?" That Jesus by these words did not intend to say of himself simply, what any honest man, who led a life in conformity with the law, might say—"Nobody could point to any sin he had committed"—is self-evident. That he, on the contrary, meant positively to affirm the purity of his moral consciousness, that his conscience was free from guilt, his inner as well as outer life unstained by sin, is irrefutably proved from those other sayings which John records of Christ, and whose meaning it is impossible to explain away, when he declares himself to be the way, the truth, and the life; when he says that it is his meat to do the will of Him that sent him; when he testifies that he does at all times the things which please the Father, that he never seeks his own will, but always the will of the Father. These are expressions which present to us the picture of a life which not only had in it no place for sin, but, more than this, which can only be thought of as an actually-perfect life. There are, especially, two significant passages which come under consideration here. The first is: "I and my Father are one." (John x, 30.) It matters not, for our purpose, whether the unity spoken of is to be understood as a unity of nature, or a moral unity, a unity of will; for where perfect unity with the Divine will exists, there must also, of necessity, be not only perfect freedom from sin, but perfect goodness. Similar is the case with regard to the other passage: "He that has seen me has seen the Father." (John xiv, 9.) Certainly we are not to restrict these words so as to mean merely that there was in Jesus *something*

Divine along with what was imperfect and sinful, as there is in every man. They must be taken in the full sense, that Jesus was morally and mentally an image of the invisible God, an expression of the Divine nature. But it is only a character of stainless purity and unsullied holiness that can be a spiritual reflection of God; where sin exists, the Holy One can not be seen; where the Holy One can be seen, there neither sin nor any imperfection can exist.

There can, therefore, be no doubt that Jesus bore within him the consciousness of being sinless and holy; and that to this consciousness he gave repeated expression. If we will not acknowledge the validity of a self-testimony of so peculiar a character, there remains nothing but to declare Jesus to have been either a fanatic or a hypocrite. If we declare him a fanatic, we must suppose that he drew no clear line of demarkation between good and evil; that he did not examine every fold of his heart, or know all the motions of his will; nay, we must believe that he was a victim to the vainest self-deception when he uttered those memorable words. And is this conceivable in the case of one who on every other occasion could distinguish with such incomparable precision between good and evil, whose keen vision pierced to the remotest depths of the nature of men, and whose feelings on all moral subjects were so singularly refined? Is it possible that he who knew others so well should have been ignorant of himself? He would thus form a strange exception even to human knowledge. For no other man, even the most darkened, would ever entertain a doubt that he is a sinner; was Jesus then a sinner, and alone ignorant of the fact? Or, if such conclusions are too absurd to be entertained, we must be prepared to accept the other more fearful alternative. He was conscious of transgressing against the Divine law, we must suppose, in thought, word, and deed, and yet he expressly denied it. But who is there that would dare to undertake the defense of such a position, to maintain that he, who in all the circumstances of his life acted from the purest conscientiousness, and who at last died for his testimony upon the cross, was, after all, nothing more than an abject hypocrite? How could it be that he, of whom even the least susceptible must confess that there breathed around him an atmosphere of purity and faith, should have fallen into an antagonism so deep and so deadly? Into such absurd and revolting self-contradictions we must land, if we refuse to acknowledge the truth of the Divine self-testimony of Jesus concerning his sinlessness.

4. There is still another argument that establishes the certainty of the perfect holiness of Jesus beyond the possibility of a reasonable doubt. The moral effects produced upon mankind by Christianity are such that the sinlessness of Jesus is their necessary condition or originating cause. In other words, it can be shown that there have been, since the appearance of Christ on earth, actual manifestations, which can be explained rationally only on one assumption; namely, that the Author of Christianity was a being of sinless holiness; and that, if we refuse to make this assumption, these manifestations must remain entirely inexplicable.

An unbiased investigation will place beyond a doubt the following facts: that Christianity produced in individual believers—that is, in those who were deservedly so called—a rich supply of virtues; and that these were, partly, virtues of which men had previously no conception whatever, or, at all events, no idea, so high and pure as Christianity imparts. Such virtues are humility, meekness, and the self-denial of compassionate love. Nor has Christianity exercised a less salutary moral influence upon the common relations of human life. In marriage and the family, in the condition of civil and political life, in the relation of ranks, castes, and nations to one another, and, in a word, in the whole condition of the race, it has laid the foundation of a state of society essentially different from what it was before. All these moral manifestations disclose to us the grand truth, that Christianity has produced something *new* in the moral world, that the individual character which is molded by its influence, and also the humanity which it forms, is a new moral *creation*. This the apostle Paul expresses in a most forcible manner, when he says: "If any man be in Christ, he is a new creature; old things are passed away, behold, all things are become new." Let us now inquire what must be the originating cause of that new creation which we find in the moral life of the Christian world. In seeking an answer to this question, we will naturally be inclined to point first to the moral ideas peculiar to Christianity—that is, to Christian ethics. Christianity has, undoubtedly, an ethical system of incomparable purity, depth, and completeness; it far transcends every thing that the heathen world has to point to; its principle and spirit far excel the loftiest ideas of the Old Testament economy, and there can be no doubt that this of itself is a fact of great importance for our purpose. For these ideas of Christian ethics are the expression and result of the moral spirit which existed in the Founder of Christianity, and thus they afford a testimony to the purity and dignity of his moral teaching. But if we are thus compelled to argue from the doctrine to its Author, this is still more the case when we look beyond the doctrine to the original source of those influences which have produced so mighty a revolution in the moral world. And this primary source is not the *doctrine* of Jesus, but his *person*. This is necessarily the case; for it is not any doctrine which calls into being a new life; it is only life which can generate life. For this we have the most decisive testimony of Christian experience. The same apostle who uttered the sublime saying concerning the new creation, says, also, when he wishes to describe the primary source and fountain of his life: "I live; but not I, but Christ liveth in me." He affirms that any one is a new creature, not because he walks according to the doctrine of Christ, but because he is "*in*" Christ—that is, personally united to him; and in this the apostle expresses only what is the experience of every true Christian in every age.

The question now arises: In what way must such a personality have been constituted to make it capable of imparting a regenerating power to Paul, and to all those whose experience has been like his? And to this question we must answer: It can not have been a personality in itself sinful, for then it would have differed from other men only in degree. It would still have partaken of the old nature. It would not have realized in itself an entirely *new creation;* and thus it could not have prepared the way for a new moral birth. On the contrary, it must have been a personality raised above all connection with the old nature; one in which the power of sin was entirely broken; which was itself in the highest sense a new creation, and was thus in a condition to produce the deep renovating effects which a perfect ideal alone could produce.* Thus, on the supposition that the Founder of Christianity was not without sin, it is impossible to understand how a morality of so pure and perfect a stamp as that which characterizes our religion could derive its origin from such a being, or how it could express its peculiar character in such words as these: "Old things are passed away, all things are become new." If, on the other hand, we suppose the Author of Christianity to have been altogether without sin, then it is easy to perceive how, within its sphere, a new creation could come to perfection in the moral world by his being formed within the individual believer.

Again, if the Christian feels in his inmost soul a consciousness that morally he is a new man, that old things are passed away and that all things are become new, then *his position with reference to God must have been changed.* The dominion of sin can not be broken, and the power of a new life can not be attained, unless its guilt has been first abolished, and the foundation laid of a right standing in relation to the holy God. Now, the words which express all that

*In reply to the objection, that the sinlessness of Jesus should have produced also in those who come within his renovating influence a perfect freedom from transgression, Ullmann observes: "We find that, in all true Christians, the principle of sin is in fact broken, and that they feel assured of its complete and final overthrow. If, in spite of this conquest of the principle of sin, it is still found operating in their lives, this circumstance only leads us to conclude that, in order to be ever more and more and at length perfectly freed from sin, all that is required is a complete surrender to the renovating influence of Christ; a conviction which can rest upon nothing else than a certainty of the fullness and boundless efficacy of that holy, sinless life which dwells in the person of Jesus."

belongs to this circle of ideas are these two: *Reconciliation* and *Redemption*. These two things constitute the fundamental consciousness of the Christian world; for the Christian world is what it is essentially because it is conscious of being reconciled and redeemed. Now, if we find this consciousness in the Christian religion alone, if Christianity is the only religion which can effect a true reconciliation between man and God by an actual redemption from sin, then it is not difficult to discover that the author of such a religion must himself be of a perfectly-sinless and holy character. The true relation of man to God can find its realization only in one in whom sin, which is the ground of separation between man and God, has no place. The real manifestation of Divine grace can exist only in one in whom the one spring of action is the fullness of love which he derives from perfect fellowship with God, and in whom this forms the principle which regulates his whole life. Were there not at the head of the Christian religion such a being, it were inconceivable how it could be the religion of reconciliation and redemption, or how the deep-rooted consciousness of being reconciled and redeemed should have come to form the fundamental belief of the Christian world. With such a being at the head of Christianity, this is at once explained. Now, if the consciousness of being reconciled and redeemed, possessed by the Christian world, has any reality, then that from which it emanated must also have had a real existence. And that that consciousness had a real foundation rests equally upon an actual fact—on a fact which every Christian practically experiences. The doctrine of the sinless holiness of Jesus is, therefore, as secure as is the truth of the efficacy of his work of reconciliation and redemption.

One point more remains to be noticed. Not only have morality and religion been both presented under a new aspect by Christianity, but it has effected an interpenetration of the moral and religious elements such as formerly did not exist. This blending of the moral and religious, which we call holiness, can only be accounted for, that it was fully realized in the person of Christ. It is Christianity alone which combines religion and morality into one, though giving each its full due; for it knows nothing of a piety which does not sanctify, which is not of an entirely *ethical* character, seeking to subdue and transfuse the whole life; or of a morality which does not rest upon a living faith, which is not thoroughly *religious.* This union gives, as has been remarked above, the idea of holiness. But it is something more than the idea that Christianity gives; it sets forth holiness not as something unattainable, far beyond the grasp of humanity, but as already really implanted in humanity—as an idea which, from the time of its first perfect manifestation in the person of its Founder, is destined to be realized ever more and more within the Christian Church. It is self-evident that the idea of holiness and the belief of its attainability by man could not proceed from any thing else than from the great fact of the life manifestation of the sinless and perfect character of Jesus.

5. When we endeavor to bring before our minds the image of the personality of Jesus in direct connection with the influences and works which originated in him, three things strike us as peculiar—unlimited perfection, unapproachable dignity, and

unconditional power of action. The character of Jesus is so constituted that we can not take away one single trait from it, or add one to it, without at once being sensible that we have not only altered but disfigured it. He includes in himself, in fact, all perfection; and, along with the highest energy, and an inexhaustible fountain of life, there is a harmony so perfect that we are compelled to exclaim: Here no improvement can be suggested by the loftiest idealizing, for the ideal itself has become real, and the life itself is stamped with the seal of perfection! In its perfection we feel, moreover, that something attaches to the person of Jesus which our thoughts and words are incapable of grasping. Art has striven in vain to find an adequate expression for the image of Christ; and so, to describe his spiritual nature and character, is a task which never has been, and never will be, accomplished to our complete satisfaction. We feel ever that he is possessed of a dignity which is unapproachable by man, of a fullness which, the more we draw from it, the greater do its treasures appear. This is perceived not only by separate individuals, but by humanity as a whole. The higher and truer the inner life of an individual becomes, the more clearly does he discern and realize the image of Jesus; and at every new step in the development of humanity the form of the Nazarene is illuminated by a fuller light. At the same time there is a distinct consciousness that it is not the image of Christ which increases by means of us, but that we, by living more deeply into it, grow in our capacity of understanding it. And however nearly we may approximate toward him, we always feel that he towers above us at a hight to which no man will ever be able fully to rise—that there is a distance between him and us which none can traverse. This eminence of Jesus is further evidenced by the unbounded power of influencing men which he manifests. The image of the serene and holy One of Golgotha sinks into the very depths of our heart, and presents itself before the soul—sometimes as a conscience warning us of sin and evil, at other times like a word of consolation coming directly from our compassionate God. And while its influence is thus felt in our own inmost life, it is no less perceptible in the ordinary course of the history of mankind. The traces there are alike notorious and indelible, and the whole development of humanity, especially in its highest aspects, would be inexplicable apart from the recognition of the presence of such a power. We can conceive it to be possible that all the great men of history should pass into utter oblivion, but we must hold it to be impossible that the memory of this image should depart, because it has become part and parcel of the inmost and truest life of humanity. Nothing like this can be affirmed of any other man. The capacity and perfection of all others are conjoined with limitation and sinfulness; eminence in every other instance is explicable on human grounds, and can be represented in human forms; all other influence on humanity, even that which deserves to be called world-wide, has its limits. The only exception is Jesus, the sinlessly-holy One.

The question now arises, whether the explanation of this phenomenon can be found within the sphere of that which is merely human; or whether it does compel us to recognize in Jesus a principle which lies beyond human nature and human powers? We, surely, can have no hesitation in denying the former and affirming the latter. If sinlessness or moral perfection were within the reach of man in his present condition, how has it come to pass that experience only furnishes one example of perfect freedom from sin? Why have not persons risen up among men, from time to time, who could lay claim to the same superiority, and compel others to acknowledge the justice of their pretensions? The only rational ground of the fact is, that a principle of sin is implanted in human nature—not, indeed, by original constitution,* but certainly, in its present state, that sin, although not the true, is still the second nature of man—that it penetrates and rules the whole race. The principle of sin being in such a manner ingrafted in human nature, in the condition in which experience presents it to us, only one supposition can render intelligible the existence of a sinless man; namely, that the chain of sin has been broken, and that, in consequence, a personality has arisen in the midst of the sinful race, whose nature is thoroughly whole and sound, to which have been given powers perfectly pure and amply sufficient for the realization of the hihger life. But this is only possible as the result of a Divine creation. Such a person could not be the product of a race subjected to sin. In this aspect he, in whom the possibility of being sinless

* "Never was there a man so purely man as the second Adam, the Lord from heaven. Never man spoke so humanly, felt so humanly, loved so humanly, lived so humanly, died so humanly. Bone of our bone, and flesh of our flesh, he had a more genuine humanity than any of the other sons of Adam, inasmuch as it was free from that demoniac adulteration which had been produced by sin. Hence he is so emphatically called, and delights to call himself, the Son of man. The term has more meaning than it seems at first view to possess. In the Syriac it is the name for humanity itself." (*Taylor Lewis's* "*The Divine Human of the Scriptures,*" *p.* 6.)

has become a reality, must be considered a totally new man, a second Adam. But this second Adam, with whose humanity begins a new career, although like the first as respects the soundness and integrity of the higher powers of life, stands in an entirely-different position toward the world. The first man was put in a world where as yet sin was not, and he had only to decide for obedience or disobedience to the plain Divine command which had been given him. The second Adam was born as a child into a world which was already under the dominion of sin, and, through all the stages of the development of his life, was exposed to its influence. In the course of such a development, independently of any natural bias in a man, sin comes upon him from all sides; it takes possession of him when he is as yet in an unconscious, or only half-conscious state; and when he awakens up to full consciousness it is already in the field, and has gained a power with which he has to struggle, not only outwardly but inwardly. Hence the impossibility of conceiving of a development, actually free from sin, being accomplished in a natural way under existing circumstances. But if, as we have found in Jesus, such a development has, notwithstanding all influences to the contrary, been brought to pass, we can not feel any hesitation in assuming the presence of something over and above, and in union with, the integrity of constitution originally given. In him whose development was thus sinless, there must have been an infallible sureness enabling him during its whole course, and even at those stages of it when he was not as yet awakened to full consciousness, to reject every thing impure, untrue, and sinful, and to appropriate for his inner life only the pure, true, and good, from that which the surrounding world presented to him. It must therefore be conceded that a Divine principle conditioned the original integrity of Jesus, and was a constituent element of his personality, and that it grew and progressed in perfect symmetry and in harmony with the human element; and that, consequently, so far from hindering, it really promoted the natural development of the latter, and secured its perfect purity and orderliness. Clearly, however, we can not understand by this Divine principle merely something akin or bearing resemblance to God, such as is in every man; for sin can and actually does coexist therewith in every man, while the sinlessness of Jesus separates him from, and constitutes him superior to, all other men. We must, therefore, consider that principle to be Divine in its uncorrupted and true essence. *In this way we are led from the sinless Son of man to the Son of God, and the recognition of the pure humanity of Jesus ends in the conviction of his true Divinity.* His personality is so constituted that, as we attentively regard it, we find it marked by those very characteristics of truth, righteousness, holiness, and love, which constitute the essential nature of God. Our thoughts, therefore, unavoidably ascend to God. We are utterly unable to understand or account for his personality otherwise. The conviction is forced upon us that, so far as it is possible to see God in human form, we have him before us in the person of Jesus. And, inasmuch as Jesus presents humanity and Divinity in complete union and interpretation, we can not conceive of him otherwise than as *God-man*.

§ 30. THE MIRACLES WROUGHT ON AND PERFORMED BY JESUS THE NATURAL AND NECESSARY OUTFLOW OF HIS HISTORICALLY-PROVED PERSONALITY, AND, AT THE SAME TIME, THE GROUND AND WARRANT OF ALL OTHER TRUE MIRACLES, PRECEDING AND SUCCEEDING HIS APPEARANCE ON EARTH.

We take it for granted that the miracles of the Gospel history are meant to be real miracles, according to the definition which we have given of a miracle in § 22. All attempts to explain them away, by putting language to the rack, or by resolving them into effects from natural causes, have so utterly failed, that those who made such attempts are ridiculed by infidelity itself. Again, the testimony of so credible men as the Evangelists, (see §§ 24, 25, 26,) may be considered sufficient to satisfy a reasonable inquiry after the verity of the miracles they record, more especially when we take into consideration that, according to their testimony, *Christ himself* claimed the power to work miracles, and appealed to it as a proof of his Divine mission; for the supposition that Jesus should have given a false testimony concerning himself, we have seen to be utterly inconceivable; and if the testimony of the Evangelists on this point were false, if the miracles they attribute to Jesus were mere fables, the product of their age, the question arises, how was it possible for them to preserve such a character as that of Christ in its perfect proportions? "If there be a greater miracle," observes Bushnell, "or a tax on human credulity more severe, we know not where it is. Nothing is so difficult, all human literature testifies, as to draw a character, and keep it in its living proportions. How much more to draw a perfect character, and not discolor it fatally by marks from the imperfection of the biographer! How is it, then, that four humble men have done this, while loading down the history of Christ with marvels and fables?"

The verity of the Gospel miracles, however, as we remarked in the introduction to this chapter, rests not simply nor chiefly on the credibility of the Evangelists. It is the moral perfection of Jesus, unparalleled and never having been conceived of by man before, that furnishes the unassailable voucher of his having performed miracles. Very boldly, but truly, Bushnell remarks: "It is no ingenious fetches of argument that we want; no external testimony, gathered here and there from the records of past ages, suffices to end our doubts; but it is the new sense opened in us by Jesus himself—a sense deeper than words and more immediate than inference—of the miraculous grandeur of his life—a glorious agreement felt between his works and his person, such that his miracles themselves are proved to us in our feeling, believed in by that inward testimony. On this inward testimony we are willing to stake every thing, even the life that now is, and that which is to come. If the miracles, if revelation itself can not stand upon the superhuman character of Jesus, then let it fall. If that character does not contain all truth and centralize all truth in itself, then let there be no truth. If there is any thing worthy of belief not found in this, we may well consent to live and die without it. Before this sovereign light, streaming out from God, the deep questions, and dark surmises, and doubts unresolved, which make a night so gloomy and terrible about us, hurry away to their native abyss. God, who commanded the light to shine out of darkness, has shined in our hearts, to give the light of the knowledge of the glory of God in the face of Jesus Christ. This it is that has conquered the assaults of doubt and false learning in all past ages, and will in all ages to come. No argument against the sun will drive it from the sky. No mole-eyed skepticism, dazzled by its brightness, can turn away the shining it refuses to look upon. And they who long after God will be ever turning their eyes thitherward, and, either with or without reason, or, if need be, against manifold impediments of reason, will see and believe."

We have shown, by a full and critical examination of the character of Jesus, that it can not have been an invention, but that such a person must have lived, else he could not be described, and that he plainly was not a mere man. This historically-proved person—a being who has broken into the world, and is not of it, but has come out from God—is himself the one central and grandest miracle that occurred in the history of the world, the ground and warrant for all other true miracles, preceding and succeeding his appearance on earth, and all the miracles, wrought on and performed by him, are only the natural outflow of that which is already contained in his personality. They are of the same significance in respect of the natural powers as sinlessness is in respect of the moral powers. A perfectly-sinless man is no whit less miraculous a phenomenon in the moral world than a man raised from the dead is in the natural world. To recognize Jesus as sinlessly holy, and yet to deny the miraculous element in his life, would be self-contradictory. It is inconceivable that he should have entered or left the world like other men. Sinful humanity could not produce out of itself the Son of Man, whom to see was to see God the Father, and the historical development of his earthly life would have had no fitting completion, if he had not risen from the dead and ascended to heaven. His supernatural conception, his resurrection and ascension can be called in question only by one who attempts to blot from the record of history the earthly life and character of Jesus, the words spoken and the influences on the minds of men exercised by him. Whoever admits these irrefutable facts of history, must expect supernatural works to proceed from this supernatural personality. The contrary would be unnatural. "Since Jesus is shown," says Bushnell, "to be a superhuman being, manifestly Nature will have a relation to him under and by her own laws, such as accords with his superhuman quality, and it would be very singular if he did not do superhuman things; nay, it is even philosophically incredible that he should not. . . . . Nay, it would be itself a contradiction to all order and fit relation if he could not. To suppose that a being out of humanity will be shut up within all the limitations of humanity, is incredible and contrary to reason. The very laws of nature themselves, having him present to them as a new agent and higher first term, would require the development of new consequences and incidents in the nature of wonders. Being a miracle himself it would be the greatest of all miracles if he did not work miracles."

Another highly-gifted American writer of our day, Tayler Lewis, in his "The Divine Human in the

Scriptures," says to the same purpose: "In the Bible even the supernatural—we may say it without a paradox—is most natural. It is in such true keeping with the times, with the events and doctrines it attests, with all the surrounding historical circumstances as they are narrated, that we almost lose the feeling of the supernatural in the admirable harmony and consistency of the ideas and scenes presented. It seems to be just what might have been expected; it would be strange that it should be otherwise; the marvelous here is the presumptive, the extraordinary becomes the easy of belief." After illustrating this thought by every part of the Old Testament, where the supernatural appears, he continues:* "But it is in the history of Christ that the idea on which we are dwelling receives its most powerful verification. A life so unearthly, so heavenly, so spiritual, so transcending nature, so full of a Divine power manifesting itself in every word and act, so spent in nights of prayer, and days of sublimest teachings—how out of all keeping does it seem, that to a state so earth-transcending in its spirituality, there should be no corresponding witness of the supernatural! . . . . There is a demand for its presence, as not only a fitting but an indispensable accompaniment. The idea can not be complete without it. Such power over the soul! it must extend to the body and the physical life; absence of this healing energy would have been the difficulty to be explained, the feature in the narrative not easy of belief. Such a life and such a death! the resurrection is the only appropriate sequence of a career on earth, yet

* We quote, leaving out all that would interrupt our argument or weaken its force.

so unearthly; the ascension into heaven is the only appropriate finale to a drama so heavenly and divine.—The serious reader can not help feeling that in the life of Christ, as given to us by the Evangelists, there is something more than a supernatural *gift*, or the occasional power of working miracles, as something imparted from without, or only exercised by himself through special effort in each particular case. We are impressed, rather, with the idea of the *constant supernatural*, as a vailed power, not so much requiring an effort for its manifestation as a restraint to prevent it beaming forth before unholy eyes that could not bear, or might profane the sight. In that earthly tabernacle there was the constant dwelling of the Shekinah, more powerfully present when alone, perhaps, or with a few chosen ones. . . . 'Thou art the Christ, the Son of the living God,' is an exclamation called out more by the overpowering effect of this constant presence, than by any great public displays of miraculous power. It is this, more than any thing else, that is attested by the holy apostle John in the words: 'That which was from the beginning, which we have heard, which we have seen with our eyes, which our hands have handled of the Word of Life, for the *Life was manifested* and we saw it, and we testify, and tell unto you of that eternal life, which was with the Father and was manifested unto us.' The reference is not so much to striking outward displays as to the constant spiritual effulgence ever beaming on the soul of the spiritual disciple, and sometimes, even to the eye of sense, surrounding the person of Christ with an outward glory. From the inward supernatural, as from a never-intermitting fountain, proceeded the outward miracle-working power, as exhibited in distinct acts. . . . . Thus, too, are we told of a constant virtue dwelling in the Savior's person; as in the story of the woman who 'touched the hem of his garment that she might be healed.' Her spiritual state, that is, her pure faith, brought her in a living relation to this power so vailed to the unbelieving or merely curious multitude; and the Savior sanctions her thought when he says: 'I know that power has gone forth from me.' . . . . It is credible, it is even to be expected that the supernatural should shine out through a natural so elevated above the ordinary condition of humanity. There is a deep mystery even in our common physical energy. The strength of the body is, in its ultimate resolution, a power of the quiescent spirit. Activity, force, yea, even in some sense, motus or *outgoing energy* are attributes of soul, even when at rest, as much as thought, or will, or emotion. The present bodily organization, instead of a necessary aid, may be, in fact, a limiting, a restraint upon a tremendous power, that needs to be confined as long as it is joined to a selfish or unholy will, even as we chain the madman in his cell. Sometimes, even in common life, there are fearful exhibitions of the loosening of these material bonds. In the last stages of bodily weakness, apparently, some delirium of the soul, if we may call it such, brings out a power of nerve and muscle irresistible to any ordinary strength, inexplicable to any ordinary physiological knowledge. The cases, indeed, are *vastly different*, and yet there is *some analogy*. Such views of the common organism do not at all account for the higher power that may dwell in a perfectly holy spirituality; but they render it credible; they prepare us to believe in it, yea, to feel it as a spiritual dissonance if there be wholly lacking some high command of nature, in connection with a perfect faith and holy will ever in harmony with the divine. It is the Scriptures, however, that must furnish our only reliable ground of argument on this mysterious subject; and here we find no small proof of such a constant indwelling glory of the supernatural as *distinguished from an occasional miraculous gift.* In certain passages there is the strongest expression of Christ's unwillingness to gratify curiosity by the display of an outward sign; in others there is shown an evident reluctance to have this holy influence the subject of any profane or gossiping rumor. But again, he exhibits it of his own accord to chosen disciples, and then it has the appearance of a manifestation, to favored souls, of a power and a spiritual glory ever more truly present in his retired than in his public life. Such is the impression left upon the mind by the account of the transfiguration. . . . . Something, too, of the same feeling comes over us as we read the account of Christ walking on the waters. . . . Why walking thus at that deep time of night over the wild and lonely waves? It was not needed, in addition to his other miracles, for the confirming of the disciples' faith. It seems, rather, the unearthly act of one filled with unearthly thoughts, and seeking a correspondence to them in the more unearthly, or, as we might even call them, supernatural aspects of the natural world. If the answer can not well be given in any thing out of himself, why should we fear to say that it was a rapt physical state, in harmony with an elevated spiritual frame, that demanded it as its fitting outward action? The ecstasy of the soul lifts up the body. There is something of this in the mere earthly human experience. There is a spiritual condition that seems comparatively, if not absolutely, to loosen the power of gravity, to set volition free, and release even the flesh from the hold of earthly bonds. How much more of this ethereal soaring must there have been in the ecstasies of Jesus? In the human spiritual power, as known to us, there is, indeed, nothing that can be strictly compared with it; and yet there *is* enough to render credible such an absolute triumph over matter in the case of one so holy and so heavenly as Christ. . . . . We think there is no irreverence in such thoughts. At all events, without any special reasoning about spiritual and physical conditions, there is in Scripture itself good evidence that the human nature in Christ was ever in connection with the supernatural, and that the special miraculous acts were unvailings of a constant hidden power, rather than special enablings or special efforts in each particular case. Christ's own words convey this thought: 'He is the resurrection and the life.' Even when vailed in human flesh, he is still the brightness of the Father, the express image of his hypostasis. 'We beheld his glory,' says John, 'the glory of the Only-Begotten, full of grace and truth.' The humanity, too, is a true humanity; no one was ever more perfectly human; and yet so wondrous is he, even in his manhood, that it forces the idea of the superhuman and the supernatural as not only the casual explanation of such an existence, but its own fitting, yea, necessary accompaniment."

While we have, as we think, presented sufficient grounds in support of our proposition, that all the miracles wrought on and performed by Christ were the natural and necessary outflow of that which is implied in his historically-proved personality—that is, that we can not, as we are compelled to do, recognize Jesus as sinlessly holy, and yet consistently deny the miraculous element in his life—we are, of course, far from permitting the unauthorized inference, that the exercise of miraculous powers necessarily involves or depends upon sinlessness on the part of every person possessed of miraculous powers. We have, on the contrary, referred to the fact that, while with all other persons to whom the Scriptures ascribe the performance of miracles, it is represented as a supernatural gift, as a power imparted from without, and exercised only occasionally through a special effort, the personality of Christ is the only one that stood in such constant connection with the supernatural; that the special miraculous acts performed by him or wrought on him were only the unvailings of a constant hidden power, requiring not so much an effort for its manifestation as a restraint to prevent its beaming forth before unholy eyes. The relation, therefore, which we have discovered between the sinlessness of Jesus and the miracles ascribed to him, admits of no application to other men who wrought miracles, except in so far as, wherever the miraculous element appears in the Holy Scriptures, it appears, in the popular sense of the word, natural, that is, "in such true keeping with the times and occasions by which it is called forth, and in such admirable harmony with the events and doctrines which it attests, that we almost lose the feeling of the supernatural." But not only this, we have remarked above that Christ himself, being the one central and grandest miracle that occurred in the history of the world, is at the same time *the ground and warrant for all other true miracles, preceding and succeeding his appearance on earth.*

This is a truth which is too much overlooked in the discussion of miracles. In section 22 we showed that miracles are not a disruption of the divinely-established order of the world, but a demonstration of Divine agency for the purpose of restoring the order of the world, which had been disordered by sin, the act of created free agents. Had there not taken place a disorder of the world by sin, there would, indeed, seem to be no demand or even place for that especial Divine agency which we call miraculous. This miraculous agency of God culminated in the incarnation of his Son, the Redeemer from sin, and it is self-evident that he, being the greatest miracle himself, should work miracles. But it is equally evident why Divine Wisdom did not see fit to confine to his person the manifestation of the miraculous agency necessary for the restoration of the moral order of the world. Mankind was to be prepared for the reception of the greatest miracles by the less. The history of the nation in which the Son of God should be born, especially the bringing the people of Israel out of the bondage of Egypt, and constituting the covenant people of God, bore, therefore, the stamp of the immediate operation of God; the Divine messengers, especially the great legislator and mediator of the first covenant, Moses, needed the authentication by miracles, and the spirit of prophecy, the continuous and most irrefutable miracle of the Old Testament, had, with the types and the shadows of the law, to point out the coming Messiah.

Nor was it proper that the manifestation of supernatural power, preparing for and culminating in the appearance of the Son of God in the flesh, should at once terminate with his ascension to heaven; for, in this case, men would have been still more slow, than they are, to believe that the greatest of all miracles had taken place. The apostles, preaching Jesus and the resurrection, needed God to bear them witness with signs and wonders and with divers miracles and gifts of the Holy Ghost, and we have credible testimony that the power of working miracles continued with the Church, to some extent, during several centuries.*

A consideration of the peculiar nature, significance, importance, and design of the miracles performed by Christ does not properly fall within the scope of our present investigation. We have considered the mira-

*In connection with these remarks it is proper to consider the question: Whether miracles are now discontinued; and, if so, why? This question we know not how to answer better than Dr. Bushnell has done: "The Scriptures no where teach, what is often assumed, the final discontinuance of miracles; and it is much to be regretted that such an assumption is so commonly made. There is no certain proof that miracles have not been wrought in every age of the Christian Church. There is certainly a supernatural and Divine causality streaming into the lives and blending with the faith of all good men, and there is no reason to doubt that it may sometimes issue in premonitions, results of guidance and healing, endowments of force, answers to prayer that closely approach in many cases, if they do not exactly meet, our definition of miracles. Again, if miracles have been discontinued, even for a thousand years, they may yet be revived in such varieties of form as a different age may require. They will be revived without fail whenever the ancient reason may return, or any new contingency may occur, demanding their instrumentality. And yet good and sufficient reasons may be given why the more palpable miracles of the apostolic age could not be continued, or must needs be interspaced by agencies of a more silent character. It may have been that they would by and by corrupt the impressions and ideas even of religion, setting men to look after signs and prodigies with their eyes, and so, instead of attesting God to them, making them unspiritual and even incapable of faith. Traces of this mischief begin to appear even in the times of the apostles themselves. Christianity, it is very obvious, inaugurates the faith of a supernatural agency in the world. Hence, to inaugurate such a faith, it must needs make its entry into the world through the fact of a Divine incarnation and other miracles. In these we have the pole of thought, opposite to nature, set before

cles of Christ in these practical aspects in our Commentary, in the introductory remarks to the eighth chapter of Matthew, where we meet the first record of a Gospel miracle. How we can distinguish true, Divine miracles from false ones, wrought by diabolic agency, we have discussed in our comment on Matthew vii, 22.

us in distinct exhibition. And then the problem is, having the two poles of nature and the supernatural presented, that we be trained to apprehend them conjunctively, or as working together in silent terms of order. For, if the miracles continue in their palpable and staring form of wonders, and take their footing as a permanent institution, they will breed a sensuous, desultory state of mind, opposite to all sobriety and all genuine intelligence. At a certain point the miracles were needed as the polar signs of a new force—but, for the reason suggested, it appears to be necessary, also, that they should not be continuous; otherwise, the supernatural will never be brought into any terms of order, as a force conjoined with nature in our common experience, but will only instigate a wild, eccentric temper, closely akin to unreason, and to all practical delusions. And yet there may be times, even to the end of the world, when some outburst of the miraculous force of God will be needed to break up a lethargy of unbelief and sensuous dullness, equally unreasoning and desultory."

PART IV.

THE ATTACKS OF MODERN CRITICISM ON THE INSPIRATION OF THE FIRST THREE GOSPELS.

PART IV.

THE ATTACKS OF MODERN CRITICISM ON THE INSPIRATION OF THE FIRST THREE GOSPELS.

§ 31. The Relation which the Authenticity and Credibility of the Gospel Records bear to their Inspiration.

The arguments by which we have established the authenticity or apostolical origin of the Gospel Records, and the Divine as well as human attestations of their credibility involve also their inspiration. To prove the trustworthiness of the Scriptures from their assumed inspiration, and then to deduce the inspiration from the testimony of the Scriptures, would be a begging of the question. Instead of this we have proved the authenticity and credibility of the Gospels, without any reference to an assumed inspiration, on simply historical grounds, and this historical argumentation is the only *outward* proof needed for their inspiration. With regard to outward proofs of inspiration Mr. Westcott remarks very justly: "To speak of the *proof* of the inspiration of the Scriptures involves, indeed, an unworthy limitation of the idea itself. In the fullest sense of the word we can not prove the presence of life, but are simply conscious of it; and inspiration is the manifestation of a higher life. The words of Scripture are spiritual words, and as such are spiritually discerned. The ultimate test of the reality of inspiration lies in the intuition of that personal faculty—πνεῦμα—by which inspired men once recorded the words of God, and are still able to hold communion with him. Every thing short of this leaves the great truth still without us; and that which should be a source of life is in danger of becoming a mere dogma." (Introduction to the Study of the Gospels, p. 45.) In Parts II and III we have met all the attacks that have been made upon the authenticity and the credibility of the Gospels, with the exception of the objections, which modern criticism has deduced from the peculiar relation in which the three first (synoptic) Gospels stand to one another and to that of John. These objections lie, indeed, not against the authenticity and credibility of the synoptic Gospels, but would, if sustained, invalidate their inspiration. For while in ordinary historians the strictest integrity is compatible with slight inaccuracy, divergence of testimony—the least discrepancy—appears formidable in a work written by Divine inspiration. It is, therefore, proper to examine these critical difficulties in connection with the question of inspiration—a question which of itself deserves a separate consideration.

Before we, however, enter upon this examination, let us glance at some of the general characteristics of the Gospel Records, which, as Mr. Westcott remarks, can only be accounted for on the assumption of their inspiration. "They are *fragmentary in form.* Their writers make no attempt to relate all the actions or discourses of our Lord, and show no wish to select the most marvelous series of his mighty works, and probably no impartial judge will find in any one of them a conscious attempt to form a narrative supplementary to those of the others. But if we know by the ordinary laws of criticism that our Gospels are the only authentic records of the Savior's life, while we believe that Providence regards the well-being of the Christian Church, are we not necessarily led to conclude that some Divine power overruled their composition, so that what must otherwise seem a meager and incomplete record should contain all that is fittest historically to aid our progress and determine our faith? Nor can it be unworthy of notice that while the Gospels evidently contain so small a selection from the works and words of Christ, so few details unrecorded by the Evangelists should have been preserved in other ways. . . . . The numerous witnesses of our Lord's works and teaching must have treasured up with affection each recollection of their past intercourse; but the cycle of Evangelical narrative is clearly marked, and it can not but seem that the same Power which so definitely circumscribed its limits determined its contents. Again, the Gospels are *unchronological in order.* We are at once cautioned against regarding them as *mere* history, and encouraged to look for some new law of arrangement in their contents, which, as I shall endeavor to prove, must result from a higher power than an unaided instinct or an enlightened consciousness. Once more, the Gospels are *brief and apparently confused in style.* There is no trace in them of the anxious care or ostentatious zeal which mark the ordinary productions of curiosity or devotion. The Evangelists write as men who see through all time, and only contemplate the events which they record in their spiritual relations. But, at the same time, there is an originality and vigor in every part of the Gospels, which become a Divine energy in the Gospel of John. As mere compositions they stand out from all other histories with the noble impress of simplicity and power; and it is as if the faithful reflection of the image of God shed a clear light on the whole narrative. The answer was once given to the Pharisees, when they sought to take Jesus, that never man spoke like that man, and those who assail the authority of the Gospels have been constrained to confess that never was history written as in them." (Introd., pp. 46–48.) On the characteristic differences of the four Gospels Mr. Westcott says further: "The three synoptic Gospels are not mere repetitions of one narrative, but *distinct views of a complex whole.* The same salient points reappear in all, but they are found in new combinations and with new details, as the features of a landscape or the outlines of a figure when viewed from various points. . . . . The only conception which we can form of the inspiration of a historic record lies in the Divine fitness of the outward dress in which the facts are at once embodied and vailed. No record of any fact can be complete. The relations of the most trivial occurrence transcend all powers of observation, and the truthfulness of special details is no pledge of the truthfulness of the whole impression. The connection and relation and subordination of the various parts, the description and suppression of particular incidents, the choice of language and style, combine to make a history true in its higher significance. This power the Evangelists possessed in the fact that they were penetrated with the truth of which they spoke. The Spirit which was in them searched the deep things of God, and led them to realize the mysteries of the faith. . . . . The contrast between the Gospel of John and the synoptic Gospels, both in substance and in individual character, is obvious at first sight; but the characteristic differences of the synoptic Gospels, which are formed on the same foundation and with common materials, are less observed. Yet these differences are not less important than the former, and belong equally to the complete portraiture of the Savior." (Introd., pp. 218–220.) The individual character of each of the four Gospels the reader may find delineated in my special introduction to the respective Gospels.

§ 32. The Peculiar Agreement and Disagreement of the First Three Evangelists in their Narratives, and the Various Explanations of this Singular Phenomenon.

The striking difference in contents and character of the first three Gospels from the fourth presents no difficulty. It is easily and satisfactorily accounted for by the difference of the individuality and scope of the Synoptists from that of John, as may be seen in my introduction to each Gospel, as well as by the fact of the later origin of John's Gospel. Owing to this later origin, we may take it for granted that the synoptical Gospels were already generally known when John wrote; that he, therefore, purposely abstaining from writing anew what they had at sufficient length recorded, only sought to complete them by narrating those portions of the life of Jesus which had been omitted by the Synoptists. The peculiar difficulties which claim our attention present themselves when we compare the synoptical Gospels with each other.

There is in them a great amount of agreement. If we suppose the history that they contain to be divided into sections, in forty-two of these all the three narratives coincide; twelve more are given by Matthew and Mark only; five by Mark and Luke only, and fourteen by Matthew and Luke. To these must be added five peculiar to Matthew, two to Mark, and nine to Luke, and the enumeration is complete. But this applies only to general coincidence as to the facts narrated; the amount of verbal coincidence, that is, the passages either verbally the same, or coinciding in the use of many of the same words, is much smaller. Without going minutely into the examination of examples, the leading facts connected with the subject may be thus summed up: The verbal and material agreement of the first three Evangelists is such as does not occur in any other authors who have written independently of one another. The verbal agreement is greater where the spoken words of others are cited than where facts are recorded, and greatest in quotations of the words of our Lord. But in some leading events, as in the call of the first four disciples, in that of Matthew, and in the transfiguration, the agreement even in expression is remarkable; there are also narratives where there is no verbal harmony in the outset, but only in the crisis or emphatic part of the story. (Matt. viii, 3, Mark i, 41, Luke v, 13; and Matt. xiv, 19, 20, Mark vi, 41–43, Luke ix, 16, 17.) The narratives of our Lord's early life, as given by Matthew and Luke, have little in common, while Mark does not include that part of the history in his plan. The agreement in the narrative portions of the Gospels begins with the baptism of John, and reaches its highest point in the account of the Passion of our Lord and the facts that preceded it; so that a direct ratio might almost be said to exist between the agreement and the nearness of the facts that sustain a close relation to the Passion. After this event, in the account of his burial and resurrection, the coincidences are few. The language of all three is Greek, with Hebrew idioms; the Hebraisms are most abundant in Mark, and fewest in Luke. In quotations from the Old Testament the Evangelists, or two of them, sometimes exhibit a verbal agreement, although they differ from the Hebrew and from the Septuagint version. (Matt. iii, 3, Mark i, 3, Luke iii, 4; and Matt. iv, 10, Luke iv, 8; and Matt. xi, 10; Mark i, 2; Luke vii, 27, etc.) Except as to twenty-four verses, the Gospel of Mark contains no principal facts which are not found in Matthew and Luke; but he often supplies details omitted by them, and these are often such as would belong to the graphic account of an eye-witness. There are no cases in which Matthew and Luke exactly harmonize, where Mark does not also coincide with them. In several places the words of Mark have something in common with each of the other narratives, so as to form a connecting link between them, where their words slightly differ. The examples of verbal agreement between Mark and Luke are not so long or so numerous as those between Matthew and Luke, and Matthew and Mark; but, as to the arrangement of events, Mark and Luke frequently coincide where Matthew differs from them. These are the leading particulars; but they are very far from giving a complete notion of a phenomenon that is well worthy of that attention and reverent study of the sacred text by which alone it can be fully and fairly apprehended.

The three Gospels exhibit themselves as three distinct records of the life and works of the Redeemer, but with *a greater amount of agreement than three wholly-independent accounts could be expected to exhibit. The agreement would be no difficulty without the differences;* it would only mark the one Divine source from which they all are derived, the Holy Spirit who spoke by the prophets. *The difference of form and style without the agreement would offer no difficulty,* since there may be a substantial harmony between accounts that differ greatly in mode of expression, and the very difference might be a guarantee of independence. The harmony *and* the variety, the agreement *and* the differences, *together,* form the problem with which Biblical critics have occupied themselves for a century and a half. To ascribe the verbal differences of the Evangelists, in their reports of sayings of our Lord and of events, in the midst of their general and substantial agreement, simply and directly to the dictation of the Holy Spirit, would make the difficulty greater instead of less. The singular phenomenon can be naturally accounted for only by assuming *the interdependence of one Evangelist upon the other, or some common source, written or oral, or a combination of these elements.*

I. The first and most obvious theory has been, *that the narrators made use of each other's works.* Accordingly, Grotius, Mill, Wetstein, Griesbach, and many others, have endeavored to ascertain which Gospel is to be regarded as the first; which is copied first; and which is copied from the other two. It is remarkable that each of the six possible combinations has found advocates, and that for the support of each hypothesis the same phenomena have been curiously and variously interpreted. This of itself proves the uncertainty of the theory. It is thoroughly refuted by Alford. If one or two of the Evangelists borrowed from the other, we must adopt one of the following suppositions: 1. That the later Evangelist, finding the earlier Gospel, or Gospels, insufficient, was anxious to supply what was wanting. But no possible arrangement of the three Gospels will suit the requirements of this supposition. The shorter Gospel of Mark can not be an expansion of the more complete Gospels of Matthew or Luke. No less can these two Gospels be considered as expansions of Mark; for his Gospel, although shorter, and narrating fewer events and discourses, is, in those which he does narrate, the fullest and most particular of the three. And again, Luke could not have supplemented Matthew; for there are most important portions of Matthew which he has altogether omitted, (e. g., chapter xxv, and much of chapters xiii and xv;) nor could Matthew have supplemented Luke, having omitted almost all of the important matter recorded by Luke, from ix, 51–xviii, 15. Moreover, this supposition leaves all the difficulties of different arrangement and minute discrepancy unaccounted for. We pass on, 2. To the supposition that the later Evangelist purposed to improve the earlier one, especially in point of chronological order. If it were so, nothing could have been done less calculated to answer the end than that which our Evangelists have done. For in no material point do their accounts differ, but only in arrangement and completeness;

and this latter difference is such that no one of them can be cited as taking any pains to make it appear that his own arrangement is chronologically accurate. No fixed dates are found in those parts where the differences exist; no word to indicate that any other arrangement had ever been published. 3. Neither does the supposition that the later Evangelists wished to adapt their Gospels to a different class of readers—incorporating, at the same time, whatever additional matter they possessed—in any way account for the phenomena of our present Gospels. For, even taking for granted the usual assumption, that Matthew wrote for Hebrew Christians, Mark for Latins, and Luke for Gentiles in general, we do not find any such consistency in these purposes as a revision and alteration of another's narrative would necessarily presuppose. We have the visit of the Gentile Magi exclusively related by the Hebraizing Matthew; the circumcision of the child Jesus, and his frequenting the Passovers at Jerusalem, by the Gentile Evangelist Luke. Had the above purposes been steadily kept in view in the revision of the narratives before them, the respective Evangelists could not have omitted incidents so entirely subservient to their respective designs. Or, 4. It may be supposed that, receiving one or two Gospels as authentic, the later Evangelist borrowed from them such parts as he purposed to narrate in common with them. But this does not represent the matter of fact. In no case does any Evangelist borrow from another any considerable part of even a single narrative. For such borrowing—unless it was with the intent of fraudulently plagiarizing from them, slightly disguising the common matter so as to make it appear original—would imply verbal coincidence. It is inconceivable that one writer, borrowing from another matter confessedly of the very first importance, *in good faith and with approval*, should alter his diction *so singularly* and *capriciously* as, *on this hypothesis*, we find the text of the parallel sections of our Gospels altered. Let the question be answered by ordinary considerations of probability, and let any passage common to the three Evangelists be put to the test. The phenomena presented will be more or less as follows: First, perhaps, we shall have three or five or more words *identical;* then as many *wholly distinct;* then two clauses or more expressed *in the same words, but differing in order;* then a clause *contained in one or two*, and *not in the third;* then several words identical; then a clause not only wholly distinct, but *apparently* inconsistent; and so forth, with recurrences of the same anomalous alterations, coincidences, and transpositions. Nor does this description apply to verbal and sentential arrangement only, but also, with slight modifications, to that of the larger portions of the narratives. Equally capricious would be the disposition of the subject-matter. Sometimes, while coincident in the things related, the Gospels place them in the most various order, each in turn connecting them together with apparent marks of chronological sequence—e. g., the visit to Gadara, in Matthew viii, 28, as compared with the same in Mark v, 1, and Luke vii, 26, sq. Let any one say, divesting himself of the commonly-received hypotheses respecting the connection and order of our Gospels, whether it is within the range of probability that a writer should thus singularly alter the subject-matter and diction before him, having *no design* in so doing, but intending, fairly and with approval, to incorporate the work of another into his own? Can an instance be any where cited of undoubted borrowing and adaptation from another, presenting similar phenomena? We see, from the above argumentation, that any theory of mutual interdependence of the three Evangelists fails to account for the appearances presented by the synoptic Gospels. We must come to the conclusion that the three Gospels arose *independently of one another.**

II. It has been assumed that there existed *a written document in the Aramaic language as the common original*, from which the three Gospels were drawn, each with more or less modification. But as this supposition, though it would account for some of the vari-

* On this point Mr. Norton makes the following remarks:

"1. The conclusion that no one of the first three Evangelists copied from either of the other two, is important as showing that their Gospels afford three *distinct* sources of information concerning the life of Jesus. The Evangelists, therefore, in their striking correspondence in the representations of his character, miracles, and doctrines must be considered as strongly confirming each other's testimony. Nothing but reality, nothing but the fact that Jesus had acted and taught, as they represent, would have stamped his character and life so definitely and vividly on the minds of individuals ignorant of each other's writings, and enabled them to give narratives, each so consistent with itself, and all so accordant with one another. A false story concerning an imaginary character would have preserved no uniform type. It would have varied in its aspects, according to the different temperaments and talents, the conceptions and purposes of its various narrators.

"2. If the notion that one Evangelist copied from another is proved to be untenable, then the accordance among the first three Gospels proves them all to have been written at an early period, when the sources of authentic information were yet fully accessible, and before any interval had elapsed, during which exaggerations, perversions, and fables, to which the wonderful history of Jesus was exposed, had had time to flow in and to change its character.

"3. If the Evangelists did not copy one from another, it follows that the first three Gospels must have all been written about the same period, since if one had preceded another by any considerable length of time, it can not be supposed that the author of the later Gospel would have been unacquainted with the work of his predecessor, or would have neglected to make use of it; especially when we take into view that its reputation must have been well established among the Christians. Whatever antiquity, therefore, we can show to belong to any one of the first three Gospels, the same, or nearly the same, we may ascribe to the other two."

ations in the parallel passages, as being independent translations, would afford no solution whatever of the more important discrepancies of *insertion*, *omission*, and *amendment*, the most complicated hypotheses have been advanced, all perfectly capricious and utterly inadequate to account for the phenomena. The supposed original is assumed to have been translated, altered, and annotated by different hands, and the synoptic Gospels are said to have been drawn from one or the other of these different forms into which the original had passed, or from a combination of them. A theory so prolific of assumptions would be admissible only if it could be proved that no other solution is possible.

The "original Gospel" is supposed to have been of such authority as to be circulated every-where, yet so defective as to require annotation from any hand, and so little reverenced that no hand spared it. If the three Evangelists agreed to draw from such a work, it must have been widely, if not universally, accepted in the Church; and yet there is no record of its existence; if of lower authority, it could not have become the basis of the three canonical Gospels. Moreover, the state of literature in Palestine, at that time, was not such as to make the assumed, repeated editing, translating, and annotating of a history a natural and probable process. (Compare §§ 5 and 6.) Happily, this hypothesis of an original Gospel, which, if true, would overthrow the Divine authority of the Gospel Records, has been found so untenable on historical and critical grounds, that it has been given up by its own inventors.

III. Having found the assumption of a common original Gospel as untenable as that of the interdependence of one Evangelist upon the other, let us examine that solution of the problem, which explains the relationship of the synoptical Gospels by deriving them from *a common oral source*, that is, from the common oral teachings of the apostles; which, from the nature of the case, we may assume to have been chiefly historical, giving an account of the discourses and acts of Jesus of Nazareth. That the written Gospels were the *result*, not the *foundation*, of the apostolical preaching, will not be called in question. On similar grounds, as the baptism of infants, in the case, was preceded by the baptism of adults, it may be said that the experience of oral teaching was required in order to commit to writing the vast subject of the life of Christ. In the first period of the apostolic age the powerful working of the Holy Spirit in the Church supplied the place of those records, which, as soon as the brightness of his presence began to be withdrawn, became indispensable, in order to prevent the corruption of the Gospel history by false teachers. The great commission given to the apostles was to *preach* the Gospel, and it was only the subsequent want of the Church, established by their preaching, which furnished an adequate motive for adding a written record to the testimony of their living words. Of the great majority of the apostles all that we know certainly is, that they were engaged in instructing, orally, the multitudes who were waiting to receive their tidings. The place of instruction was the synagogue and the market-place, not the student's chamber. "The elders refrained from writing," it is said by Clemens, "because they would not interrupt the care which they bestowed in teaching orally, by the care of composition." Besides, the *written* evidence for the facts of the Gospel was found already in the Old Testament. All the prophets spoke of Christ, and to them the apostles constantly referred, by showing them fulfilled in the life of Christ. That the apostolic preaching consisted chiefly in relating the wondrous life, the teaching and the acts, the suffering, death, and resurrection of our Lord, we learn from the conditions of apostleship propounded by Peter himself, (Acts i, 21, 22;) that, in order to give a proper testimony of the resurrection of Christ, an apostle must have been an eye and ear-witness of what had happened from the baptism of John till the ascension, that is, during the whole official life of our Lord; and, accordingly, Paul claims to have received an independent knowledge, by direct revelation, of at least some of the fundamental parts of the Gospel history, (Galatians i, 12; 1 Cor. xi, 23; xxv, 3,) to qualify him for his calling as an apostle. That the apostolic preaching was chiefly historic, is confirmed by Luke, who, in the preface to his Gospel, expressly designates the oral apostolical testimony as the source of the Evangelical narratives, which many had taken in hand to draw up; and, as far as the records of apostolic preaching in the Acts of the Apostles go, they confirm this view. Peter, at Cæsarea, and Paul, at Antioch, preach alike the facts of the Redeemer's life and death. As to the Epistles, they were evidently not designed for primary instruction, but for the further instruction of those who were familiar with the great outlines of the "mystery of godliness," (1 Tim. iii, 16,) and had professed their belief by baptism.

We are then led to the inquiry, in what manner

the synoptic Gospels are connected with the oral Gospel preached by the apostles? Before showing the relation of the written to the oral Gospel, we remind the reader that the Gospel history was *first orally* delivered by the apostles *at Jerusalem*, where they formed the mother Church, and remained till dispersed by the first persecution. And is it not to be presumed that the very portions of that Gospel history, which form the common subject-matter of the synoptical Gospels, would be more frequently and fully dwelt upon by the apostles in their preaching at Jerusalem, than those incidents which had taken place there, and were therefore well known to those to whom the apostles first addressed themselves? This explains to us, in part, (compare my introductory remarks to § 8 in the Gospel of Matthew,) why it is that the ministry of Jesus in Galilee is almost exclusively recorded to us by the three Evangelists in a manner so singularly similar. There is nothing unnatural in the supposition that the oral narratives of the apostles at Jerusalem, concerning the words and deeds of our Lord, would be delivered, for the most part, in the same form of words; on the contrary, it was in the highest degree desirable for the teachers whom the apostles were sending forth into the world, and it became the most fitting means to secure and make manifest the purity of the subsequent written Gospel. The particular points, especially in sayings of Christ, were always reproduced; unusual expressions were the more firmly retained, since, when they were uttered, they had the more strongly attracted the attention of the disciples. Sermons and sayings were naturally retained with more care, and reported with more uniformity than incidents; although even in the latter, in the same degree that the incident was surprising and peculiar, a fixed type of narration had involuntarily formed itself. Thus it was that the authors had often heard the points, both of incidents and sayings, narrated in substantially the same words. There were, moreover, peculiar circumstances which naturally contributed to the uniformity in question. While modern taste aims at a variety of expression, and abhors a repetition of the same phrases as monotonous, the simplicity of the men, and their language, and their education, would all lead us to expect that the apostles would have no such feeling. They were from the humblest ranks of society in a nation destitute of polite literature. Their abilities and education were nearly alike. Their susceptibilities for apprehending the scenes they had witnessed were similar, while the poverty of the Aramaic Greek, in which they reported what they had seen and heard, did not admit of much variety. The first preachers aimed at fidelity and truth in their reports of the events they had witnessed, rather than at ornament. They had no wish to dress out their descriptions, even if they had been capable of doing so, and the genius of the dialect they employed had allowed a wider scope and variety. Besides, they had been accustomed, as Jews, to treasure up and hand down traditionally the interpretations of their fathers respecting the law, and must have been disposed to follow the same method in regard to the Christian religion. Nor would the immediate disciples desire to depart from the expressions they had learned from their instructors. On the contrary, they would studiously attach themselves to the form in which the Gospel narratives had orally been delivered to them. Such were the circumstances that contributed to produce and perpetuate a stereotype form of the Evangelical history, and to bring the oral narratives into an archetypal form, which was subsequently transferred to the written Gospels. It is supposed, then, that the preaching of the apostles, and the teaching whereby they prepared others to preach, as they did, would tend to assume a common form, more or less fixed; and that the portions of the three Gospels which harmonize most exactly owe their agreement to the fact that the apostolic preaching had already clothed itself in a settled or usual form of words, to which the writers inclined to conform without feeling bound to do so; and the differences which occur, often in the closest proximity to the harmonies, arise from the feeling of independence with which each wrote what he had seen and heard, or, in the case of Mark and Luke, from what apostolic witnesses had told them. But if the uniformity of the synoptic Gospels is ascribed to the oral narratives of the apostles, it may be asked why the accounts of the death and resurrection of Christ given in the three Gospels present so few correspondences compared with the other narratives? Was not this history of the highest interest and importance? Could it have failed to be repeated and dwelt upon? Should it not, therefore, have presented the most marked similarities in the historic cycle? Whence, then, arise the very great discrepancies running through the description of this event in the four canonical Gospels? To this it may be answered, that these facts took place at Jerusalem, and were so well known that the apostles could insist upon them as indubitable facts without dwelling on the minor circumstances. And, as regards the resurrection, it is possible that the divergence arose from the intention of each Evangelist to contribute something toward the weight of evidence for this central truth. Accordingly, each of the four Evangelists mentions distinct acts and appearances of the Lord to establish that he was risen indeed.

The supposition that the singular correspondence in matter and language, which exists among the first three Gospels, is to be attributed to the oral teaching of the apostles is strikingly confirmed by Luke, who, in his preface, expressly declares the information derived from the eye-witnesses of the ministry of Christ, that is, the oral narratives of the apostles, to be the only authentic source of his own Gospel, and of the other narratives that had been attempted. While Matthew, the apostle, committed to writing the narratives as he and the other apostles had been accustomed to communicate them orally, Mark and Luke, who derived their knowledge from the apostles, would record those narratives as they had heard them. There would, of course, be variations of language, and minor circumstances would be omitted or inserted, as it was orally related by different individuals, or by the same individual at different times. It is not probable that the apostles recited in a systematic series of discourses all the transactions of the ministry of Jesus related by any one of the first three Evangelists. According to the particular occasion presented, or the special object which they had in view, they would group together events, sayings, and discourses particularly adapted to their purpose. They would class their accounts of the life of Christ, but they did not narrate them chronologically. Thus we may account for the agreements and disagreements in the chronological arrangement of the Synoptists.

As an objection to the foregoing explanation of the coincidence of language among the Synoptists, it has been urged as highly improbable that the apostles, whose native language was Hebrew, or rather its Aramaic dialect, would have addressed the Jews at Jerusalem in Greek. But we must remember that many Hellenists—Jews born and educated in foreign countries, to whom the Greek was more familiar than the language of their own nation—dwelt in Jerusalem, or resorted thither during the great national feasts, and that the Greek was at the time so widely spread, (Josephus, Antiq., XVII, 11, 4; Bell. Jud., III, 9, 1,) that most of the natives of Palestine were sufficiently acquainted with it. Though the apostles may, at first, have preached the Gospel at Jerusalem, more or less, in Aramaic, it is evident that the Greek language was soon substituted; for it is certain that a considerable portion of the early Christians in Jerusalem was composed of Hellenists, (Acts vi, 1;) with Hellenists Paul disputed after his conversion, (Acts ix, 29;) we find mention of various synagogues in that city of foreign Jews who associated together according to the countries from which they came, (Acts vi, 9.) As the Hellenists, with the converts from Greek Gentiles, soon outnumbered the Christians of Palestine, the Greek language was adopted as the regular medium of the Church to promulgate the Gospel. That this could be done even in Jerusalem without provoking popular prejudice, appears from the circumstance that, when Paul spoke in Hebrew, (Acts xxii, 2,) it was unexpected, and produced unusual attention. From this the inference may be drawn, that public addresses were commonly made in Greek.

It is now generally admitted that the oral teaching of the apostles was the archetype, the original source of the common parts of the synoptic Gospels; but, at the same time, it has been considered as not of itself sufficient to account for all the phenomena which they present, without assuming the existence of some written documents embodying portions of that oral teaching, such as Luke refers to. Of this opinion is Alford, who says: "I believe that the apostles, in virtue not merely of their having been eye and ear-witnesses of the Evangelical history, but especially in virtue of *their office,* gave to the various Churches their testimony in *a narrative of facts;* such narrative being modified in each case by the individual mind of the apostle himself, and his sense of what was requisite for the particular community to which he was ministering. While they were principally together, and instructing the converts at Jerusalem, such narrative would naturally be *for the most part the same,* and expressed in the same, or nearly the same words; coincident, however, *not from design or rule,* but because *the things themselves were the same,* and the teaching naturally fell for the most part into one form. It would be easy and interesting to follow the probable origin and growth of this cycle of narratives of the words and deeds of our Lord in the Church at Jerusalem—for both the Jews and the Hellenists—the latter under such teachers as Philip and Stephen, commissioned and authenticated by the apostles. In the course of such a process *some por-*

tions would naturally be written down by private believers for their own use or that of friends. And as the Church spread to Samaria, Cæsarea, and Antioch, the want would be felt, in each of these places, of similar cycles of oral teaching, which, when supplied, would thenceforward belong to and be current in those respective Churches. And these portions of the Evangelic history, oral or partially documentary, *would be adopted under the sanction of the apostles*, who were as in all things, so especially in this, the appointed and Divinely-guided overseers of the whole Church. This *common substratum of apostolic teaching, I believe to have been the original source of the common part of our three Gospels.* . . . . Delivered, usually, in the same or similar terms to the catechumens in the various Churches, and becoming the text of instruction for their pastors and teachers, it by degrees underwent those modifications which the various Gospels now present to us. And I am not now speaking of any considerable length of time, such as might suffice to deteriorate and corrupt mere traditional teaching, but *of no more than the transmission through men apostolic, or almost apostolic, yet of independent habits of speech and thought, of an account which remained in substance the same.* Let us imagine the modifications which the individual memory, brooding affectionately and reverently over each word and act of our Lord, would introduce into a narrative in relating it variously and under differing circumstances; the Holy Spirit, who brought to their remembrance whatever things he had said to them, (John xiv, 26,) working in and distributing to each severally as he would; let us place to the account the various little changes of transposition or omission, of variation in diction or emphasis, which would be sure to arise in the freedom of individual teaching, and we have, I believe, the only reasonable solution of the arbitrary and otherwise unaccountable coincidences and discrepancies in these parts of our Gospels."

§ 33. A Consideration of the Inspired Character of the Synoptical Gospels, on the Ground of their being chiefly the Result of the Oral Teaching of the Apostles.

It is a postulate of reason to assume that, if the Author and object of our Christian faith was, as is historically proved, God manifest in the flesh, the Son of man in whom dwelt the fullness of the Godhead bodily, this fact involves another fact; namely, that the records of his life, his discourses, and acts were written under Divine direction and preserved to us by Divine Providence. That they were written under Divine direction, or by inspiration, is, moreover, a necessary inference from the promise of the gift of the Holy Spirit, given by Christ to his apostles *in connection with their commission* to preach the Gospel to all the world, and to build up his Church.

It was at their first mission (Matt. x) that Christ referred his apostles to the assistance of the Holy Spirit in certain emergencies of their apostolic calling; namely, when they should be called upon to give an account of their doctrine and ministry. In such cases he would teach them what and how they should speak, (Luke xii, 11, 12;) yea, their Father's Spirit would speak in them, (Matt. x, 19, 20.) It was in his last conversations with them, preparatory to the time when they should carry on his work on earth without his personal presence, that he promised them the Comforter, the Holy Ghost, who should not only bring his teaching to their remembrance, but complete it, and guide them into all truth, even into those truths which they could, as yet, not bear. (John xiv–xvi.) Announcing to them after his resurrection their future mission in the words, "As my Father has sent me, even so send I you," and granting them the power to forgive and retain sins, he breathed upon them—an act emblematical of the Holy Ghost, which they were to receive, (John xx, 21–23;) but while instructed to become his witnesses in Jerusalem, in Samaria, and unto the uttermost parts of the earth, they are commanded to tarry at Jerusalem till they should be endued with the Spirit from on high. (Luke xxiv, 49; Acts i, 8.) This promise was fulfilled to its whole extent on the day of Pentecost, and from this day we see the hitherto timid apostles engage in the public preaching of the Gospel with power and success through the Holy Ghost, that had been sent them from heaven. (Acts ii, 33; 1 Peter i, 12.) To the Holy Ghost they ascribe their doctrines and precepts. (Acts xv, 28; v, 3, 4; 1 Cor. xiv, 37; Eph. iii, 5; 1 Thess. ii, 13; iv, 8.) They claim (1 Cor. ii) that they do not speak in human wisdom and skill, but in a higher wisdom given unto them from God, through his Spirit, that searches all things, (v. 10;) that the Holy Ghost imparts unto them a knowledge which is altogether foreign to the world and the natural man, (vs. 8, 14,) being part of that knowledge with which God knoweth himself, (vs. 11, 12,) but by which they are enabled to know the mind of the Lord as such that have the mind of Christ, (v. 16;) that what they know in this way they speak not in words which human wisdom teacheth, but which the Holy Ghost teacheth, (v. 13,) comparing spiritual things with spiritual. For this very reason the apostles place themselves not only on an equal footing with, but even above "the prophets," the sacred writers of the Old Testament. (2 Peter iii, 2; Rom. xvi, 25, 26; 1 Cor. xii, 28; Eph. iv, 11; ii, 20.)

From all this we learn two truths: First, that the men chosen by Christ for the preaching of his Gospel acted, both in their oral teachings and in their writings, not in the capacity of merely-human witnesses, but that their testimony was united with that of the Holy Ghost, (John xv, 26, 27;) secondly, that the Spirit promised and given by Christ personally to the eleven had reference not so much to them individually, but *to the apostolical office and all its functions*, as we clearly see in the case of the apostle Paul, inclusive of those assistants in their work whom the Lord raised up, and who were also partakers of the gifts of the Holy Ghost.

The Holy Ghost must be conceived of as the Agent, who begets, guides, and governs the Church. In this capacity he is Christ's representative on earth. For this very reason it was necessary that he should preëminently manifest his power in those who were to be the chief organs through which the new life was to flow from the head into the whole body; that is, in those who were, to use Paul's expression, the apostle of Jesus Christ *by the will of God.* But from the relation of the Holy Ghost to the *apostolic office* we learn, also, why we may place the writings of the Evangelists, Mark and Luke, on an equal footing with those of the apostles, and consider them as inspired. We need not attach much importance to the tradition that they belonged to the seventy whom Jesus first sent forth to preach in Judea, or to the one hundred and twenty disciples on whom the Holy Ghost fell on the day of Pentecost. It is enough to know that the apostles had received the power to impart the gift of the Holy Spirit by the imposition of their hands, and that they made use of this power. (Acts viii, 14–17; xix, 6.) Are we, then, not authorized to take it for granted that Mark and Luke, whom Peter and Paul had chosen for their special co-workers out of the great number of Evangelists whom the Lord had already raised up from among Jews and Gentiles, received through the apostles the gift of the Holy Spirit necessary to give to the Church an inspired record of the discourses and acts of the Lord? Besides, though they had not been eye and ear-witnesses of the life and ministry of Christ, yet they were the companions of those that had been eye-witnesses, and they heard continually from their lips the sayings and doings of Christ, having the best opportunity to obtain the fullest information. Again, though they had not been commissioned by Christ himself to teach the nations and to feed his lambs, yet they had been made by the apostles their partners and fellow-laborers for the kingdom of God, (2 Cor. viii, 23; 1 Thess. iii, 2; Philem., 24;) they were engaged in the same work of the Lord as the apostles, (1 Cor. xvi, 10,) and had to perform apostolical functions, (Titus i, 5; 2 Tim. iv, 1–5.) Although they did not plant, yet they did water; although they did not lay the foundation, yet they built upon it, and have transmitted to us records of unadulterated truth through the same Spirit that was also in them, (2 Tim. i, 14,) and we have to honor them next to the apostles as the Divine instruments in the building up of his Church, and as stewards of the mysteries of God, (1 Cor. iv, 1.) Lastly, it must not be forgotten that the Gospels of Mark and Luke, having been written, if not before the death of Peter and Paul, at least before that of the apostle John, must have had the sanction of at least one of the apostles whom the Head of the Church had authorized to bind and to loose.

But the important question arises: *In what sense*, or *to what extent* were the historical books of the New Testament inspired, especially the records of the two Evangelists who were not themselves apostles? There has been much unnecessary controversy on the definition of the term "inspiration;" different modes and degrees of inspiration have been assumed. The most important distinction appears to us that between *inspiration* and *revelation:* two terms which, though totally different, are often used as synonyms. *Revelation is a purely-Divine act*—it is God revealing himself to man, either by supernatural, external facts, such as the miracles recorded in Scripture, or by supernatural, internal communications, such as when the Spirit of God imparts to man the infallible foreknowledge of future events, or reveals to him doctrines which lie beyond the reach of human reason. In the reception of such a supernatural, internal communication, the human mind is perfectly passive, not thinking its own thoughts, or speaking its own words, but only the thoughts and words of the Spirit of God. *Not so in inspiration.* That demands *human as well as Divine agency.* The Spirit of God in inspiration acts simply *on* man but *through* man, using the faculties not of man according to their natural law. God, who gives the message, selects also the messenger, so that the traits of individual character and the peculiarities of manner and purpose, which are displayed in the composition and language of the sacred writings, are essential to the perfect exhibition of their meaning. By inspiration the human mind is enabled correctly to apprehend, and then authentically and authoritatively to make known, orally or in writing, a revelation which God has given of himself. The duty and qualification authentically and authoritatively to make known a self-revealing act of God is evidently to be distinguished from that Divine act. This distinction is overlooked when it is assumed that, in recording the facts of revelation, the sacred writers wrote down every word just as it was dictated to them by the Holy Ghost, in the same manner in which God revealed to the prophets future events. This is what is called *verbal inspiration* in the strict sense of the word; but the term itself, as we have seen, is a misnomer—it would be revelation, not inspiration. Such Divine influence as takes place in revelation was not needed for an authentic and authoritative record of revelation, nor do the Evangelists claim it; nor would it have been in accordance with Divine Wisdom to have excluded human agency in the communication of his revelation. The very evidences, for instance, of this human agency, which the apparent or trifling discrepancies in the statements of the different Evangelists present, answer a wise purpose; they convince us that they were independent witnesses, and that the whole story did not arise from some well-concerted plan to deceive the world; the homely style of some of the writers proves to us that they were really fishermen, and not philosophers; thus we have a convincing evidence that the deepest system of theology, and the noblest code of ethics ever propounded—the one stirring the depth of the whole human heart, the other guiding all human life—came, not from the profound speculations of the wisest of mankind, but either from God himself, or else from a source more inexplicable and absolutely impossible. The theory of what is called verbal inspiration, on the contrary, far from being essential to the Divine authority of the Gospel Records, is, indeed, as we shall further show, the only ground on which an objection can be brought against their claim of being authentic and authoritative records of a Divine revelation; and though this theory of verbal inspiration has been received as if it were tantamount to plenary inspiration, it rests on no Scripture authority and is supported by no historical testimony, if we accept a few ambiguous metaphors of the Fathers. "Much might be said," says Alford, in his Prolegomena to the Gospels, "of the *a priori* unworthiness of such a theory, as applied to a Gospel whose character is the freedom of the spirit, not the bondage of the letter; but it belongs more to my present work to try it by applying it to the Gospels as we have them. And I do not hesitate to say, that, being thus applied, its effects will be to destroy the credibility of our Evangelists. Hardly a single instance of parallelism between them arises where they do not relate the same thing, indeed, in substance, but expressed in terms which, if literally taken, are incompatible with each other. To cite only one obvious instance: The title over the cross was written in Greek. According, then, to the verbal-inspiration theory, each Evangelist has recorded *the exact words* of the inscription; *not the general sense*, but the *inscription itself*—not a letter less or more. This is absolutely necessary to the theory. Its advocates must not be allowed, with convenient inconsistency, to take refuge in a common-sense view of the matter wherever their theory fails them, and still to uphold it in the main. Another objection to the theory is, if it be so, the Christian world is left in uncertainty what her Scriptures are, as long as the sacred text is full of various readings. Some one manuscript must be pointed out to us which carries the weight of verbal inspiration, or some text whose authority shall be undoubted must be promulgated. But manifestly neither of these things can ever happen. The fact is, that this theory uniformly gives way before an intelligent study of the Scriptures themselves; and is only held, consistently and thoroughly, by those who never have undertaken that study. *When put forth by those who have, it is never carried fairly through; but, while broadly asserted, is in detail abandoned.*"

Verbal inspiration, *in the sense explained*, is utterly irreconcilable with the peculiar coincidences and differences which the compositions of the Synoptists present; but, in rejecting the verbal dictation of the Gospel Records, we are far from calling in question their "*plenary* inspiration." By plenary inspiration we mean such an influence of the Holy Spirit on the minds of the Evangelists as prevented them from expressing an error or untruth, in any thing essential to the Divine revelation, of which they were to give an authentic and authoritative record, both with regard to its facts and the doctrines involved in them—yet, so that, on the one hand, the human element was not neutralized by the Divine agency, and, on the other hand, the truth of God remained unimpaired by the individual mind. The relation of the human to the Divine element in the inspired writings is very beautifully and cautiously set forth by Mr. Elliott, (Aids to Faith, page 479:) "As in the case of the Incarnate Word, we fully recognize in the Lord's humanity all essentially-human limitations and weakness—the hunger, the thirst, and the weariness on the side of the body, and the gradual development on the side of the human mind—in a word, all that belongs to the essential and original characteristics of the pure form of the nature he vouchsafed to assume, but plainly deny the existence therein of the faintest trace of sin, or of moral or mental imperfection—even so in the case of the written Word, viewed on its purely-human side, and *in its reference to matters previously admitted to have no bearing on Divine Truth*, we may admit therein the existence of such incompleteness, such limitations, and such imperfections as belong even to the highest forms of purely-truthful *human* testimony, but consistently deny the existence of mistaken views, perversion, misrepresentation, and any form whatever of consciously-committed error or inaccuracy."

Plenary inspiration, then, properly understood, does not forbid the Evangelists to draw from natural sources of information, as Luke, in the preface to his Gospel expressly asserts to have done, or to quote from other inspired writers without giving their words literatim, and according to their individuality to differ from each other in the selection, in the manner and in the arrangement of the events which they relate, nor is it inconsistent even with *inaccuracies* in matters which all agree in regarding as wholly unimportant, which have no reference to the purpose of their writings, to give an authentic and authoritative record of Divine revelation. Such alleged inaccuracies have not yet been incontestably proved; but even if we admit their existence, they are, like some alleged contradictions, (see § 21,) due either to our ignorance of some simple fact, which, if known, would explain all; or they furnish only an illustration of one of those very conditions and characteristics of human testimony, however honest and truthful, without which it would cease to be human testimony at all. Moreover, there is no need of ascribing to the inspired writers a perfect knowledge of geography, profane history, science, etc.; it is sufficient for their inspired character to maintain that whatever they affirm to be true, if it has the remotest reference to religion, is the truth, the whole truth, and nothing but the truth, and that they never declare any thing to be *scientifically* true that is *scientifically* false. This is a point which concerns not so much the Evangelists as the other inspired writers, especially of the Old Testament; yet, as it is a vital point in the question of inspiration, we may dwell on it for a moment. Though the writers of the Old Testament, compared with the most enlightened sages of heathen antiquity, show a superior knowledge of physical science, which nothing short of Divine inspiration can account for; and though recent discussions of the subjects of controversy by men of acknowledged scientific attainments have tended to show that the oppositions of Scripture and of science are far more doubtful than they are assumed to be; yet—even if the charge of error in matters of human knowledge should be substantiated against any of the sacred writers—this would not militate against their plenary inspiration for the purpose of giving us an infallible depository of religious truth. Scripture was not given to teach us science; it was, therefore, not needful to render the sacred writers infallible in matters of science.

Alford, who arrives, as we have shown, at substantially the same results with regard to the origin of the synoptical Gospels we have tried to reach, lays down the following propositions respecting their inspiration, which are in full harmony with the definition of inspiration given above, and may serve as a summary of our whole investigation:

"1. The results of our inquiries may be thus stated: That our three Gospels have arisen independently of one another from sources of information possessed by the Evangelists; such sources of information, for a very considerable part of their contents, being the narrative teaching of the apostles; and in cases where their personal testimony was out of the question, oral or documentary narratives, preserved in and received by the Christian Church in the apostolic age; that the three Gospels are not formal, complete accounts of the whole incidents of the sacred history, but each of them fragmentary, containing such portions of it as fell within the notice, or the special design, of the Evangelist.

"2. The important question now comes before us: *In what sense are the Evangelists to be regarded as having been inspired by the Holy Spirit of God?* That they *were so, in some sense*, has been the concurrent belief of the Christian body in all ages. In the *second*, as in the *nineteenth* century, the ultimate appeal in matters of fact and doctrine has been to these venerable writings. It may be well, then, first to inquire on what grounds their authority has been rated so high by all Christians?

"3. And I believe the answer to this question will be found to be: *Because they are regarded as authentic documents, descending from the apostolic age, and presenting to us the substance of the apostolic testimony.* The apostles being raised up for the special purpose of *witnessing to the Gospel history*, and these memoirs having been universally received in the early Church as embodying their testimony, I see no escape left from the inference that they come to us with *inspired authority*. The apostles themselves, and their cotemporaries in the ministry of the Word, were singularly endowed with the Holy Spirit for the founding and teaching of the Church; and Christians of all ages have accepted the Gospels and other writings of the New Testament as the written result of the Pentecostal effusion. The early Church was not likely to be deceived in this matter. The reception of the Gospels was *immediate* and *universal*. They never were placed for a moment, by the consent of the Christians, in the same category with the spurious documents which soon sprang up after them. In external history, as in internal character, they differ entirely from the apocryphal Gospels; which, though in some cases bearing the name and pretending to contain the teaching of an apostle, were *never recognized as apostolic.*

"4. Upon the authenticity, that is, the apostolicity of our Gospels, rest their claims to inspiration. Containing the substance of the apostles' testimony, they carry with them that special power of the Holy Spirit which rested on the apostles in virtue of their office, and also on other teachers and preachers of the first age. It may be well, then, to inquire of what kind that power was, and how far extending.

"5. We do not find the apostles transformed, from being men of individual character, and thought, and feeling, into mere channels for the transmission of infallible truth; we find them, humanly speaking, to have been still distinguished by the same characteristics as before the descent of the Holy Ghost. We see Peter still ardent and impetuous, still shrinking from the danger of human disapproval; we see John still exhibiting the same union of deep love and burning zeal; we find them pursuing different paths of teaching, exhibiting different styles of writing, taking hold of the truth from different sides.

"6. Again, we do not find the apostles *put in possession at once* of the Divine counsel with regard to the Church. Though Peter and John were full of the Holy Ghost immediately after the ascension, neither at that time, nor for many years afterward, were they put in possession of the purpose of God regarding the Gentiles, which in due time was specially revealed to Peter, and recognized in the apostolic council at Jerusalem.

"7. These considerations serve to show us in what respects the working of the Holy Spirit on the sacred writers was analogous to his influence on every believer in Christ; namely, in the retention of individual character, and thought, and feeling, and in the gradual development of the ways and purposes of God to their minds.

"8. But their situation and office was *peculiar* and *unexampled.* And for its fulfillment peculiar and unexampled gifts were bestowed upon them. One of these, which bears very closely upon our present subject, was the *recalling by the Holy Spirit of those things which the Lord had said to them.* This was his own formal promise, recorded in John xiv, 26. And, if we look at our present Gospels, we see abundant evidences of its fulfillment. What unassisted human memory could treasure up sayings and parables, however deep the impression at the time, and report them in full at the distance of several years, as we find them reported, with every internal mark of truthfulness in our Gospels? What invention of man could have devised discourses which, by common consent, differ from all sayings of men—which possess this character unaltered, notwithstanding their transmission through men of various mental organization—which contain things impossible to be understood or appreciated by their reporters at the time when they profess to have been uttered—which inwrap the seeds of all human improvement yet attained, and are evidently full of power for more? I refer to this latter alternative only to remark, that all considerations, whether of the apostles' external circumstances, or their internal feelings respecting Him of whom they bore witness, combine to confirm the persuasion of Christians that they have recorded as said by our Lord *what he truly did say*, and not any words of their own imagination.

"9. And let us pursue the matter further by analogy. Can we suppose that the light poured by the Holy Spirit upon the *sayings* of our Lord would be confined to such sayings, and not extend itself over the other parts of the narratives of his life on earth? Can we believe that those miracles, which, though not uttered in words, were yet *acted parables*, would not be, under the same gracious assistance, brought back to the minds of the apostles, so that they should be placed on record for the teaching of the Church?

"10. And, going yet further, to those parts of the Gospels which were wholly out of the cycle of the apostles' own testimony, can we imagine that the Divine discrimination which enabled them to detect the 'lie to the Holy Ghost,' should have forsaken them in judging of the records of our Lord's birth and infancy, so that they should have taught or sanctioned an apocryphal, fabulous, or mythical account of such matters? *Some account* of them must have been current in the apostolic circle; for Mary, the mother of Jesus, survived the ascension, and would be fully capable of giving undoubted testimony to the facts. Can we conceive, then, that, *with her among them*, the apostles should have delivered other than a true history of these things? Can we suppose that Luke's account, which he includes among the things *delivered by those who were eye-witnesses and ministers of the Word* from the first, is other than the true one, and stamped with the authority of the witnessing and discriminating Spirit dwelling in the apostles? Can we suppose that the account in the still more immediately-apostolic Gospel of Matthew is other than the history seen from a different side, and independently narrated?

"11. But if it be inquired *how* far such Divine superintendence has extended in the *framing of our Gospels as we at present find them*, the answer must be furnished by no preconceived idea of what ought to have been, but by *the contents of the Gospels themselves.* That those contents are *various*, and *variously arranged*, is token enough that in their selection and disposition we have human agency presented to us, under no more direct guidance, in this respect, than that *general leading* which, in main and essential points, should insure entire accordance. Such leading admits of much variety in points of minor consequence. Two men may be equally led by the Holy Spirit to record the events of our Lord's life for our edification, though one may believe and record that the visit to the Gadarenes took place before the calling of Matthew, while the other places it after that event; though one, in narrating it, speaks of two demoniacs—the other only of one.

"12. And it is observable that in the only place in the three Gospels where an Evangelist speaks of himself, he expressly lays claim, not to any supernatural guidance in the arrangement of his subject-matter, but to a diligent tracing down of all things from the first; in other words, to the care and accuracy of a faithful and honest compiler. After such an avowal on the part of the writer himself, to assert an immediate revelation to him of *the arrangement to be adopted* and the *chronological notices to be given*, is clearly not justified, according to his own showing and assertion. The value of such arrangement and chronological connection must depend on various circumstances in each case; on their definiteness and consistency; on their agreement or disagreement with the other extant records; the preference being, in each case, given to that one whose account is the most minute in details, and whose notes of sequence are the most distinct.

"13. In thus speaking, I am doing no more than even the most scrupulous of our harmonizers have, in fact, done. In the case alluded to in paragraph 11, *there is not one of them who has not altered the arrangement*, either of Matthew or of Mark and Luke, so as to bring the visit to the Gadarenes into the same part of the Evangelic history. But *if the arrangement itself were matter of Divine inspiration*, then have we *no right to vary it* in the slightest degree, but must maintain—as the harmonists have done in other cases, but never, as I am aware, in *this—two distinct visits to have been made at different times, and nearly the same events to have occurred at both.* I need hardly add that a similar method of proceeding with all the variations in the Gospels, *which would on this supposition be necessary*, would render the Scripture narrative a heap of improbabilities, and strengthen, instead of weakening, the cause of the enemies of our faith.

"14. And not only of the arrangement of the Evangelic history are these remarks to be understood. There are certain minor points of accuracy or inaccuracy, of which human research suffices to inform men, and on which, from want of that research, it is often the practice to speak vaguely and inexactly. Such are sometimes the conventionally-received distances from place to place; such are the common accounts of phenomena in natural history, etc. Now, in matters of this kind, the Evangelists and apostles were not supernaturally informed, but left, in common with others, to the guidance of their natural faculties.

"15. The same may be said of citations and dates from history. In the last apology of Stephen—which he spoke, being full of the Holy Ghost, and with Divine influence beaming from his countenance—we have at least two demonstrable historical inaccuracies. And the occurrence of similar ones in the Gospels does not in any way affect the inspiration or the veracity of the Evangelists.

"16. It may be well to mention one notable illustration of the principles upheld in this section. What can be more undoubted and unanimous than the testimony of the Evangelists to *the resurrection of the Lord?* If there be one fact rather than another of which the apostles were witnesses, *it was this;* and in the concurrent narratives of all four Evangelists it stands related beyond all cavil or question. Yet, of all the events which they have described, *none is so variously put forth in detail,* or with so many minor discrepancies. And this was just what might have been expected on the principles above laid down. The great fact that the Lord *was risen*—set forth by the ocular witness of the apostles, who had seen him—became from that day first in importance in the delivery of their testimony. The *precise order* of his appearances would naturally, from the overwhelming nature of their present emotions, be a matter of minor consequence, and perhaps not even of accurate inquiry till some time had passed. Then, with the utmost desire on the part of the women and apostles to collect the events in their exact order of time, some confusion would be apparent in the history, and some discrepancies in versions of it which were the results of separate and independent inquiries; the traces of which pervade our present accounts. But what fair-judging student of the Gospel ever made these variations or discrepancies a ground for doubting the veracity of the Evangelists as to the fact of the resurrection, or the principal details of the Lord's appearances after it?" (Alford's Prolegomena to the Greek Testament, Ch. I, Sec. 6.)

PART V.

REMARKS ON THE GOSPEL HISTORY.

PART V.

REMARKS ON THE GOSPEL HISTORY.

§ 34. The Condition of the World, Jewish, Greek, and Roman, at the Advent of Jesus Christ.

Christ being "the center and turning-point, as well as key of all history," it seems to us not out of place, in concluding this argument, to glance at the preparation which existed in the moral and religious condition of the world for the appearance of the Redeemer on earth. Upon this process of preparation Neander, the father of modern Church history,* threw more light than any of his predecessors; and, upon the foundation which he had laid, his worthy successors, Guericke, Kurtz, Jacobi, and Schaff, built their deeply-interesting researches. The most lucid as well as comprehensive discussion of this subject we find in Dr. Schaff's Church History, and

*"By birth and early training an Israelite, and a genuine Nathanael too, full of childlike simplicity and of longings for the Messianic salvation—in youth an enthusiastic student of Grecian philosophy, particularly of Plato, who became for him a scientific schoolmaster to bring him to Christ—he had, when in his seventeenth year he received Christian baptism, passed through in his own inward experience, so to speak, the whole historical course by which the world had been prepared for Christianity; he had gained an experimental knowledge of the workings of Judaism and heathenism in their direct tendency toward Christianity; and thus he had already broken his own way to the only proper position for contemplating the history of the Church—a position whence Jesus Christ is viewed as the object of the deepest yearnings of humanity, the center of all history, and the only key to its mysterious sense." (Dr. Schaff's History of the Apostolic Church, p. 96.)

quote, therefore, from him, with some modification and abridgment, and with the exception of what is said "on the moral and religious state of the Pagan world among the Greeks and Romans," on which we have preferred the statement of Guericke.

With the incarnation of the Son of God commences, and on it rests, the fullness of time. (Gal. iv, 4.) It is the end of the old world, and the beginning of the new, which is dated from his birth. The entire development of humanity, especially of the religious ideas of all nations, before the birth of Christ, must be viewed as an introduction to this great event. The preparation for it began indeed with the very creation of man, who was made in the image of God, and destined for communion with him through the eternal Son, and with the promise of deliverance by the seed of the woman, some vague memories of which promise survived in the heathen religions. With the call of Abraham, some two thousand years before the birth of Christ, the religious development of humanity separates into two independent and antagonistic lines, Judaism and heathenism. In the former the development was influenced and directed by a continuous course of Divine coöperation; in the latter it was left to the unaided powers and capacities of man. These two parallel lines continued side by side with each other till, in the fullness of time, they merged in Christianity, which they were mutually to serve by their appropriate fruits, and results, and respectively-peculiar developments; but with which, also, the ungodly elements of both would enter into a deadly conflict. As Christianity is the reconciliation and union of God and man in and through Jesus Christ, the God-man and Savior, it must have been preceded by a twofold process of preparation—an approach of God to man, and an approach of man to God. In Judaism the preparation is direct and positive, proceeding from above downward, and ending with the birth of the Messiah. In heathenism it is indirect, and mainly, though not entirely, negative, proceeding from below upward, and ending with a helpless cry of mankind for redemption. There we have a special revelation or self-communication of the only true God by word and deed, ever growing clearer and plainer, till at last the Divine nature appears in the human to raise it to communion with itself; here man, guided indeed by the general providence of God, and lighted by the glimmer of the *Logos* shining in the darkness, (John i, 5,) yet unaided by direct revelation, and left to his own ways, (Acts xiv, 16,) if haply he might feel after the Lord and find him. In Judaism the true religion was prepared for mankind, and in heathenism mankind was prepared for its reception. There the Divine substance is begotten; here the human forms are molded to receive it. The former is like the elder son in the parable, who abode in his father's house; the latter like the prodigal, who squandered his portion, yet at last shuddered before the gaping abyss of perdition, and penitently returned to the bosom of his father's compassionate love. The flower of paganism appears in the two great nations of classic antiquity, Greece and Rome. With the language, morality, literature, and religion of these nations Christianity came directly into contact. These, together with the Jews, were the chosen nations of the ancient world, and shared the earth among them. While the Jews were chosen for things eternal, to keep the sanctuary of the true religion, the Greeks prepared the elements of natural culture, of science and art for the use of the Church, and the Romans developed the idea of law, and organized the civilized world in a universal empire, ready to serve the spiritual universality of the Gospel. On the one hand God endowed the Greeks and Romans with the richest natural gifts, that they might reach the highest civilization possible without the aid of Christianity, and thus both provide the instruments of human science, art, and law for the use of the Christian Church, and yet at the same time show the utter impotence of these alone to bless and save the world. On the other hand, the universal empire of Rome was a positive groundwork for the universal empire of the Gospel. It served as a crucible, in which all contradictory and irreconcilable peculiarities of the ancient nations and religions were dissolved into the chaos of the new creation. The Roman legions razed the partition-walls among the ancient nations, brought the extremes of the civilized world together in free intercourse, and united North and South, and East and West in the bonds of a common language and culture, of common laws and customs. Thus they evidently, though unconsciously, opened the way for the rapid and general spread of that religion which unites all nations in one family of God by the spiritual bond of faith and love. In addition to this general survey, let us consider more particularly:

1. *The moral and religious state of the pagan world among the Greeks and Romans.* The religious ideas that lie at the bottom of all pagan religions sprang originally from Divine revelation, either internal or external. Having been darkened by human apostasy,

they could not, however, in the distorted form which they assumed in heathenism, avail to check even the grossest manifestations of unbelief and superstition. Resting upon myths and the vague intimations and feelings of the human soul, *the ancient popular religion of the Greeks and Romans*, in particular, naturally came in conflict with the increasing education and refinement of these highly-civilized nations, but could not vanquish the skepticism that was engendered thereby. Hence, notwithstanding the efforts of the Government and the patriotic citizen to prop up the declining State religion, an utter disbelief in every thing religious and Divine gradually spread among the cultivated and noble classes, and passed over from them into the mass of society, bringing with it a dreadful corruption of morals and manners. A species of philosophy that set up pleasure as the highest good, and wholly denied the reality of any objective truth, became the prevalent mode of thinking, and if here and there a man of more earnest religious temper felt constrained to resist the godless spirit of his age in its extreme forms, yet religion even for him lost its vitality, and God himself became the product of the human understanding. But on the other hand, this very unbelief, groping about in vain for a satisfying object, carried the germ of a reaction. Many, with a sense of inward emptiness and a dim intimation of a higher world, despairing of any satisfaction from the various conflicting philosophical systems, yearned after the old religion of their fathers, and boldly grasped it again with glowing zeal, and the "barbaric" religions of Asia and Egypt were brought in to impart a new decoration and interest to the effete ancestral system, and amulets, talismans, and magicians found a welcome reception. Such was the general state of the religion of the Greeks and Romans at the time of the advent of the Redeemer. Reckless infidelity and horrible superstition, both alike fostered by the reigning dissoluteness of morals, contended for the mastery, and the great mass of the people lay sunk in absolute godlessness.

A deeper religious need was awakened in some few minds, and these sought satisfaction in the *two better* philosophical systems of the time; neither of which, however, was fitted to meet this immortal longing of the heart. The *Stoic* philosophy, through its ideal of a perfect virtue, could indeed flare a clearer light over the prevailing corruption of morals, but could give no disclosures respecting the unseen world and man's future relations to God. Stoicism, moreover, left its disciples to the isolated strain of their own wills. Blindly and coldly they subjected themselves, for life or for death, to the unalterable law of the universe; to despise pleasure and pain, and, in case of necessity, to put an end to an existence which had missed its aim—such was the climax of their wisdom. The principles of *Platonism* did not, indeed, minister to the self-reliant pride of human nature. On the contrary, they tended to produce the sense of dependence upon a higher Power, and to lead men to seek communion therewith, as the only source of enlightenment and moral excellence. But they could only teach them to *seek*, not to find. This consummation could be effected only by a mediator who "was come from God and went to God." Platonism, in thus hinting at a perfect religion that was itself the substance, while all others were the shadows, and in spiritualizing the popular religions of the time, dimly looked toward Christianity.

We have to survey, 2. *The religious condition of the Jewish people.* This wonderful people was chosen by Sovereign Grace to stand amid the surrounding idolatry as the bearer of the knowledge of Jehovah, the only true God, of his holy law, and of his comforting promise, and thus to become the cradle of the Messiah. It arose with the calling of Abraham, and the covenant of Jehovah with him in Canaan, the land of promise; grew to a nation in Egypt, the land of bondage; was delivered, and organized into a theocratic State, on the basis of the law of Sinai, by Moses in the wilderness; was led back into Palestine by Joshua; became, after the Judges, a monarchy, reaching the hight of its glory in David and Solomon, the types of the victorious and peaceful reign of Christ; split into two hostile kingdoms, and, in punishment of internal discord and growing apostasy to idolatry, was carried captive by heathen conquerors; was restored, after seventy years' humiliation, to the land of its fathers, but fell again under the yoke of heathen foes; yet in its deepest abasement fulfilled its highest mission by giving birth to the Savior of the world. Judaism was, among the idolatrous nations of antiquity, like an oasis in a desert, clearly defined and isolated; separated and inclosed by a rigid moral and ceremonial law. The Holy Land itself, though in the midst of the three grand divisions of the ancient world, was separated from the great nations of ancient culture by deserts south and east, by sea on the west, and by mountains on the north; thus securing to the Mosaic religion freedom to unfold itself and to fulfill its great work without disturbing influences from abroad. And Israel carried in its bosom from the first, the large promise, that in Abraham's seed all the nations of the earth should be blessed.

The outward circumstances, and the moral and religious condition of the Jews at the birth of Christ, would indeed seem, at first and on the whole, to be in glaring contradiction with their divine destiny. But, in the first place, their very degeneracy proved the need of Divine help. In the second place, the redemption through Christ appeared by contrast in the greater glory, as a creative act of God. And finally, amid the mass of corruption, as a preventive of putrefaction, lived the succession of the true children of Abraham, longing for the salvation of Israel, and ready to embrace Jesus of Nazareth as the promised Messiah and the Savior of the world.

Since the battle of Philippi, (B. C. 42,) the Jews had been subject to the heathen Romans, who heartlessly governed them by the Idumean Herod and his sons, and afterward by procurators. Under this hated yoke their Messianic hopes were powerfully raised, but carnally distorted. Misapprehending the spirit of the Old Testament, vain-gloriously boasting themselves to be the people of God, utterly blinded as to the cause of the terrible national judgments they were suffering, the mass of the Jewish nation desired nothing but deliverance from temporal distresses, and hoped greedily for the advent of a Messiah who should free them from the Roman yoke by supernatural power, and give *them* the supreme dominion on earth. Their morals were *outwardly* far better than those of the heathen; but under the garb of strict obedience to their law they concealed great corruption. They are pictured in the New Testament as a stiff-necked, ungrateful, and impenitent race, a generation of vipers. Their own priest and historian, Josephus, who generally endeavored to present his countrymen to the Greeks and Romans in the most favorable light, describes them as at that time a debased and ungodly people, well deserving their fearful punishment in the destruction of Jerusalem. As to religion, the Jews, especially after the Babylonish captivity, adhered most tenaciously to the letter of the law, and to their traditions and ceremonies, but without knowing the spirit and power of the Scriptures. They cherished the most bigoted horror of the heathen, and were therefore despised and hated by them as misanthropic. After the time of the Maccabees, (B. C. 150,) they fell into two mutually-hostile sects. The *Pharisees* represented the traditional orthodoxy and stiff formalism, the legal self-righteousness and the fanatical bigotry of Judaism. The bitter opponents of the Pharisees were the skeptical, rationalistic, and worldly-minded *Sadducees.* Their religious creed was confined to the mere letter of the Pentateuch, and contained only such tenets as they deemed to be explicitly taught in it. The sect of the Essenes came into no contact with the Gospel history. They were a mystic, ascetic sect, and lived in monkish seclusion on the coasts of the Dead Sea.

Degenerate and corrupt though the mass of Judaism was, yet the Old Testament economy was the Divine institution preparatory to the Christian redemption, and as such received the deepest reverence from Christ and his apostles, while they sought by terrible rebuke to lead its unworthy representatives to repentance. *Law* and *prophecy* were the two great elements of the Jewish religion by which it was made *a direct Divine introduction* to Christianity. (1.) The law of Moses was the clearest expression of the holy will of God before the advent of Christ. It set forth the ideal of righteousness, and was thus fitted most effectually to awaken the sense of man's great departure from it, the knowledge of sin and guilt. It acted as a schoolmaster to lead men to Christ that they might be justified by faith. The same sense of guilt and of the need of reconciliation was constantly kept alive by daily sacrifices, at first in the Tabernacle and afterward in the Temple, and by the whole ceremonial law, which, as a wonderful system of types and shadows, perpetually pointed to the realities of the new covenant, especially to the one all-sufficient atoning sacrifice of Christ on the cross. For, inasmuch as God requires absolute obedience and purity of heart, under promise of life and penalty of death, and as he can not cruelly sport with man, there is hidden in the moral and ritual law, as in a shell, the sweet kernel of a promise, that he will one day exhibit the ideal of righteousness in living form, and give the miserable sinner power to fulfill the law. Without such assurance the law were bitter irony. (2.) The law was, as already hinted, the vehicle of the Divine promise of redemption, and became by prophecy a religion of hope. While the Greeks and Romans put their golden age in the past, the Jews looked for theirs in the future. Their whole history, their religious, political, and social institutions and customs pointed to the coming of the Messiah, and the establishment of his kingdom on earth. Prophecy begins with the promise of the Serpent-bruiser immediately after the fall. It predominates in the patriarchal age, and Moses, the lawgiver, was at the same time a prophet pointing the people to a greater successor. Without the comfort of the Messianic promise, the law must have driven the earnest soul to despair. From the time of Samuel, some eleven centuries before Christ, prophecy took an organized form in a permanent prophetical office and order. In this form it accompanied the Levitical priesthood and the Davidic dynasty down to the Babylonish captivity, survived this catastrophe, and directed the return of the people and the rebuilding of the Temple; interpreting and applying the law, reproving abuses in Church and State, predicting the terrible judgments and the redeeming grace of God, warning and punishing, comforting and encouraging, with an ever plainer reference to the coming Messiah, who should redeem Israel and the world from sin and misery, and establish a kingdom of peace and righteousness on earth.

This is the Jewish religion as it flowed from the fountain of Divine revelation and lived in the true Israel, the spiritual children of Abraham, in John the Baptist, his parents and disciples, in the mother of Jesus, her kindred and friends, in the venerable Simeon, and the prophetess Anna, in Lazarus and his pious sisters, in the apostles and the first disciples, who embraced Jesus of Nazareth as the fulfiller of the law and the prophets, the Son of God and the Savior of the world.

We have to glance, 3. *At the influence which Judaism and heathenism mutually exerted upon one another.* (1.) The Jews, since the Babylonish captivity, had been scattered over all the world. In spite of the antipathy of the Gentiles, they had, by their judgment, industry, and tact, risen to wealth and influence, and had built their synagogues in all the commercial cities of the Roman Empire. They had thus sown the seeds of the knowledge of the true God, and of Messianic hope in the field of the idolatrous world. The Old Testament Scriptures were translated into Greek two centuries before Christ, and were read and expounded in the public worship of God, which was open to all. Every synagogue was, as it were, a mission-station of monotheism, and furnished the apostles an admirable place and a most natural introduction for their preaching of Jesus Christ as the fulfiller of the law and the prophets. Then, as the heathen religions had been hopelessly undermined by skeptical philosophy and popular infidelity, many earnest Gentiles, especially multitudes of women, came over to Judaism either wholly or in part. The thorough converts, called "proselytes of righteousness," were commonly still more bigoted and fanatical than the native Jews. The half-converts, "proselytes of the gate," or "God-fearing men," who adopted only the monotheism, the principal moral laws, and the Messianic hopes of the Jews, without being circumcised, appear in the New Testament as the most susceptible hearers of the Gospel. (2.) On the other hand, the Græco-Roman heathenism, through its language, philosophy, and literature, exerted no inconsiderable influence to soften the fanatical bigotry in the higher and more cultivated classes of the Jews. Generally the Jews of the dispersion, who spoke the Greek language, the Hellenists, as they were called, were much more liberal than the proper Hebrews, or Palestinian Jews, who kept their mother tongue. This is evident in the Gentile missionaries, Barnabas of Cyprus, and Paul of Tarsus, and in the whole Church of Antioch, in contrast with that at Jerusalem. The Hellenistic-Jewish form of Christianity was the natural bridge to the Gentile. The most remarkable example of a traditional, though very fantastic and Gnostic-like combination of Jewish and heathen elements meets us in the educated circles of the Egyptian metropolis, Alexandria, and in the system of Philo, who was cotemporary with the founding of the Christian Church, though he never came in contact with it. This Jewish theologian sought to harmonize the religion of Moses with the philosophy of Plato by the help of an ingenious but arbitrary allegorical interpretation of the Old Testament; and from the books of Proverbs and of Wisdom he deduced a doctrine of the *Logos* so similar to that of John's Gospel, that some have imputed to the apostle an acquaintance with the writings of Philo. But Philo's speculation is to the apostle's "Word made flesh," as a shadow to the body, or a dream to the reality. The Theraputæ, or Worshipers, a mystic, ascetic sect in Egypt, akin to the Essenes in Judea, carried this Platonic Judaism into practical life; but were, of course, equally unsuccessful in uniting the two religions in a vital and permanent way. Such a union could only be effected by a new religion revealed from heaven.

Thus was the way for Christianity prepared on every side, positively and negatively, directly and indirectly, in theory and practice, by truth and by error, by false belief and by unbelief, by Jewish religion, by Grecian culture, and by Roman conquest;

by the vainly-attempted amalgamation of Jewish and heathen thought, by the exposed impotence of natural civilization, philosophy, art, and political power, by the decay of the old religions, by the universal distraction and hopeless misery of the age, and by the yearnings of all earnest and noble souls for the unknown God.

In the fullness of time, when the fairest flowers of science and art had withered, and the world was on the verge of despair, the Virgin's Son was born to heal the infirmities of mankind. Christ entered a dying world as the author of a new and imperishable life.

§ 35. The Chronology and Harmony of the Gospel Narratives.

It is very difficult to arrange in their proper chronological order the events of our Lord's life, many of which are narrated by one or more of the Evangelists in a different order. Alford thinks that it is impossible to combine the narratives given by the Evangelists into one continuous history, without doing considerable violence to the arrangement of some one or more of the Evangelists. We readily acknowledge that we can not gather from the Gospel Records *that* knowledge of the real process of the transactions themselves, which alone would enable us to give a satisfactory account of the different order in which they appear in our Gospels, and *with certainty* to assign to each event its proper chronological place; nevertheless, there is light enough to show us the chronological order of the Gospel narratives in the main, and modern harmonists have arrived at the same conclusions on almost every essential point, except with regard to the beginning of the Galilean ministry proper and the insertion of Luke ix, 51–xviii, 14. The late Dr. E. Robinson has given, in his "Harmony of the Four Gospels," a digest of the many learned disquisitions on the various difficult points, and the conclusions which he has arrived at in common with the leading harmonists of Germany, and upon which he builds his harmonistical arrangement of the Gospel narratives, have been accepted by all the later commentators; their synoptical and harmonistical table does not vary from that of Robinson. But there has now appeared a work whose thorough researches have brought out a different and far more satisfactory result with regard to the two important points mentioned above. We refer to "*The Life of Our Lord upon the Earth*," by the Rev. Samuel J. Andrews, who has done the Church a great and lasting service by setting the desigh of our Lord's Judean ministry, and its relation to the Galilean, as well as his last journey to Jerusalem, in a light which has an important bearing upon the exegesis of the Gospels. We have no doubt that, henceforward, Mr. Andrews will be the standard authority on the chronology and harmony of the Gospels, as Dr. Robinson has been hitherto. To his "Life of Our Lord," our readers will be indebted for much of the light which we have been enabled to throw upon the chronological and harmonistical questions in the Gospel history. By having adopted the results of Mr. Andrews's researches, and arranging them in tabular form, we hope to contribute something toward giving his valuable work a more general circulation. The chronology and harmony of the Gospels is of so much importance that it ought to be made a subject-matter of study for itself, apart from all other questions, and the Bible student will find in Mr. Andrews's work all he needs for this purpose.

Referring the reader to that work, and to our comments on the respective passages to which the chronological and harmonistical questions refer, for details, and for the reasons that have led us to our conclusions, we will here only present a summary of the data we have for ascertaining the year of our Lord's birth, and death, and consequently the duration of his ministry, in order to obtain a basis for a chronological arrangement of the events narrated in the Gospels.

A. THE DATE OF THE BIRTH OF CHRIST.

According to the received chronology, which is that of Dionysius Exiguus, in the sixth century, Jesus was born in the year of Rome 754. But it is now admitted, on all hands, that this calculation places the nativity some years too late. It can be proved satisfactorily that it could not have occurred after 750, nor before 747.

1. It is certain that Jesus was born before the death of Herod the Great, (Matt. ii, 1–6.) Almost all chronologists agree in putting his death in the year 750, shortly before the Passover, (between the 13th of March and the 4th of April.) But how long before Herod's death was Christ born? The answer to this question depends upon the length of time which the events between his birth and Herod's death—the presentation of the child at the Temple forty days after the nativity, the visit of the Magi, the flight into Egypt, and the remaining there till

Herod was dead—may have required. So much is certain, that the nativity can not be fixed later than the month of January, 750.

2. Another note of time occurs in Luke iii, 1, 2, where John the Baptist is said to have entered upon his ministry in the fifteenth year of Tiberius. The rule of Tiberius may be calculated either from the beginning of his sole reign, after the death of Augustus, August 19, 767, or from his joint government with Augustus, near the end of 764 or the beginning of 765. It is admitted by most chronologists as almost certain, that Luke computed the reign of Tiberius from his colleagueship. If so, the fifteenth year of Tiberius and the beginning of John's ministry is 779. From the fact that the Levites were not allowed to enter upon their full service till the age of thirty, (Num. iv, 3,) it has been generally supposed—although there is no express law to that effect—that the priests began their labors at the same age. Hence it has been inferred that John must have reached the age of thirty ere he began his ministry. That his ministry may have continued about six months, when the Lord came to be baptized, is in the highest degree probable. If, then, John entered upon his ministry in the year 779, being thirty years old, and about six months elapsed ere the Lord, whose birth took place six months after that of John, came to him to be baptized, it follows that the birth of John is to be fixed in the Summer of 749, and that of our Lord toward the close of the same year or in the beginning of 750.

3. The baptism of Jesus was followed by a Passover, (John ii, 13,) at which certain Jews mention that the restoration of their Temple had been in

progress for forty-six years, Jesus himself being at this time "about thirty years of age," (Luke iii, 23.) The statement of Luke, "And Jesus himself began to be about (ὡσεὶ) thirty years of age," has been variously interpreted. According to some it is to be understood as a round or indefinite number, permitting a latitude of at least two or three years. But this is highly improbable. The most natural meaning is, that the Lord was some months more or less than thirty. He was not just thirty, nor twenty-nine, nor thirty-one. This is confirmed by the remark of the Jews, at the Passover which our Lord visited two or three months after his baptism, that that the Temple was then in building forty and six years. This building, or rather rebuilding, of the Temple was begun by Herod in the eighteenth year of his reign, or during the year from Nisan, 734–Nisan, 735. The forty-sixth year following was from Nisan, 780–81. If the forty-sixth year is to be taken as completed, it was that of 781; if it is to be taken as current, it was that of 780. This calculation, like the former points, would fix the birth of Jesus toward the close of 749, or beginning of 750. But this calculation is made somewhat uncertain by the consideration that Josephus assigns the length of Herod's reign at thirty-seven or thirty-four years, according as he reckons from his appointment by the Romans, or from the death of Antigonus.

4. Astronomy is also brought under contribution to settle the date of the birth of Christ. Whether the star seen by the Magi was the conjunction of the planets Jupiter and Saturn, which occurred in the year 747, the reader will find discussed in our notes on Matthew ii, 1–10. We do not enter here upon

this question, because, owing to our not knowing whether the first appearance of the constellation was designed to signify the annunciation of the incarnation or the actual birth, nor at which of the successive appearances of the constellation the Magi set out on their journey, we can not reach any precise chronological results, except this, that the conjunction of the planets in 747 defines the earliest period at which the Lord's birth can be placed.

In respect to the time of the year when Jesus was born there is still less certainty. Mr. Andrews says: "The only direct datum which the Gospels give us is found in the statement of Luke, (i, 5,) that Zacharias 'was of the course of Abia.' It is known that the priests were divided into twenty-four classes, each of which officiated at the Temple in its turn for a week, (1 Chron. xxiv, 1–19.) This order, originally established by David, was broken up by the captivity. The four classes that returned from Babylon were divided anew by Ezra into twenty-four, to which the old names were given. Another interruption was made by the invasion of Antiochus, but the old order was restored by the Maccabees. Of these courses that of Jehojarib was the first, that of Abia the eighth. We need, therefore, only to know a definite time at which any one of the courses was officiating, in order to be able to trace the succession. Such a datum we find in the Talmudical statements, supported by Josephus, (Bell. Jud., VI, iv, 5,) that, at the destruction of the Temple by Titus, on the 5th of August, 823, the first class had just entered on its course. Its period of service was from the evening of the 4th of August, which was the Sabbath, to the evening of the following Sabbath, on the 11th of

August. We can now easily compute backward, and ascertain at what time in any given year each class was officiating. If we take the year 749 as the probable year of Christ's birth, the appearance of the angel to Zacharias announcing John's birth must be placed 748. In this year we find, by computation, that the course of Abia officiated during the weeks from April 17th to 23d, and again from October 3d to 9th. At each of these periods, therefore, was Zacharias at Jerusalem. If the annunciation of the angel was made to him during the former, the birth of John may be placed near the beginning of 749, and the Lord's birth about six months later, or near the middle of 749; if the annunciation was made during the latter, John's birth was near the middle of 749, and the Lord's birth near its end. The fact that we do not know how soon after the completion of the ministry of Zacharias the conception of John is to be placed prevents any very exact statement of dates. Luke (i, 24) uses only the general expression, 'After those days his wife Elisabeth conceived.' Yet the tenor of the narrative leads us to believe that it was soon after his return to his home, and may be placed in either of the months, April or October. Counting onward fifteen months, we reach June and December, in one of which the birth of Christ is thus to be placed." To the month of December the objection is made, that, in the night when the Lord was born, shepherds were in the field keeping watch over their flocks, and that, if we place the birth of Christ in that season, his baptism would fall in January, a month considered by some as unfavorable for the work of baptism. But the most reliable testimonies concerning the climate of Palestine show the groundlessness of the objection made on this ground. Considering the time most probably required for the events that took place between our Lord's baptism and his first Passover, we are almost forced to the conclusion that he was baptized by John early in January, and that, therefore, his birth is to be placed in the month of December.

B. THE DURATION OF OUR LORD'S MINISTRY, AND THE DATE OF HIS DEATH.

We have shown the grounds upon which we may assume that the Baptist began his ministry in midsummer of the year 779, and that our Lord was baptized about six months afterward, that is in January, 780. Immediately after his baptism he was led by the Spirit into the wilderness to be tempted of the devil, and was there forty days. From John i, 29, we learn that after the temptation he returned to Bethabara the day after John had been visited by a deputation of priests and Levites from Jerusalem. As he sees Jesus coming he bears witness to him as the Lamb of God. The day following he repeats this testimony to his disciples. Two of them—Andrew, and no doubt John, the narrator of the fact—followed Jesus and staid with him the whole day. Andrew brings his brother Simon to see him also, and he receives the name of Cephas. The succeeding day Jesus departs to Galilee. Two days seem to have been spent on the way to Cana, during which time he meets with Philip and Nathanael. On the third day (from the departure to Galilee) the marriage-feast took place at Cana, where our Lord performed his first miracle. From Cana he went down with his mother and brethren, and disciples, to Capernaum, and remained there (John ii, 12, 13) till it was time to go up to Jerusalem to attend the Passover, which, in the year 780, fell upon the 9th of April; the whole interval between his baptism and his first Passover was, consequently, about three months.

The duration of our Lord's ministry can best be determined by the number of Passovers which took place between his baptism and death, and which we have to ascertain from the Gospel of John. This Evangelist mentions six feasts, at five of which Jesus was present; the Passover that followed his baptism, (ii, 13;) a feast of the Jews, (v, 1;) a Passover, during which Jesus remained in Galilee, (vi, 4;) the feast of tabernacles to which the Lord went up privately, (vii, 2;) the feast of dedication, (x, 22;) and, lastly, the Passover at which he suffered. There are, therefore, certainly three Passovers, and if the feast mentioned in chap. v, 1, be also a Passover, four. The reasons for regarding it as a Passover may be found in our comments on John v, 1; they are so preponderating that a great majority of commentators and harmonists have declared in favor of it, and we, therefore, assume this conclusion as the most probable. Accordingly, our Lord's ministry from his baptism embraced three years and about three months, and the Passover on which he died was that of 783.

With regard to the day of the month on which he died, we meet the much-disputed point whether he was crucified on the 14th or 15th Nisan. According to the Synoptists, Jesus partook of the Paschal Supper at the same time with the Jews in general, and at the time appointed in the law, on the evening following the 14th Nisan, Thursday evening, and on the next day, Friday, the 15th Nisan, he was crucified. But according to John (xviii, 28, and xix, 14) it seems that Christ was crucified on the 14th Nisan, the same day on the evening of which the supper was to be legally eaten, and that, consequently, the supper eaten by him and his disciples the evening previous to his death was not the legal Paschal Supper. How John's statement is to be harmonized with that of the Synoptists, is considered at the proper place in our Commentary. This point is mentioned here only on account of its bearing on the year in which our Lord died. We assume here that our Lord died on the 15th Nisan. As it is almost universally admitted that he died on Friday, the question arises, in what year following 780 the 15th Nisan fell on a Friday. According to Wieseler this was the case in 783. Those who place the crucifixion on the 14th Nisan, find that it fell on a Friday in 782 and 786. Seyffarth contends that he died on the 14th Nisan in the year 785, and that this day was Thursday, not Friday.

Inasmuch as the duration of our Lord's ministry can not be ascertained with absolute certainty, from the number of Passovers which took place between his baptism and death, the following data have been made the basis of computing the year of the death of Christ. 1. The tradition of the Talmudists, that the power to inflict capital punishment was taken from the Jews forty years before the Temple was destroyed, which occurred in 823, is adduced as corroborative of the crucifixion having taken place in the year 783. 2. It has been inferred from the parable of the barren fig-tree, (Luke xiii, 6–9,) that Christ's ministry dated three years from the Passover of 780. 3. The prophetic half-week of Daniel (ix, 27) has been interpreted as referring to the length of our Lord's ministry; but this is a mere conjecture. 4. The great eclipse of the sun, reported by Phlegon to have taken place in the fourth year of the 202d Olympiad—from July, 785 to 786—has been considered by some as identical with the darkening of the sun at the crucifixion; but this supposition is of no weight, because the darkening of the sun occurring at the time of the full moon could not have been an eclipse. Besides, the eclipse spoken of by Phlegon occurred, according to astronomical calculations, in November, 782. 5. Some of the Fathers were induced by the passage, Isaiah lxi, 2, where mention is made of "the acceptable year of the Lord," quoted by the Lord at Nazareth, (Luke iv, 19,) to limit his ministry to a single year, or a year and some months. But this supposition is entirely untenable. No less preposterous is the inference of Irenæus, from John viii, 57, and ii, 20, that our Lord was between forty and fifty years old when he died. 6. According to Tertullian, Christ suffered under Tiberius Cæsar, R. Geminus and P. Geminus being Consuls, on the eighth day before the calends of April—March 25th. This statement, although it seems to have obtained general currency, is inexplicable. The Gemini were Consuls during the year beginning January, 782. Our Lord's death could not have taken place in that year on the 25th of March, for he was crucified on the 14th or 15th Nisan; and these days, in 782, fell on the 16th and 17th of April. Besides, Tertullian is not consistent with himself, assigning to our Lord's ministry in one place, one year, and in another place, three years.

In consideration of all the data, though none of them leads to absolute certainty, the majority of *modern* commentators and harmonists have arrived at the conclusion that the ministry of our Lord embraced four Passovers, having a duration of three years and about three months from his baptism in the beginning of January, 780, to the 7th of April, 783.

THE END.

www.ingramcontent.com/pod-product-compliance
Lightning Source LLC
LaVergne TN
LVHW010133110826
845151LV00002B/340

9781425540098